WORSHIP
Old &
NEW

WORSHIP Old & NEW

A BIBLICAL, HISTORICAL, AND PRACTICAL INTRODUCTION
REVISED EDITION

ROBERT E. WEBBER

ZondervanPublishingHouse
Grand Rapids, Michigan

A Division of HarperCollinsPublishers

Worship Old and New: A Biblical, Historical, and Practical Introduction Revised Edition
Copyright ©1994 by Robert E. Webber
Requests for information should be addressed to:
Zondervan Publishing House
Grand Rapids, MI 49530

Library of Congress Cataloging in Publication Data
Webber, Robert
    Worship, old and new / Robert Webber. — Rev. and expanded ed.
    p. cm.
    Includes bibliographical references and index.
    ISBN 0-310-47990-8
    1. Public worship. 2. Evangelicalism. I. Title
BV15.W4 1994
94-12730

          264 — dc20
          CIP

Edited by Matthew Maloley
Cover design by Mary Cantu

Printed in the United States of America

00 01 /❖ DC/ 20 19 18 17 16 15 14 13 12 11 10 9 8

This edition is printed on acid-free paper and meets the American National Standards Institute Z39.48 standard.

Dedicated to my sister and her husband

Eleanor and Nelson Entwistle

*in appreciation for the warm hospitality
they have shown to many people and
especially for the love and tender
care given to our parents in their
maturing years.*

CONTENTS

Preface

In the preface to the first edition of *Worship Old and New*, I wrote: "the primary value of the book is as a classroom text in seminary and college courses on worship. However, it should also be of interest to pastors, Christian education directors, worship committees, and laypersons who wish to be more informed on the subject."

In this second edition of *Worship Old and New*, I have resisted the temptation to write a simplistic and popular introduction to worship. Instead, I have maintained the scholarly flavor of the book and continue to see it as an academic introduction to the vast field of worship studies.

Since *Worship Old and New* was published eleven years ago, an enormous quantity of books covering every aspect of worship has emerged. Additionally, the fires of worship renewal have spread in every direction. I have interacted with this renewed interest in worship in this revised edition. While a good portion of the original text has been maintained, the entire work has undergone significant revision.

The material has been reorganized into four major divisions: The Biblical Foundations of Worship, A Biblical Theology of Worship, A Brief History of Worship, and The Practice of Worship.

The biblical portion of the book has been strengthened with the addition of a new chapter on the biblical themes of worship and with a more thorough chapter on Old Testament worship.

I have also reorganized the theological material and expanded the historical material to include a chapter on the renewal movements of the twentieth century.

The section on the practice of worship contains the most significant changes. Here, I have attempted to provide not only an academic understanding of worship but a perspective through the eyes of the worship leader and the worshipers.

I hope these improvements in *Worship Old and New* will make the work more useful for classroom study and a helpful guide for the practitioners of worship who wish to improve the worship of the local church.

Finally, I wish to add a word of thanks to my editor, Matthew Maloley, and to Dr. Richard Leonard, who offered many suggestions for the improvement of this second edition of *Worship Old and New*.

— Robert Webber

Chapter 1

Introduction

On a recent visit to San Francisco I had a Sunday open to visit the church of my choice. Looking in the yellow pages I found an advertisement for St. Gregory Nyssen Episcopal Church that asserted "we follow an early church model of worship with full congregational participation and involvement."

A visit to this church validated the advertisement. This church had a highly participatory and engaging style of worship. The congregation first gathered around a large table at the east end of the church. There we practiced the "Alleluias" we were to sing in the service. Worship then began with an entrance hymn and we all processed in a dance movement to the worship space for the service of the Word. After completing the entrance rites, we sat facing each other and listened to the Word of God read from a lectern flanked by African flags. After each Scripture reading a Tibetan gong was rung, and as its sound passed through the room, we meditated on the words we had heard. After the sermon, which was preached sitting down (an ancient custom), the congregation was invited to respond. One by one the people stood and responded. Some asked questions and received an answer. Others spoke of needs met or awakened. Still others spoke of how God had spoken to them through the sermon or how God was present in their struggles. After the service of the Word we processed with congregational dance back to the table. Standing around the table, we passed the peace of Christ, gave thanks over the bread and wine, partook, and then sang and danced around the table. Finally, a benediction was given and then bread, cheese, and fruit were brought to the table for all to eat and enjoy.

A similar experience occurred at Christ Church in Nashville, a large Pentecostal church that is moving toward what it believes to be the worship of the early church. Every Sunday morning this church celebrates a special Eucharist during the Sunday School hour for those wishing to participate. On the first Sunday of every month the entire congregation celebrates the Eucharist.

The service of the Eucharist began with spirited singing — hymns, choruses, psalms, and songs particular to the Pentecostal tradition. The singing was followed by a time of prayer during which we gathered in small circles, held hands, and prayed for each other. We then heard and responded to two Scripture readings that were followed by a brief sermon. Then the pastor called the people to gather around the table of the Lord. Again we sang and sang. The pastor led us through a confession of sin using the *Book of Common Prayer* and then asked if anyone present was in need of healing. Several people came and knelt for the anointing with oil and the laying on of hands by the pastor. The congregation then received the bread and wine while songs of resurrection and exaltation were sung. As we left, we greeted each other with the peace of Christ.

I have described two Christian traditions on opposite ends of the Protestant spectrum — one a liturgical church and the other a Pentecostal church. Yet both of them have moved from the particular style of their tradition to a new style, a style that has numerous common elements. This phenomenon, which is happening in nearly every denomination and all around the world, can be explained by three interrelated statements:

1) Churches of nearly every tradition are discovering the worship of the biblical and historical traditions.

2) Churches of nearly every denomination are discovering each other and are recognizing that elements of worship preserved in other traditions are relevant to today's worship.

3) What is happening is the convergence of worship traditions, a blending of worship old and new.[1]

WORSHIP OLD AND NEW

Currently, the worship of many local congregations stands at an uncertain crossroad. One of the major reasons for this uncertainty is the breakdown of distinct denominational worshiping styles. The interdenominational character of many denominations and the freedom of worship leaders to draw from the many styles of worship is changing the worship of many churches. For this reason, there seems to be a great deal of anxiety among pastors and other worship leaders. What kind of worship could possibly meet the changes that are taking place in the church?

There are three responses to this question. First, there are the traditionalists who want worship to be as it was. These are the people who resist change or are so deeply committed to a particular historical model of worship that talk of incorporating new styles of worship is intolerable. Second, there are those who wish to jettison traditional worship as irrelevant and go in search of a worship that is contemporary. Contemporary worship is difficult to pinpoint since there are so many forms of creative contemporary worship, ranging from the guitar mass to entertainment models of worship.

A third approach, which I support in this book, blends both the old and the new, a worship that respects the tradition yet seeks to incorporate worship styles formed by the contemporary church. I refer to this approach as worship old and new.

General Characteristics

Worship old and new first of all examines old questions about worship. The Reformational theme of *Semper Reformanda* (always reforming) is taken seriously. Ecumenical worship recently has questioned the essence of and reasons for worship; this book addresses these questions from the biblical, historical, theological, and social science perspectives.

Second, worship old and new learns from the entire worshiping community. Consequently, this book will look sympathetically at liturgical worship as well as the worship of the Reformers, the free church movement, and Pentecostals and charismatics. Worship old and new identifies what worshiping communities can learn from traditions other than their own.

Third, worship old and new has a healthy respect for the past. This work recognizes the way worship has remained faithful to its Jewish and early Christian roots, and how it has been adapted in various time periods and diversified cultures.

Finally, worship old and new is fully committed to contemporary relevance. Because worship is an act of communication between God and his people, worship must touch the lives of people, stimulate personal and spiritual formation, and bring healing to relationships.

Specific Characteristics

Worship old and new is committed to the Scriptures as the foundation for worship studies. Worship is not a human invention but a God-given gift. Consequently, research into the origins of worship in both the Old and New Testaments is not a matter of choice but of necessity. If God gifted the peoples of Israel and the early church with worship, then the Scriptures will relate principles and patterns of worship that will not only inform the church about worship but guide it in its concern to be faithful to the biblical tradition.

Worship old and new approaches the history of the church's worship with great respect. Throughout the history of the church, God's worshiping people have sought with varying degrees of success to give shape to a worship faithful to the biblical tradition. As a result of the work of the Holy Spirit throughout history, the church has been blessed by a great variety of worshiping styles. These styles are not mere artifacts of the past but a rich treasury of resources from which we can learn and even borrow for today's worship.

Worship old and new recognizes theology as a discipline that reflects on its experience, particularly the experience of worship. From a theological point of view worship constitutes the gospel in motion. Worship celebrates God's great acts of salvation. During worship God communicates to the worshipers his salvation and healing, to which the people respond with faith, praise, prayer, thanksgiving, and a life of service in the world.

Finally, worship old and new presents the practice of worship in its fullness — Sunday worship, the role of music and the arts, the services of the Christian year, the sacred actions of worship, and the ministries of worship.

The Practice of Worship Old and New

This section demonstrates how old and new can be blended into a joyful experience of worship. Consequently, the four acts of worship are presented: acts of entrance, the service of the Word, the service of the Eucharist, and the acts of dismissal. Leaders of convergence worship recognize that these four acts are characterized by a narrative quality, which tells and acts out the story of God's saving deeds. These acts also draw the worshiper into the experience of symbolizing a relationship to God through a joyful entrance that brings the worshiping community into God's presence, the reading and preaching of Scripture that speak to felt needs, a eucharistic response that celebrates Christ's healing presence at the table, and a mission-oriented dismissal that sends the people forth into the world to love and serve the Lord.

The practice of a worship old and new draws on a broad range of musical content and style. For example, the gathering may be characterized by friendly folk songs or contemporary choruses while the entrance hymn may be an ancient processional hymn accompanied by stringed and brass instruments, a joyful procession of people led by a dancer, and banners and flags that express the festive nature of coming before God. The responsorial psalm may be led by a cantor with the people responding with a compelling refrain. The communion songs may be a mixture of Taizé music and appropriate contemporary choruses.

A worship old and new also draws on the arts. In worship renewal today much attention is given to the artists and to the use of their artistic gifts. The power of visual symbol, congregational movement and physical participation, appropriate uses of drama, the recovery of the senses, and the engagement of the whole person in worship have all been rediscovered.

The practice of a worship old and new also calls for the recovery of the feasts of the Christian year. The services of the Christian year are not mere rituals but real feasts. They feature the great dramatic events of redemptive history in which God brings salvation to the people: Advent, Christmas, Epiphany, Lent,

Holy Week, Easter, and Pentecost. The recovery of the evangelical nature of these services holds the power to not only revitalize faith but to order the spirituality of the congregation.

The practice of worship old and new may be enriched by the sacred actions that bring us into the church, nourish us, sustain us, and bring healing into our lives. Today's renewal of worship boasts new insights into the meaning and practice of the sacraments and a rediscovery of how the evangelical practice of ordinances and sacraments renew faith.

CONCLUSION

The kind of worship presented in this book should be greeted as a challenge and not a threat. It builds on the best of the biblical, historical, and traditional elements of worship. It is concerned that worship be authentic and real and characterized by a sense of fullness, the feeling of deep joy, and the experience of comfort and healing.

It is, in a word, post-Enlightenment worship that is in tune with the dynamic faith of biblical Christianity and the changing cultural patterns of modern life. This is the kind of worship that will attract and hold people in the church and give direction to their confused lives.

For these reasons, convergence of worship old and new stands as a signpost at the uncertain crossroad of future worship. It says, "Here is a way to preserve the best of the past and to walk with confidence into the future."

---

1. The preceding material was adapted from Robert E. Webber, "The Future of Christian Worship," *Ex Auditu* 8 (1992): 113 – 14.

Inspiring examples of two churches on opposite ends which share common elements of worship.

3 interrelated themes on page 12.

3 possible respones on pp. 12-13

Semper reforandum = always reforming.

PART I

The Biblical Foundations of Worship

It is a strange and curious matter that so little has been presented in most worshiping communities about the biblical foundations of worship. While biblical students have labored over the Hebrew and Greek to interpret the Scriptures in their original language and historical setting, little attention has been paid to the language of worship in the Scriptures. While students of Scripture have examined the development of biblical thought concerning God's initiative in revelation and redemption, few have been interested in the response of the people in worship. While students have done theology and reflected on the character of God, the sinfulness of the human condition, and the rescuing work of Jesus Christ, little thought has been given to how all this theology is put into motion in the institution of worship. Consequently, students have graduated and become pastors who direct the attention of the congregation to Scripture but have little knowledge about how to lead that congregation in the worship of God.

But all of this is now changing. One of the most important topics on the lips of both pastor and people is worship. Congregations not only want to know how to worship better; they want to know what Scriptures teach about worship.

Part I addresses these questions and grounds contemporary worship in the Scripture. Chapter 2 presents biblical themes of worship that span the testaments, chapter 3 examines the worship of the Old Testament, chapter 4 discusses the worship of the New Testament church, and chapter 5 focuses upon the worship of the early church to A.D. 200.

Chapter 2

Biblical Themes in Worship

Worship is not something tangential to the Christian story but a matter that lies at the very heart of the Christian Scriptures from the beginning to the end.[1] The importance of worship is expressed as early as the story of Cain and Abel, who brought offerings to the Lord (Gen. 4:3–5), and as late as the book of Revelation, which not only depicts a heavenly scene of worship (Rev. 4–5) but is filled with songs of praise and images of worship. Between the pages of Genesis and Revelation the Scriptures portray a moving story, which depicts the themes of worship, of how God worked in human history to initiate a saving relationship with the people of the world.

God initiated a relationship with Abraham and Sarah; entered into a covenantal relationship with Israel at Mount Sinai; continually called wayward Israel back to relationship through the prophets; and culminated the great act of redemption in the life, death, and resurrection of Jesus Christ. And God called the church into being as the people of this saving event. God now requires the church to remember his saving deeds, to rehearse the covenant, and to live in total obedience to his will.

This story of God initiating a relationship and of the people responding in faith is not only the story of salvation and redemption, but it comprises the very essence of worship. What lies at the heart of worship is God's continual movement toward the peoples of the world and the continual response of the people of God in faith and obedience. This chapter explores the themes of this two-way relationship and shows how worship is inextricably interwoven with the theme of salvation.

THE EVENT ORIENTATION OF BIBLICAL WORSHIP

Although God initiated a relationship with Abraham and the patriarchs, and they responded with obedience and worship, the turning point of salvation history in the Old Testament is found in the great saving events of the Exodus. Here, what is true of the Old Testament is also true of the New Testament; an event stands at its center—the Christ event. These great acts of salvation point to the fundamental nature of biblical worship—the epicenter from which all the facets of worship proceed is an event. From that event a covenant is made with the people of God; central to the covenant is obedience to the Word of the Lord and the ratification of the covenant by sacrifice. Beyond this, at least in the Old Testament, the worship of God is to occur at a prescribed time and place with particular rituals. These are the themes we will examine in search of the biblical foundations of worship.[2]

The event orientation of worship in the Old Testament is clearly seen in the meeting that took place between God and his people after God had miraculously delivered them from the hands of the pharaoh.

The full context of this event, known as the Sinai event or the Exodus event, is described in chapters 19–24 of the book of Exodus. The most pertinent part of this event for worship is the public meeting that took place between God and Israel at the foot of Mount Sinai.

> Then he said to Moses, "Come up to the LORD, you and Aaron, Nadab and Abihu, and seventy of the elders of Israel. You are to worship at a distance, but Moses alone is to approach the LORD; the others must not come near. And the people may not come up with him."
> When Moses went and told the people all the LORD's words and laws, they responded with one voice, "Everything the LORD has said we will do." Moses then wrote down everything the Lord had said.
> He got up early the next morning and built an altar at the foot of the mountain and set up twelve stone pillars representing the twelve tribes of Israel. Then he sent young Israelite men, and they offered burnt offerings and sacrificed young bulls as fellowship offerings to the LORD. Moses took half of the blood and put it in bowls, and the other half he sprinkled on the altar. Then he took the Book of the Covenant and read it to the people. They responded, "We will do everything the LORD has said; we will obey."
> Moses then took the blood, sprinkled it on the people and said, "This is the blood of the covenant that the LORD has made with you in accordance with all these words."
>
> Exodus 24:1–8

This meeting between God and Israel is important because *it contains the most basic structural elements for a meeting between God and his people.* These elements, the very substance of public worship, are found later in the more detailed descriptions of Judaic and Christian worship.

First, the meeting was convened by God. It was God who called the people out of Egypt and brought them to Mount Sinai. God called the people to meet at the foot of the mountain where they became the *q'hal Yahweh*, the "assembly of God." In this is seen the prerequisite of true worship—a call from God to worship.

Second, the people were arranged in a structure of responsibility. Although the role of leadership was given to Moses, other parts of the drama were to be played by Aaron, Nadab, Abihu, the seventy elders of Israel, the young Israelite men, and the people. The picture is not that of leaders and an audience but of full participation of those congregated. Each had his or her own part to play. The full orchestration brought every person together in a harmonious whole. This points to *participation* as a fundamental aspect of worship.

Third, the meeting between God and Israel was characterized by the *proclamation of the Word*. God spoke to the people and made his will known to them, thus showing that worship is not complete without hearing from the Lord.

Fourth, the people accepted the conditions of the covenant, thus signifying a subjective commitment to hear and to obey the Word. An essential aspect of worship in both the Judaic and Christian traditions is the *continuous renewal of personal commitment*. In worship, the community renews their covenant with God.

Finally, the meeting was climaxed by a *dramatic symbol* of ratification, a sealing of the agreement. In the Old Testament, God always used a blood sacrifice to demonstrate the sealing of a relationship with people. These sacrifices pointed to the definitive sacrifice of Jesus Christ. After his sacrifice, the Lord's Supper became the sign of the relationship between the church and God.[3]

While the New Testament does not contain a comparable description of God's convening a public meeting with the church, it is clear that the New Testament writers see the connection between the Exodus event and the Christ event. Peter summarizes the comparison in these words:

> But you are a chosen people, a royal priesthood, a holy nation, a people belonging to God, that you may declare the praises of him who called you out of darkness into his wonderful light.
>
> 1 Peter 2:9

Absolutely fundamental to Christian worship is the praise of God, "who called you out of darkness into his wonderful light." The Exodus event stood at the center of Israelite worship. As Israel was in bondage to Pharaoh, so all people are in bondage to the power of evil (Eph. 2:2). As God sent Moses to deliver Israel from its bondage, so God sent Jesus to deliver us from our bondage to sin (Matt. 1:21). As God entered into a covenant with Israel, so God enters into covenant with the church (Heb. 8:8–12). As God established a tabernacle for worship with a high priest, so also God has established a new high priest and an entrance into the Holy of Holies through Jesus Christ (Heb. 9:11–14). As the tabernacle was characterized by sacrifices, so also the new covenant with the church is characterized by the once-for-all sacrifice of Jesus Christ (Heb. 10:15–18). As Israel looked forward to the Promised Land, so the church looks forward to the new heavens and the new earth (Rev. 21–22). Consequently, Peter confesses with confidence,

> Once you were not a people, but now you are the people of God; once
> you had not received mercy, but now you have received mercy.
>
> 1 Peter 2:10

God's people are the people of a saving event. And it is this event, and all that it represents, that lies at the heart of biblical worship.

THE COVENANTAL NATURE OF BIBLICAL WORSHIP

At the heart of the relationship between God and Israel expressed in the public meeting at Mount Sinai was the *covenant.* The covenant was an agreement or treaty between God and his people Israel. Frequently, the terms of this relationship were expressed in shortened form in a brief formula, such as, "I will be their God, and they will be my people" (see Jer. 31:33; cf. Gen. 17:7; Lev. 26:12; Deut. 29:10–13; Ezek. 37:27, etc.). These simple, straightforward words expressed the agreement: The Lord agreed to be the God of Israel, and Israel agreed to worship and obey the Lord.

God's covenant with Israel was similar to treaties that ancient emperors sometimes made with the client kings and officials who governed parts of their empire. In these treaties, the emperor or "great king" identified himself as the one who had granted a favored position to his treaty partner or "servant." In return for complete loyalty, the king promised to protect the servant. He also laid down stipulations by which the relationship would be maintained. For example, the servant had to treat as brothers all others who were in covenant with his ruler, and he had to appear before the great king at specific times to bring tribute.

These treaties included acts by which the agreement was ratified, such as the servant's solemn oath of loyalty to the great king, or a sacrifice. The agreement often concluded with the promise of benefits that would come to the servant if he kept its terms, such as prosperity and peace for his region. Conversely, various curses would take effect if the servant violated the great king's commandments, such as drought, famine, and disease.

Treaties of this type were probably well known to the ancient Israelites because they were part of their cultural background. To make clear what kind of relationship he was establishing with them, God seems to have included many features of these treaties in his covenant with Israel on Mount Sinai. He began by identifying himself as the one who had shown favor to his people: "I am the LORD your God, who brought you out of Egypt, out of the land of slavery." He then demanded their complete loyalty: "You shall have no other gods before me" (Ex. 20:1–2).

God then set forth the terms of the agreement—the Ten Commandments and other stipulations of the Book of the Covenant. As we have seen, the covenant was sealed by an act of sacrificial worship in which all the people participated. In other parts of the books of Moses we find recitals of the blessings that would come from faithfulness to the covenant (Lev. 26:1–13; Deut. 28:1–14) and the curses that would take effect if the servant people disobeyed their King (Lev. 26:14–39; Deut. 28:15–68). Finally, God gave specific instructions for worship as part of his covenant, not only in the directions for constructing tabernacle and consecrating the priesthood (Ex. 25–31), but also in the detailed description of sacrifices and offerings in the following chapters of Exodus and Leviticus. Through sacrificial worship on specified occasions, God's people were to offer their tribute to their Great King.

In this way the covenantal nature of worship was laid down in the establishment of the covenant itself. Through worship, Israel was to maintain its identity as the people of God, for it was in worship that Israel continually recalled and celebrated its relationship to their God. Through this worship, Israel was also to offer its tribute as the loyal servant of the Great King. The story of the events on Mount Sinai is the basic narrative of the covenant worship ceremony, but the covenantal basis of worship is clear throughout the Old Testament. It was affirmed in the words of the prophets of Israel, who repeatedly announced God's judgment on a people whose worship had turned false because of their neglect of the covenant. And it is seen clearly in the Psalms, in which worshipers proclaim the majesty of the Great King, offer the tribute of their praise, and affirm their loyalty to God as his trusting servants. Through worship based on the covenant, Israel was to reflect the glory of God to the nations.

Thus the covenantal nature of worship continued to be seen throughout Israel's history. Whenever the Israelites lapsed into sin and apostasy, they forgot their covenant and their worship was lost, ritualized, or corrupted by pagan influences. But, whenever there was a renewal of Israel's relationship to God, the restoration of the covenant and of the true worship of God went hand in hand. Examples of this principle include the covenant renewal under Joshua (Josh. 23:1–16); David's reforms based on his consultation with the Book of the Covenant (1 Chron. 15:11–16:43); the renewal movements under Solomon (1 Kings 8:1–9:9), Hezekiah (2 Chron. 29:1–31:1), and Josiah (2 Chron. 34:14–35:19); and the rediscovery of Deuteronomy under Ezra the priest and

Nehemiah the governor when the remnant of Israel returned to Jerusalem from its captivity in Babylon (Ezra 9:1–10:17; Neh. 12:27–13:31).

The covenantal theme of the Old Testament is continued in the New Testament. Just as God entered into covenant with Israel, so also God entered into covenant with the church. While the covenant stipulations with the church are similar to the covenant stipulations with Israel ("I will be your God and you will be my people"), there is a difference. The difference is Jesus Christ. Israel was not able to keep the covenant. Israel fell away from the agreements again and again. But in the new covenant, Jesus Christ does for Israel and for the church—for us and for everyone—what we cannot do for ourselves. He keeps the agreement. He fulfills the covenant. And in his absolute obedience, death, and resurrection, he establishes for us and for all people an eternal relationship with God. Nowhere is this truth more clearly expressed than in the book of Hebrews (see especially chap. 8).[4]

So, biblical worship is rooted in an event and based on a covenant. And as one examines the covenant, it becomes clear that the covenant has two central foci: obedience to the Book of the Covenant and ratification of the covenant through an act of sacrifice.

Obedience to the Book of the Covenant

The Book of the Covenant may be identified with the Ten Commandments and the regulations for obedience found in Exodus 20–23 as well as the later laws of Leviticus. What was central to the covenant was the agreement that the Israelites live by the book, an agreement they made with God in the public meeting that took place at Mount Sinai.

Before the actual meeting between Israel and God occurred at the foot of the mountain, the text informs us that "When Moses went and told the people all the LORD's words and laws, they responded with one voice, 'Everything the LORD has said we will do'" (Ex. 24:3). Then again in the context of the meeting itself, Moses "took the Book of the Covenant and read it to the people. They responded, 'We will do everything the LORD has said; we will obey'" (Ex. 24:7).

This Book of the Covenant containing the laws and regulations for Israel was pivotal throughout Israel's history of worship. A place of particular prominence was given to it in the renewal under Ezra the priest and Nehemiah the governor after the people returned from their Babylonian captivity to rebuild Jerusalem. The reading of the Book of the Covenant was the central act of worship. The reading of God's Word struck at the hearts of the people so that they were "weeping as they listened to the words of the Law" (Neh. 8:9).

Like the Israelites, Christians have always regarded the Scriptures highly and given the Word of God a place of supreme importance in worship. Paul wrote to Timothy that "all Scripture is God-breathed and is useful for teaching, rebuking, correcting and training in righteousness, so that the man of God may be thoroughly equipped for every good work" (2 Tim. 3:16–17). Early Christians "devoted themselves to the apostles' teaching" to hear the Word of the Lord and to live in obedience to God's word (Acts 2:42). Throughout the history of the church the reading and preaching of Scripture has always been central to Christian worship.

So, biblical worship is rooted in an event, established in a covenant, and characterized by the centrality of God's Word and the ratification of the covenant by a sacrifice.

The Sacrificial Nature of Biblical Worship

In the Scriptures, covenants between God and his people were always secured with a sacrifice (see, for example, Noah [Gen. 8:20–9:17], Abram [Gen. 15:9–21], Isaac [Gen. 26:24–25], and Jacob [Gen. 31:43–55, 35:6–12]). The covenant made with Israel was no exception. Exodus 24:5–6 says "they offered burnt offerings and sacrificed young bulls as fellowship offerings to the LORD. Moses took half of the blood and put it in bowls, and the other half he sprinkled on the altar."

In the sacrifices of the tabernacle God gave the Israelites acts that symbolized their approach to God. A fundamental sign of relationship with God was expressed in the sacrifices of the tabernacle and in the very setting of time, space, and ritual in which these sacrifices were accomplished.

A central feature of the entire sacrificial system was the notion of atonement, expressed particularly in the sacrifices on the day of atonement. On this day, once a year, the high priest entered into the Holy of Holies carrying the blood of the sacrifice, which was sprinkled on the lid of the ark to make atonement for the entire nation (Lev. 16:1–34). In this act the sacrificial animal was understood to be a substitution for the people of the nation. This blood atoned for Israel's sins symbolically. Although the sin of Israel remained, it had been covered by the blood of the sacrifice, so that God no longer looked upon it.

Just as the concept of sacrifice was central to the worship of Israel, so the concept of sacrifice is central to the worship of the church. Hebrews clearly sets forth the sacrificial nature of the work of Jesus Christ (see especially chap. 9). Jesus Christ is the new propitiation (Rom. 3:25). He stands between God and the covenant people. His sacrifice is for them. He is their covering, their atonement. While sacrifice is now unnecessary in Christian worship, the Lord's Supper was given as a perpetual sign of the culminating sacrifice of Christ and of his victory over the powers of evil.[5]

Finally, biblical worship that is rooted in an event, expressed in a covenant, characterized by a book, and ratified by sacrifice is to occur at specific times and places.

THE APPOINTED TIMES AND PLACES
OF BIBLICAL WORSHIP

God not only instituted worship as a central feature of the covenant, but he set aside one day of the week as a day of worship and rest.

> The Israelites are to observe the Sabbath, celebrating it for generations to come as a lasting covenant. It will be a sign between me and the Israelites forever, for in six days the LORD made the heavens and the earth, and on the seventh day he abstained from work and rested.
>
> Exodus 31:16–17

While the Sabbath is a day to remember God's act of creation, it is also a day to remember God's work of redemption in delivering Israel from Egypt (Deut. 5:15).

As Israel moved through history, various festivals were also established to remember God's great acts of salvation and goodness. Chief among these festivals was the Passover, which signified the passing over of the houses of Israel when the firstborn sons of the Egyptians were slain and the subsequent delivery of the people of Israel from the hands of Pharaoh took place (Ex. 12).

In addition to the times appointed for worship, God also established a specific place for worship—first the mobile tabernacle and then the temple. While Israelites could worship God in their hearts anywhere and anytime, specific gatherings for public worship occurred at a particular time and place.

In the New Testament, the church assembled for worship on the Jewish Sabbath (cf. Acts 17:1–2; 18:4). But sometime in the first century the church designated the first day of the week to remember the resurrection of the Lord. The *Didache* or *Teaching of the Twelve Apostles*, a noncanonical document dated as early as A.D. 50 by some scholars and generally regarded as no later than the early second century, directs that the church "on every Lord's Day—his special day—come together and break bread and give thanks."[6] This day, mentioned in Revelation 1:10, is a distinctly Christian institution, the day on which God's great act of salvation is remembered.

The church also has established feast days to remember God's saving deeds. The worship of the Christian year, with feasts celebrating the birth of Christ (Advent, Christmas, and Epiphany) and feasts recalling the death and resurrection of Christ (Lent, Holy Week, Easter, and Pentecost) stands in the biblical tradition of marking time by God's saving events.

While Christians have marked time by the saving events, they have also built places of worship where God's saving events are remembered. While Christians have created these appointed times and places for worship, they have done so more out of inference from God's relationship with Israel than out of divine injunction given to the church.

Thus far in chapter 2 we have surveyed the origins of biblical worship from God's perspective. What we have seen is that God always initiates a relationship with humanity. This principle is profoundly expressed in the saving events of the Exodus and in the life, death, and resurrection of Christ. Through events God established a covenantal relationship with Israel and then with the church. Worship in the covenantal relationship is characterized by a willingness to be obedient to the Book of the Covenant and a commitment ratified in a sacrifice. The worship of Israel was to take place at a particular time and a particular place with particular rituals. While Christians have no prescribed time or place, they do have the ritual of the Lord's Supper, they have adopted the first day of the week to celebrate the death and resurrection, and they have established places of worship.

THE RESPONSE OF THE PEOPLE

While the first fundamental theme of salvation history and of worship is that God initiates a relationship, the second is that the people of God must respond to God's initiative. God speaks and acts and the people respond.

These responses are done in public worship through institutions of worship such as the tabernacle, the temple, the synagogue, and the church. Worship in and through these institutions proclaims, recalls, and enacts the great saving deeds of God. And, the people respond by remembering, anticipating, celebrating, and serving.

The People Remember

The theme of remembering (*anamnesis*) is central to biblical worship. The people of God remember his saving deeds by telling and acting out the story of redemption.[7]

This rationale of worship was expressed by Moses in a dialogue with God. The people wanted to know how to tell their children about all the laws that they had. The answer God gave Moses, and the answer that Moses handed down to the people, was to tell them the story of redemption. God instructed Moses to tell the children the following story:

> We were slaves of Pharaoh in Egypt, but the LORD brought us out of Egypt with a mighty hand. Before our eyes the LORD sent miraculous signs and wonders—great and terrible—upon Egypt and Pharaoh and his whole household. But he brought us out from there to bring us in and give us the land that he promised on oath to our forefathers. The LORD commanded us to obey all these decrees and to fear the LORD our God, so that we might always prosper and be kept alive, as is the case today. And if we are careful to obey all this law before the LORD our God, as he has commanded us, that will be our righteousness.
>
> Deuteronomy 6:21–25

This concept of remembering God's saving deeds, which was fundamental to Old Testament worship, is equally fundamental to New Testament worship. Preaching as in the kerygma tells the story of redemption (see Acts 2:22–36), and the Lord's Supper is an act that the church does in remembrance (1 Cor. 11:24). But biblical worship not only remembers, it anticipates.

The People of God Anticipate

Biblical religion is not only a religion of historical events, which it remembers in worship, it is also a religion of promise. The promise is first found in the covenant with Abram and then in all succeeding covenants. The promise was the land. For the Lord appeared to Abram and said, "To your offspring I will give this land" (Gen. 12:7). When Israel was called out of bondage in Egypt, it was to possess the land. For as God said to Moses, "I will bring you to the land I swore with uplifted hand to give to Abraham, to Isaac and to Jacob. I will give it to you as a possession. I am the LORD" (Ex. 6:8).

Christians have always seen the promise of the land in the Old Testament as a type of the promise of the new heavens and the new earth, the kingdom of God. Baptism is an initiation into the new kingdom, the church is a type of the kingdom on earth, and the Eucharist is a continual renewal of the initial foretaste of God's kingdom.

Worship is not only grounded in past redemptive events but in an anticipation of what is to come. Consequently, God's people gather to remember his saving events and anticipate his ultimate salvation in the new heavens and the new earth. One may speak of this kind of worship as a celebration.

The People Celebrate

The concept of celebration is implicit in the idea of remembrance. A true celebration, whether it be of a birthday, anniversary, or a national event, has three main characteristics. A celebration remembers a past event. A celebration makes the past event contemporaneous. Past events are remembered and celebrated through story, song, drama, and feasting.

The Old Testament worship festivals were celebrations. They remembered the past, made the past contemporaneous, and they were characterized by story, song, drama, and feasting. For example, the Passover actually recalled and relived the immediate moments of preparation in the home as the family prepared itself to escape from Egypt.

Both the Jewish Passover and the Christian Eucharist are great dramas of God's saving deeds. They are not mere rituals to be repeated in a bland sort of way, but the epicenter of faith and worship, which the people of God celebrate through sacred acts of recollection and remembrance.

But these great acts of salvation cannot be remembered apart from the symbols that bespeak them.

THE PEOPLE OF GOD WORSHIP THROUGH SIGN-ACTS

Biblical worship involves numerous signs and symbols that proclaim and enact the original saving event and thus act as "presence carriers" of God's saving action.

These sacred actions of worship were clearly visible in the Old Testament tabernacle, temple, and festivals, with their concept of sacred space, sacred ritual, and sacred ministry. While these sacred actions are less obvious in the New Testament, they are clearly implied in the rituals of baptism and Eucharist.

Through these sacred actions God both speaks and acts and brings the power of the saving event to the worshiping community. The worshipers then respond in faith, remembering and celebrating God's saving deeds through these sacred actions. Consequently, the sacred actions become the meeting point for God's saving presence and the worshipers response of praise and thanksgiving.

The People of God Worship from the Heart

Public worship in the Scripture is always defined by the visible and tangible characteristics mentioned above—the people assemble to remember, anticipate, and celebrate through particular acts of worship. But the Scripture goes deeper than the outward acts of worship and prescribes the inner, heartfelt response of the people of God. God wants more than ritual. God wants the worship of the inner person.

The people of God are to remember God's deeds of salvation and his promise of the land by being grateful and by committing their lives. And they are to come before him with a particular attitude of homage and reverence in the presence of their King. This aspect of worship is expressed by some of the biblical words for worship.[8]

The Hebrew word most commonly translated as "worship" is the verb *shachah*, in what grammarians call the reflexive form. This verb means "to bow down" or "to prostrate oneself." It denotes the gesture of a subject's bowing down to a ruler or master. It points to both an inner and an outer homage to God as a token of awe and surrender. When Abraham's servant found a wife for Isaac, for example, he "bowed down and worshiped the LORD, saying, 'Praise be to the LORD'" (Gen. 24:26–27). His worship was a heartfelt thanksgiving in response to God's provision. This is the attitude God desires in response to his acts of salvation. The psalmist declares, "All the earth bows down to you" (Ps. 66:4), using the same verb.

The corresponding Greek word is *proskuneo*. Matthew used this verb when he told how the Magi from the east, when they found the infant Jesus in Bethlehem, "bowed down and worshiped him" (Matt. 2:11). John used the same word in recording Jesus' statement to the Samaritan woman about true spiritual worship (John 4:21–24).

Another Hebrew word signifying worship is *'avad*, which literally means "to serve." When God called Moses to lead the people of Israel out of their slavery to the Egyptian pharaoh, it was for the purpose of worshiping: "When you have brought the people out of Egypt, you will worship God on this mountain" (Ex. 3:12). This same word is used in the familiar invitation to "worship the LORD with gladness." What the psalmist meant in this context is explained by the following phrase, "come before him with joyful songs" (Ps. 100:2). The concept of worship as service implies a total lifestyle in allegiance to God (Deut. 10:12–13). This idea is captured by the corresponding Greek verb *latreuo* (cf. Acts 24:14). Paul used the noun form, *latreia* "service") when he urged the Roman Christians to offer themselves in "spiritual ... worship" (Rom. 12:1). Such worship demanded the service of God with all of one's heart and soul. Worship is, therefore, not only an inner heartfelt response of thanksgiving; it also indicates a life totally committed to serving God.

Another verb often used for worship is the Hebrew *yare'*; its New Testament Greek equivalent is *phobeomai*. These verbs denote the awe and respect with which God's people approach him. To fear God and to have reverence and respect for him is to obey his voice (1 Sam. 12:14), to walk in his ways (Deut. 8:6), to keep his commandments (Eccl. 12:13), and to turn away from evil (Job 1:1; Prov. 3:7). The early church was characterized by a corporate lifestyle of "living in the fear of the Lord" (Acts 9:31). Gentiles who worshiped in the synagogue and who responded readily when the apostles proclaimed Jesus as the Messiah are called "God-fearers" (*phoboumenoi*) (Acts 13:16). To fear God is to worship him and give him glory (Rev. 14:7).

Finally, an important Hebrew word associated with worship is *hodah*, "to give thanks." Several times the Psalms invite us to "give thanks to the LORD, for he is good" (Ps. 136:1). This word conveyed more than what we understand by gratitude. It meant "to make confession," in the sense of affirming the Lord as God. For biblical worshipers, giving thanks was directly related to covenantal worship, Israel's pledge of loyalty to the Great King. The comparable Greek word is *exomologeo*, the verb used by Paul when he declared "that at the name of Jesus every knee should bow ... and every tongue confess that Jesus Christ is Lord, to the glory of God the Father" (Phil. 2:10–11). Paul's image is a powerful picture of the purpose of Christian worship.

Conclusion

In this chapter we have seen that worship in the biblical tradition is oriented around two primary foci. The first is the initiative taken by God to bring salvation to fallen creatures. The second is the response of the people toward God.

The epicenter for worship with Israel was the central saving event of the Exodus, and with the church it is the life, death, and resurrection of Christ. Through these events God offers a covenant, an agreement with binding stipulations and ritual acts of worship, which under the old covenant occurred at appointed times and places through specific sacred acts. Also, worship is the response of the people to God's saving initiative. Through prescribed acts the people remember the past saving event; and through commemorative time and ritual acts the power of this saving event is communicated again and again. The inner person receives God's acts of salvation communicated in public worship with humility and in reverence and demonstrates his or her continued response to God in a life of service and devotion.

These are the basic biblical themes of worship which are expressed in both the Old and New Testaments. And it is to the study of these themes that we turn in chapters 3–5.

---

[1] See E. H. Van Olst, *The Bible and the Liturgy* (Grand Rapids: Eerdmans, 1991), especially chapter 1.

[2] For an excellent presentation of the themes of biblical worship see David Peterson, *Engaging With God: A Biblical Theology of Worship* (Grand Rapids: Eerdmans, 1992).

[3] See Conrad Antonsen, "Jewish Sources of Christian Worship," *Modern Liturgy* 3, no. 4 (April, 1976): 4–6.

[4] See Janice Leonard "The Concept of the Covenant in Biblical Worship," *The Biblical Foundations of Worship* (Nashville: Abbot Martyn, 1993), 56–65.

[5] See Peterson, *Engaging With God*, 36–42.

[6] *The Didache*, 14. See Cybil Richardson, *Early Christian Fathers* (Philadelphia: Westminster, 1953), 178.

[7] For a discussion of remembrance see Van Olst, *The Bible and the Liturgy*, 15–20.

[8] See Peterson, *Engaging With God*, 55–74, and Richard Leonard, "The Old Testament Vocabulary of Worship," *The Biblical Foundations of Worship* (Nashville: Abbott Martyn, 1993), 3–9.

Chapter 3

Old Testament Worship

In chapter 2 we saw that Old Testament worship was grounded in the Exodus event, the event that shaped the entire religious life of Israel. Through this event God brought the children of Israel out of their slavery to the Egyptian pharaoh and entered into a covenantal relationship with them, making them the servants of God. Central to their service of God was worship.

God gave worship to Israel as the means to express its relationship to God. This worship included a sacred enclosure (the tabernacle, and later the temple) with its sacrifice and ritual and a sacred priesthood. Israel's worship also entailed a number of festivals. Later, after the Exile, the people began to worship in synagogues. This chapter looks at these institutions of worship, but does not seek to develop the history of Israel's worship, a subject beyond the scope of this work.[1]

SACRED SPACE, SACRED RITUALS, AND SACRED MINISTRY

In Exodus 25–31 God gave Israel explicit instructions regarding the building of the tabernacle. The primary purpose of the tabernacle was to provide God with a place to dwell in the midst of Israel (Ex. 25:8). Unlike the pagan nations that had an image or idol of their god, the God of Israel was actually present among his people. Within the tabernacle, in the Holy of Holies, the ark that contained the Book of the Covenant was positioned. The ark containing God's Words was a powerful expression not only of God's presence with Israel, but of God's kingly rule over Israel (Ex. 25:10–22; Deut. 10:1–5). So intense was God's presence with the ark that God was described as one "enthroned between the cherubim" of the ark (2 Sam. 6:2; 1 Kings 19:15; Ps. 80:1).[2]

The tabernacle was to stand at the very center of the camp of Israel as a continuing symbol not only of God's presence but of God's kingly rule over the people. Whenever Israel moved, the tabernacle was moved with them and was always kept at center stage.

Worship in the tabernacle set the Israelites apart from the pagans and accentuated their relationship to God (Deut. 12). It also symbolized Israel's relationship to God through sacred space, sacred rituals, and a sacred ministry. Israel knew of God's glory and holiness, and they knew that they could only approach God on his terms. Here, through the space, rituals, and ministry of the tabernacle, Israel had a clearly defined way to approach the Holy One and live in the presence of God.

The tabernacle employed much symbolism in its use of space. The arrangement of the outer court, the inner court, and the Holy of Holies communicates the distance between the worshiper and God, who dwells in the Holy of Holies. All of the pieces of furniture such as the altar, the laver, the golden lampstands, the table with the bread of the Presence, the altar of incense, and the ark were laden with symbolic meaning as they depicted an encounter with God. Nothing in the temple furniture or layout was randomly selected or haphazardly placed.

Furthermore, a number of sacred rituals took place in the tabernacle. General rules governed the offering of a sacrifice: presentation of the victim, placing hands on the victim, slaying the victim, sprinkling the blood, and burning the sacrifice. Sacrifices such as the burnt offering (the daily offering of a lamb was entirely consumed to indicate complete consecration to God), the fellowship offering (a voluntary offering symbolizing communion and fellowship between persons and God), the sin offering (offered for sins of omission among other things), and the trespass offering (offered for sins of commission) were offered at various times. The important feature of these sacrifices was that they were visible signs that expressed the relationship between God and his people. They grew out of the act of ratification at Sinai, and they anticipated the sacrifice of Christ (Heb. 10).

Worship in the tabernacle necessitated a sacred ministry. Ministers of the sacred ritual represented the entire nation. They were the mediators between Israel and God. Not just anyone could be a priest, only the Levities. They were called by God and consecrated to his service in an elaborate ceremony (Ex. 29). They wore garments fitting to their service (Ex. 28; 39:1–31) and were given stringent requirements for holy living (Lev. 21–22:6).

Here in the tabernacle the glory of God dwelt with the people of Israel. John captured this theme when he wrote, "The Word became flesh and made his dwelling [tabernacled] among us. We have seen his glory, the glory of the one and only Son, who came from the Father, full of truth" (John 1:14). In the life of Jesus the glory of God that was present in the tabernacle became enfleshed and participated in humanity.

WORSHIP DURING DAVID'S TIME

When Israel entered into the land and settled, it was inevitable that a center for worship would be established. When David became the king over Israel and brought the ark into Jerusalem, Jerusalem became the center of Israel's life and worship.

The history of the temple is the chief concern of 1 and 2 Kings. The temple differed from the tabernacle only in its size and magnificence. Like the tabernacle, the temple continued to represent God's rule over Israel; stood as a continued reminder of God's presence; and continued to represent Israel's approach to God through sacred space, sacred rituals, and sacred ministry.

The New Testament describes how Jesus Christ supersedes the temple cult (Mark 14:58; 15:38; John 2:19–21), and how the church (his body) becomes the new dwelling place (temple) of God (1 Cor. 3:16–17; 6:19; 2 Cor. 6:16; Eph. 2:21–22). The sense that *there is a physical side to spiritual life and activity*, a sense that came from the temple, continued in New Testament worship. Early Christians rejected the nonphysical spirituality of the Gnostics and continued to express their spirituality through physical means. For that reason the sense of sacred place (church buildings), sacred rituals (the Eucharist), and sacred ministers (ordained persons) all stand in the tradition of temple worship.

Since the temple was not completed until Solomon's reign, David needed a place of worship. In Zion, David erected a tent for worship, a tent that is sometimes called David's tabernacle. The worship in David's tabernacle differed substantially from the worship in Moses' tabernacle. In David's tent there were no animal sacrifices. Levites led the people day and night in praising the Lord through song, musical instruments, and dance (1 Chron. 16:4). Even musical prophecy, both vocal and instrumental, was a feature of Davidic worship (1 Chron. 25:1).

Worship in the tabernacle of David may be seen as a type of the worship of the church. Here was a model of the people of God entering into God's gates with thanksgiving and offering their sacrifices of praise and thanksgiving night and day (Heb. 13:15).[3]

THE FESTIVALS

Davidic worship clearly demonstrated that Israel's worship involved more than the sacrificial system. It also illustrated the freedom, joy, and celebrative nature of nonsacrificial worship. These same themes of celebration and joy are expressed in the festivals of Israel.[4]

The most recurring of the festivals was the Sabbath, which was instituted as a special sign of God's relationship with Israel (Ex. 31:2–17). The Sabbath not only entailed a weekly celebration but a full year of rest for the land every seventh year (Lev. 25:1–7). That praise, thanksgiving, and celebration stood at the very heart of Israel's religion was demonstrated not only by the Sabbath but by the cycle of joyous feasts celebrated throughout the year.

The Israelites struggled to keep their religion undefiled by the influences of their pagan neighbors and their religion. A feature of paganism was the religious relation it sustained with nature. Consequently, Israel established nature festivals that acknowledged God's hand in the seasons of nature and in the fruitfulness of the earth. In these festivals, the people were able to celebrate God's goodness with sacrifices and feasting. The three nature festivals were the "Barley Harvest," celebrated with Passover and the seven days of Unleavened Bread (Ex. 12:6; Lev. 23:5–8; Num. 28:16–25; Deut. 16:1–18); the "Wheat Harvest," celebrated by the Feast of Weeks, also known as Pentecost (Ex. 34:26; Lev. 23:10–14; Num. 28:26–31); and the "General Yearly Harvest Festival" celebrated with the Feast of Tabernacles (Ex. 23:16; Lev. 23:33–36; Deut. 16:13–15).

These feasts were deep expressions of joy offered to God for his continual preservation and nourishment. Through these feasts the Israelites professed God's ownership of the fruits of the earth and their dependence upon him. Therefore, Israel did not receive the gifts of the earth through any right of its own but only as a divine gift. Consequently, when the people offered to the Lord part of their harvest and shared the harvest with others, they were fulfilling the command to love and obey God (Deut. 6:5).

Of the three major festivals—Passover, Pentecost, and Tabernacles—two played a major role in the worship of the early church. Jesus introduced the Lord's Supper during the celebration of the Passover. This not only put emphasis on Jesus as the Passover Lamb (1 Cor. 5:7), but it also established the Lord's Supper as the central rite of the new covenant. Pentecost (literally "fifty") concluded the cycle of time that began at Passover. It was a feast of joy and thanksgiving for the completion of the harvest season. People came from all over to Jerusalem to celebrate. After the coming of the Holy Spirit (see Acts 1–2), Christians looked to Pentecost as the birth of the church.

THE SYNAGOGUE

The synagogue (literally "gathering place" or "place of assembly") originated as a result of the destruction of Jerusalem and the temple and the subsequent dispersion of the Jewish people during the Exile. A motivating concern was the preservation and propagation of the Word of the Lord in the context of the Jewish community. Thus the synagogue became the religious, educational, and social center of Jewish life. Through it the traditions of ancient Israelite religion were preserved and passed down from generation to generation.

Worship in the synagogue differed greatly from temple worship. It had no sacred rituals and did not support a sacred ministry. Its focus was on reading and understanding the Word of God.[5]

Synagogue worship consisted of an affirmation of faith, prayer, and the reading of the Scriptures. The affirmation of faith was expressed in the *shema* (Deut. 6:4–9). The Shema proclaims the unity of God and sets forth the primary duty of the children of Israel to "love the LORD your God with all your heart and with all your soul and with all your strength" (v. 5).

Synagogue worship also stressed prayer. The *tefillah*, a series of prayers divided into three sets, was recited in a standing posture. The first set was a series of three prayers concentrating on the praise of God by paying homage to him as the God of Abraham, Isaac, and Jacob and revering him as the one "who nourishes the living, quickens the dead, and is the Holy One of Israel."[6] The next series contained thirteen "congregational petitions for such matters as wisdom and understanding, forgiveness of sins, restoration of Israel, good health and sustenance." Specifically, the prayers addressed repentance; forgiveness of sins; the ability to study the Torah; and the deliverance from misfortunes such as persecution, famine, and sickness. They also mentioned the coming of the Messiah and asked for God's acceptance of the prayers of Israel. The three concluding prayers of the final series expressed personal thanksgiving to God and desires for peace.

The third element of synagogue worship was the study of the Torah.[7] A thoroughgoing reverence was given to the Scriptures because they embodied the traditions of ancient Israel. A primary duty of every Jew was to study the Torah and to pass on its teachings to the next generation. "Impress them on your children. Talk about them when you sit at home and when you walk along the road, when you lie down and when you get up" (Deut. 6:7). This notion that a common people could understand and learn the tradition was a revolutionary concept. In other religions the tradition was secret, known only to the priestly class. But in the religion of Israel the tradition of the people and their relationship with God were to be known and taught by all.

The reading of the Torah was followed by a sermon (see Luke 4:16–30). Usually the reading of the Torah was accompanied by a translation. The translation was necessary because many people spoke only the language of the culture in which they resided. Here is a tenth-century description of the reading that had remained unchanged for centuries:

The one called to the Torah reads and another translates, verse by verse . . . and a third person stands between the reader and the translator, and to prompt them before they read or translate . . . If there is one who does not know how to read well, or is shy, then the third one helps him. But if he doesn't know at all how to read, he may not be called to read or to translate. . . And if the reader erred, the translator may not correct him. Similarly if the translator erred, the reader may not correct him. Only the third one may correct the reading or the translating.[8]

The sermon interpreted and applied the Scripture reading to the daily life of the people. It was known as the *derashah*, an act of "searching" in the Torah for its teachings. The preacher was called the *darshan*, or the one who "searched." The objective of the preachers was moral and theological instruction. They offered the people comfort and hope as they taught the doctrines and laws by which the people were to live.[9]

The influence of the synagogue on early Christian worship was remarkable. The whole sense of affirming faith, of offering prayer for specific concerns, and reading and preaching from the sacred writings was easily transferred from the synagogue to the Christian assembly, as Christians began to form their own separate worshiping communities.

CONCLUSION

The biblical themes of worship developed in chapter 2 are clearly seen in the worship of the Old Testament. God continued to initiate a relationship with Israel based on the Exodus event through the worship of the tabernacle and later the temple. The sacrifices in these institutions of worship as well as the festivals of Israel and later the worship of the synagogue demonstrated that remembrance, anticipation, celebration, and service lay at the heart of Israel's response to God. In spite of the fact that Israel frequently fell away from God, these institutions of worship provided a continual way for the people to renew their faith.

These institutions of worship foreshadowed the worship of the New Testament. Some falsely assume that the worship of Israel was physical and the worship of the church should be spiritual. This is a false dichotomy that fails to recognize the overlap between the content of the Old Testament (the Exodus event) and the content of the New Testament (the Christ event). Worship in the Old and the New Testament has both spiritual and physical aspects. As we develop the physical side of Christian worship, we will see how Old Testament principles are still found in Christian worship. The radical difference is that they are informed by the event of Jesus Christ, the main content of the Christian faith.

1. For a survey of Old Testament worship see "An Historical Survey of the Study of Old Testament Worship," in Hans-Joachim Knaus, *Worship in Israel,* trans. Geoffrey Buswell (Richmond: John Knox, 1966), 1–25.

2. See Charles Feinberg, "The Tabernacle," *The Biblical Foundations of Worship* (Nashville: Abbott Martyn, 1993), 112–118.

3. See Richard and Janice Lenoard, "The Tabernacle of David," in *The Biblical Foundations of Worship,* 120–22.

4. For a thorough discussion of the festivals of Israel see Carmine Di Sante, *Jewish Prayer: The Origins of Christian Liturgy* (New York: Paulist, 1991), 189–224.

5. For a discussion of synagogue worship see Di Sante, *Jewish Prayer,* 169–188. See also Abraham Millgram, *Jewish Worship* (Philadelphia: Jewish Publication Society, 1971).

6. Millgram, *Jewish Worship,* 102.

7. Millgram, *Jewish Worship,* 103.

8. Millgram, *Jewish Worship,* 103.

9. See Israel Bettar, "Early Preaching in the Synagogue," *Studies in Jewish Preaching* (Cincinnati: Hebrew Union College, 1939).

Chapter 4

New Testament Worship

The study of worship in the New Testament is more difficult and complex than a study of worship in the Old Testament because of the fragmentary nature of the sources. There is no single highly developed statement on worship in the New Testament. Rather, brief descriptions provided by hymns, confessions, benedictions, doxologies, and subtle hints in words descriptive of worship are scattered throughout the New Testament documents. Changing and somewhat confusing patterns force us to remember the simple but necessary principle of *the process of development*. Thus, allowance must be made for a certain degree of flexibility in forming all the loose ends together into a coherent whole.[1]

However, it is certain that the worship of the New Testament was born in the crucible of those events surrounding Jesus that were recognized as the fulfillment of the Old Testament prophecies to Israel. At first there was no hint that a new people of God, one including the Gentiles, was being formed as a result of these events. Therefore, early Christians worshiped in the synagogue until the growing conflict over the messiahship of Jesus forced them to go elsewhere. In this context, Christian worship developed characteristics that were distinct from Jewish worship.[2]

In this chapter we will reflect in a systematic way on the beginnings of Christian worship in the first century by concentrating on two questions: What is the basis of New Testament worship? and what descriptions of worship emerge? Other issues such as prayer, hymns, confessions, and the like will be treated elsewhere.

THE BASIS OF NEW TESTAMENT WORSHIP

The basis of New Testament worship may be discovered by examining the attitude of Jesus toward worship and the meaning of the Christ event.

Jesus' Attitude Toward Worship

First, *Jesus supported Israelite worship.* An examination of his relationship to the temple, the synagogue, and the feasts confirms this conclusion. Luke and John tell of Jesus' teaching in the temple (Luke 19:47; John 7:14; 10:22–24), and all four Gospels describe the cleansing of the temple, in which Jesus demonstrated his concern for the purity of temple worship (Matt. 21:12–13; Mark 11:15–17; Luke 19:45–46; John 2:13–16). Jesus went regularly to the synagogue on the Sabbath (see Luke 4:16: "on the Sabbath day he went into the synagogue, *as was his custom*").[3] Jesus attended the feasts of Israel, and the detail with which he celebrated his last Passover displays his knowledge and appreciation of the major feast of Israel (Matt. 26:17–30; Mark 14:12–26; Luke 22:7–23).

Second, *Jesus believed that he superseded the Old Testament institutions of worship.* He saw himself as fulfilling the temple cult. He was "greater than the temple" (Matt. 12:6; see also John 2:19) and rendered its rituals obsolete. When Jesus celebrated his final Passover he viewed himself as the final sacrifice and the true Lamb of God: "Take and eat; this is my body. . . . This is my blood of the covenant, which is poured out for many for the forgiveness of sins" (Matt. 26:26, 28).

Also, *Jesus assumed the right to reinterpret the customs of Jewish worship.* For example, in the confrontations Jesus had with the Pharisees over the Sabbath, Jesus asserted, "The Sabbath was made for man, not man for the Sabbath. So the Son of Man is Lord even of the Sabbath" (Mark 2:27–28). Jesus' willingness to break the strict rules of the Sabbath as developed by the Pharisees carried over into his attitude toward the regulations that governed cleanness and uncleanness (Mark 7:1–23), as well as the rules regarding fasting and prayer (Matt. 6:5–8, 16–18). The point in each of these cases is that Jesus is proclaiming himself—his lordship, his place in the kingdom, his place in the revelation of God in history—as superior to everything before him. In this manner Jesus prepared the way for the significant changes that occurred in worship as the new people of God gradually developed a worship depicting the fulfillment of the Old Testament rituals in Jesus Christ.

The Christ Event

In the same way that Old Testament worship celebrated the Exodus event, New Testament worship proclaims the story of the second Exodus—Christ's leading his people out of their bondage to sin.[4]

The birth of Christ generated a significant amount of worship literature that praised God for fulfilling the Old Testament prophecies.[5] The keynote of the birth narratives is struck by Mary in the *Magnificat* (Luke 1:46–55). This note of worship is recognized as one of the earliest hymns of the church. The events of Jesus' death and resurrection produced a worship response that stressed the destruction of the powers of sin and death. This theme is the focus of baptism, preaching, and the Lord's Supper. Jesus Christ, as Paul stated to the Colossians, has "disarmed the powers and authorities" and has "made a public spectacle of them, triumphing over them by the cross" (2:15). The power of God that was demonstrated in the Cross has been evident in the church since the Ascension and Pentecost. The outpouring of the Spirit is manifested in the lives of God's new people who by the Spirit act in his name and worship him. The fact that Jesus is now seated at the right hand of God and will return in judgment focuses worship not only on past events but also on the completion of those events in the consummation. In this way the events associated with Christ have formed the content of Christian worship.

Baptism is an identification with the death and resurrection of Christ, whereby the new Christian passes from death to life (Rom. 6:1–4). It is possible that the contrasts between the old life and the new life that so frequently appear in Scripture are actual remnants of baptismal instructions given to new believers and worshipers (see Rom. 6:18 "set free from sin . . . slaves to righteousness"; Col. 3:5 "put to death . . . your earthly nature"; Ga. 5:16 "live by the Spirit, and you will not gratify the desires of the sinful nature."

These themes are so pervasive in the literature of the New Testament that some scholars view portions of the New Testament as products of early worship.[6] "At an early date liturgical and catechetical forms began to be developed for the worship and teaching of various churches and soon spread widely among the rest."[7] Although there is no absolute proof that elements of early Christian worship are incorporated in the New Testament documents, the idea itself is fascinating and has provoked scholarly inquiry that demands attention.

For example, these scholars make a case that the *Magnificat* (Luke 1:46–55), the *Benedictus* (Luke 1:68–79), the *Gloria in Excelsis Deo* (Luke 2:14), and the *Nunc Dimittis* (Luke 2:29–32) were all hymns of the church, known and used by the church before their incorporation into the gospel text. The same has been said for the Christ hymns such as John 1:1–18, Philippians 2:6–11, and Colossians 1:15–20, and the many psalms and doxologies such as those found in Revelation (4:8, 11; 7:12; 11:17–18; 15:3–4). It seems reasonable to assume that worship traditions would have developed and spread rapidly among the various Christian communities. Since the Gospels were not written for a number of years after Pentecost, the development of hymns, doxologies, and baptismal catecheses that predate the literature of the New Testament seems natural.

EMERGING CHRISTIAN WORSHIP

Christianity began as a movement among Palestinian Jews, and then spread to the Jewish community of the Diaspora and, through it, to the Gentiles. Christian worship evolved as part of this process of expansion. While the New Testament mentions some features of this emerging worship in various Christian communities, we can trace its chronological development only in a broad sense.

Worship in the Jerusalem Church

The first Christian community was the church in Jerusalem. It was made up of both Aramaic- and Greek-speaking Jews (the latter are called "Hellenists" or "Grecian Jews" in the New Testament; Acts 6:1). Because Jerusalem with its temple was the center of Judaism, devout Jews from Greek-speaking areas often visited as pilgrims, and many lived there permanently. Both Aramaic- and Greek-speaking Jews responded to the apostles' proclamation of Jesus' messiahship, and the Jerusalem church grew rapidly after the events of the day of Pentecost (Acts 2:37–41). The Acts of the Apostles gives us some insights into the worship of this first Christian community.

First, *the Jerusalem Christians continued to be related to the temple.* Their connection with the Jewish sacrificial rites is not clear, although Luke reports that "a large number of priests became obedient to the faith" (6:7). But the temple was the scene of many other activities; for example, a number of synagogues met within its precincts. Acts records the claim of the Jerusalem Christian leaders that "many thousands of Jews have believed, and all of them are zealous for the law" (21:20). Acting on the advice of these leaders, Paul himself took part in traditional purification rites.

While it is true that the new believers "broke bread in their homes," yet "every day they continued to meet together in the temple courts" (Acts 2:46), and they used these courts as a place to proclaim the gospel (Acts 3:11–26).[8] Luke describes the life of the Jerusalem community in this way: "They devoted themselves to the apostles' teaching and to the fellowship, to the breaking of bread and to prayer" (Acts 2:42). The Christ-centered content of this worship is clear, but the word for "prayer" is plural in Greek ("the prayers") and probably refers to the traditional Jewish hours of prayer. In fact, Luke tells us that the apostles continued to observe the regular hours of prayer (Acts 3:1).

Nevertheless, *the Jerusalem Christians were aware that the temple and its rites had been fulfilled in Christ.* This is clear from the account of Stephen, a Greek-speaking Jewish Christian who had become an effective preacher of Christ. Members of the Synagogue of the Freedmen, an organization of Jews from outside Palestine, accused Stephen before the Council of the Jews, saying, "This fellow never stops speaking against this holy place and against the law. For we have heard him say that this Jesus of Nazareth will destroy this place and change the customs Moses handed down to us" (Acts 6:13–14). Confronting his opponents, Stephen launched into a narrative of the history of Israel's disobedience to the Lord. The most inflammatory part of this speech was Stephen's rejection of the temple, expressed in a quotation from Isaiah: "Heaven is my throne, and the earth is my footstool. What kind of house will you build for me? says the Lord. Or where will my resting place be? Has not my hand made all things?" (7:49–50). Here Stephen struck a prominent note of early Christian preaching: because the Old Testament cult was fulfilled in Christ, the temple and its sacrifices were no longer necessary.[9]

Worship in the Diaspora Churches

As Christianity expanded into the Jewish Diaspora, this theme was amplified. *Jewish ceremonies were reinterpreted as having been fulfilled in Christ and his church.* For example, Christ was seen as the Passover lamb who had been sacrificed (1 Cor. 5:7; see also Rom. 3:25; Eph. 5:2; 1 Peter 1:19). The temple was replaced by the body of Christ: "Don't you know that you yourselves are God's temple and that God's Spirit lives in you? If anyone destroys God's temple, God will destroy him; for God's temple is sacred, and you are that temple" (1 Cor. 3:16–17; see also Eph. 2:19–22; 1 Peter 2:4–5). The people who make up the church, the new temple, were designated a "royal priesthood" (1 Peter 2:9). Because Jerusalem, Judaism's religious center, was "in slavery with her children," it was displaced by the "Jerusalem that is above" as the true mother of Christian believers (Gal. 4:25–26). The worshiping community in the midst of which God now lived was "the new Jerusalem, coming down out of heaven from God" (Rev. 21:2–3). These reinterpretations of Jerusalem, the temple, the sacrifices, the Passover lamb, and the priesthood, along with their application to the emerging church, were radical and new. They reached into the very essence of Judaism and struck at the heart of Jewish worship. It was becoming evident that Jewish and Christian worship did not mix.

Christian differentiation from Jewish worship was clearly set forth in the letter to the Hebrews, which was probably written from a Diaspora location (see Heb. 13:24). The author struck his keynote in 7:18, in the discussion of the priesthood. "The former regulation," he insisted, "is set aside because it was weak and useless." The Jewish cultic practices had served their purpose. They were obsolete now, since a new and better way had come (see Heb. 7–10). Christians, the author declared, have not come to Mount Sinai, "a mountain that can be touched." Rather, they have come "to Mount Zion, to the heavenly Jerusalem," through Jesus, who has mediated a new covenant in his blood (see 12:18–24). In the sacrificial rites of the old covenant, worshipers were sprinkled with the blood of the victim in order to be prepared to enter God's presence. The blood of Jesus has now taken the place of these sacrifices.

Already in Palestine, the Christian movement came to include people who were not Jewish, such as an Ethiopian official (Acts 8:26–39) and a Roman officer and his household (Acts 10). The number of Gentile converts increased markedly in the Diaspora setting, where many non-Jews seeking God attended the synagogues in their cities. When these people heard the apostles announce the new covenant through Jesus the Messiah, many responded with enthusiasm. Now they could be part of God's covenant without having to become Jews by undergoing circumcision and other Jewish rites. Indeed, the prophets and psalmists of Israel had foretold that non-Jews (i.e., "the nations") would be part of God's kingdom and worship him (see Isa. 2:2–5; 11:1–10; 42:6; Dan. 7:27; Zech. 8:23; Pss. 22:27–28; 117:1–2). Saul of Tarsus, persecutor of the church, was called by Jesus to be "my chosen instrument to carry my name before the Gentiles" (Acts 9:15). As Paul the apostle, he viewed the inclusion of the Gentiles in God's purpose as the "mystery" now revealed, of which he was a steward (Eph. 2–3). Early Jewish Christian opposition to the free acceptance of Gentiles was overcome (Acts 15), and most churches of the New Testament seem to have included both Jewish and Gentile members.

The life of one of the Diaspora churches, the church in Corinth, is reflected in Paul's letters to that congregation. In 1 Corinthians, the apostle deals extensively with issues related to corporate worship, sometimes directly and sometimes indirectly. This material, verified in other liturgical sources from the period, includes such things as the form of blessing (1 Cor. 1:3; 16:23), worship on Sunday or "on the first day of each week" (16:1–2), the possible celebration of Pentecost (16:8) and Passover (5:7), the use of the holy kiss (16:20), and church discipline with an emphasis on excommunication (5:5; 16:22).

Most helpful for our purposes are Paul's explicit teachings about worship. First, *Paul emphasized the need for order in corporate worship.* Many Corinthian Christians apparently were not used to the structured type of gathering found in the synagogue and needed to learn how to conduct themselves "in a fitting and orderly way" (14:40) in their assembly. Paul emphasizes order with reference to the exercise of spiritual gifts, especially tongues and prophecy. It seems that worship was sometimes filled with confusion: "If the whole church comes together and everyone speaks in tongues, and some who do not understand or some unbelievers come in, will they not say that you are out of your mind?" (14:23). Paul did not instruct the Corinthians to stop speaking in tongues; he simply asked that they recognize the proper place of tongues in worship, and that all tongue-speaking and interpretations should proceed in an orderly manner. The same was true for prophecy. Two or three prophets might speak, and the others were to evaluate what was said. No one was to monopolize the prophetic gift if another worshiper had something to say (14:29–32).

Order was also a matter of concern with regard to the Lord's Supper. Paul commented on conditions in Corinth in these words: "When you come together, it is not the Lord's Supper you eat, for as you eat, each of you goes ahead without waiting for anybody else. One remains hungry, another gets drunk" (11:20–21). Even in this central rite of the Christian faith, the Corinthians had to be taught how to focus on the death of Christ and to examine their motives with respect to fellow believers (11:23–32).

The issue of order, with respect to both the Lord's Supper and the assembly where tongues and prophecy were practiced, had to do with recognizing that Christian worship was a corporate, not just an individual, action. Paul reminded the Corinthians that the bread they broke together was "a participation in the body of Christ," and that therefore "we, who are many, are one body, for we all partake of the one loaf" (10:17). For that reason a worshiper should not observe the Lord's Supper as a selfish, individual act, "without recognizing the body of the Lord" (11:29). And a worshiper who speaks in tongues without recognizing the need to edify other members of the assembly is misusing his gift. For this reason, Paul included his well-known exhortation about love in his discussion of spiritual gifts (chapter 13). The love Paul describes here is *agape*, a love that is recognized by loyalty to one's brothers and sisters within the relationship of God's covenant.

Second, *Paul's teaching about worship had to do with content.* Paul does not give us an order of service, but he does mention some of the major aspects of Christian worship, especially in 1 Corinthians 12 and 14. "When you come together," he wrote, "everyone has a hymn, or a word of instruction, a revelation, a tongue or an interpretation" (14:26). Paul also refers to praying, singing, giving thanks, and responding with the "Amen" (14:13–17). Indicating that "the manifestation of the Spirit is given for the common good," he mentions among other gifts the word of wisdom, the word of knowledge, prophecy, the ability to distinguish between spirits, the ability to speak in different kinds of tongues, and the interpretation of tongues (12:7–11).

Paul's discussion reveals a great variety in the worship activities of the Diaspora churches where Gentiles worshiped alongside Jewish Christians. To what Paul mentions in this letter must be added singing of Psalms and other music (Eph. 5:19), baptism (Rom. 6:4; Eph. 1:5; Col. 2:12), and preaching of the kerygma or gospel proclamation. As to preaching, Paul reminded his readers in Corinth of the message that had been handed down in the church. Some of them did not believe in the resurrection of the dead (1 Cor. 15:12–58). So Paul reviewed (in confessional form) the tradition of the church that he had received and passed on to them: "that Christ died for our sins according to the Scriptures, that he was buried, that he was raised on the third day according to the Scriptures, and that he appeared to Peter, and then to the Twelve" (15:3–5). This basic confession lies at the heart of the kerygma, and it must be at the center of Christian preaching.

The Apostolic Period

It is imperative to keep in mind that the period until A.D. 100 was a highly formative period in the life of the early church as shown through signs of *maturation in the increased organization of the church.*

By now the mission of the church had extended throughout most of the Roman Empire and beyond. Along with the spread of the Gospel, heretical groups arose and challenged the church. Consequently, the church was put under external pressure to define itself more clearly. This it did through a growing literature (the Gospels and Epistles), a more fixed and precise organization of the church (see 1 Tim. 3:1–13), the emergence of creedal statements (see 1 Tim. 3:16; 1 Cor. 15:3–5), and a more highly developed liturgical consciousness.

An increasing number of scholars recognize the presence of worship materials in the literature of the apostolic period. The argument presupposes the incorporation of the church's hymns, baptismal catechetical literature, creedal statements, confessions, doxologies, and benedictions in the writings of the apostles. For example, it is thought that hymns of the church are sometimes used as arguments to make a particular doctrinal point or that large sections of the Epistles are elaborations on existing worship materials already known to the church. Even the Gospels do not escape the setting of worship. Oscar Cullmann has attempted to set forth "the connection between the contemporary Christian worship and the historical life of Jesus" in the gospel of John.[10] And others, like Massey Shepherd, have argued for the structure of a Christian worship service as the organizing principle for the revelation of the apostle John in the Apocalypse.[11]

An examination of this vast amount of material leads to the conclusion that *the apostolic period included an increasing emphasis on the ordered approach to worship.* For example, the Pastoral Epistles emphasize the role of the office of ministry in the worship of the church. At the same time the church attempted to find a balance between Corinthian enthusiasm and Jewish forms of and concern for order. Thus, in the apostolic period worship became more fixed. That this seems to be the case is suggested by the study of the worship forms known to us from the second century, the subject of the next chapter.

CONCLUSION

The purpose of this chapter has been to trace the *development* of New Testament worship. Although there are many gaps in the fragmentary documents on worship, it is evident that we are dealing with a *process* and with a *variety* in the earliest Christian communities.

However, three summary statements can be made with a degree of certainty.

1) Christ superseded the temple cult and Jewish ritual.

2) The common source of Christian worship is rooted in the Christ event.

3) The New Testament does not provide a complete picture of worship.

Because the New Testament does not provide a systematic picture of Christian worship, guidance may be sought regarding worship from the practice of the early church.

On the conviction that God is the Lord of the church, that God has given his Spirit to guide the church into all truth, and that the immediate successors to the apostles were careful to maintain apostolic practice, we turn in the next chapter to compare the earliest noncanonical descriptions of worship with the New Testament sources.

---

1. For a brief but comprehensive view of the various approaches to worship in the New Testament see Ferdinand Hahn, *The Worship of the Early Church* (Philadelphia: Fortress, 1973).

2. See Ralph P. Martin, *Worship in the Early Church* (Grand Rapids: Eerdmans, 1974), chap. 2; Eric Werner, *The Sacred Bridge: Liturgical Parallels in Synagogue and Early Church* (New York: Schocken, 1970).

3. Italics added. See C. F. D. Moule, *Worship in the New Testament* (Nottingham: Grove, 1977), 1:9–10.

4. See Hahn, *Worship of the Early Church*, chap. 4.

5. See "Hymns and Spiritual Songs" in Martin, *Worship in the Early Church*, 43–45.

6. For an example see John C. Kirby, *Ephesians, Baptism, and Pentecost* (Montreal: McGill Univ. Press, 1968).

7. James D. G. Dunn, *Unity and Diversity in the New Testament* (Philadelphia: Westminster, 1977), 141–49. Dunn argues against this position.

8. See Ernst Haenchen, *The Acts of the Apostles: A Commentary*, trans. R. McL. Wilson, et al., from the 14th German ed., 1965 (Philadelphia: Westminster, 1971).

9. See Hahn, *Worship of the Early Church*, chaps. 6–7.

10. Cullmann, *Early Christian Worship* (Philadelphia: Westminster, 1978), 37; see also 31–119.

11. See Massey H. Shepherd, *The Paschal Liturgy and the Apocalypse* (Richmond: John Knox, 1960).

Chapter 5

Early Christian Worship

The time lapse between the letters of Paul and Justin Martyr's description of worship in the second century may be filled in with references to Peter, the Book of Hebrews, and the Apocalypse, as well as several noncanonical writings. In this chapter we will examine worship practices recorded by Pliny, the *Didache*, and Justin and then consider their New Testament origins as we observe the normative picture of Christian worship emerging in the second century.

DESCRIPTIONS OF SECOND-CENTURY WORSHIP

Elaborate descriptions of worship are not found in either the New Testament or the writings of the second-century church. This, however, does not mean that worship was unimportant to the early church. Worship was of such vital importance to the early Christians that they *consciously withheld information* lest they cast their pearls before the swine. The Lord's Supper in particular was deliberately protected from pagans.[1]

The Letter of Pliny

The secrecy of worship in the second century provoked an inquiry on the part of Pliny, the Roman governor of Bithynia-Pontus (A.D. 111–113). He wanted to know what Christians did when they gathered together for worship. In a letter addressed to the Emperor Trajan, Pliny described his findings. From this report we gain some small insight into worship, especially the secrecy surrounding Christian worship. He informed the emperor that "the substance of their fault or error was that they were in the habit of meeting on a fixed day before daylight and reciting responsively among themselves a hymn to Christ as a god."[2] Some think that the word translated "hymn" means "religious formula" and may refer to the Lord's Supper.

Pliny also told the emperor that Christians "bound themselves by an oath not to commit any crime but to abstain from theft, robbery and adultery, that they should not break their word or deny a deposit when called upon to pay it." While it is not absolutely clear how this oath was expressed, it is generally believed to be what liturgical scholar Joseph Jungmann describes as "a distant parallel to the Sunday confession of sins."[3] Perhaps the recital of the Decalogue was used.

A third part of Pliny's statement reported that "when they had performed this it was their custom to depart and to meet together again for a meal, but of a common and harmless kind. They said they had even given up doing this since the promulgation of my edict, by which, in accordance with your commands, I had forbidden the existence of clubs." The reference to this meal as "common" and "harmless" indicates a fair amount of knowledge on Pliny's part about the meal. That it was probably not the Lord's Supper is suggested by the fact that it was held separately from the "hymn" and that the Christians "gave it up" as a concession to Pliny. More than likely it was the *agape* feast, a common meal eaten together by the church, but set apart from the Lord's Supper.[4]

The Didache

A second document coming from the same period of time is the *Didache* (ca. A.D. 100). This short document, an early church manual, contains among other things instructional material for the early church. For our purposes the most striking feature of the *Didache* is the full text of prayer used in a common meal that led to the celebration of the Eucharist.

> Regarding the Eucharist. Give thanks as follows: First concerning the cup: "We give Thee thanks, our Father, for the Holy Vine of David Thy servant, which Thou hast made known to us through Jesus, Thy Servant." "To Thee be the glory forevermore."
>
> Next, concerning the broken bread: "We give Thee thanks, our Father, for the life and knowledge which Thou hast made known to use through Jesus, Thy Servant." "To Thee be the glory forevermore." "As this broken bread was scattered over the hills and then, when gathered, became one mass, so may Thy Church be gathered from the ends of the earth into Thy Kingdom." "For Thine is the glory and the power through Jesus Christ forevermore." Let no one eat and drink of your Eucharist but those baptized in the name of the Lord; to this,

too, the saying of the Lord is applicable: Do not give to dogs what is sacred.

After you have taken your fill of food, give thanks as follows: "We give Thee thanks, O Holy Father, for Thy holy name which Thou hast enshrined in our hearts, and for the knowledge and faith and immortality which Thou hast made known to us through Jesus, Thy Servant." "To Thee be the glory forevermore." "Thou, Lord Almighty, hast created all things for the sake of Thy name and hast given food and drink for men to enjoy, that they may give thanks to Thee; but to us Thou hast vouchsafed spiritual food and drink and eternal life through (Jesus) Thy Servant." "Above all, we give Thee thanks because Thou art mighty." "To Thee be the glory forevermore." "Remember, O Lord, Thy Church: deliver her from all evil, perfect her in Thy love, and from the four winds assemble her, the sanctified, in Thy kingdom which Thou hast prepared for her." "For Thine is the power and the glory forevermore." "May grace come, and this world pass away!" "Hosanna to the God of David!" "If anyone is holy, let him advance; if anyone is not, let him be converted. Maranatha!" "Amen." But permit the prophets to give thanks as much as they desire.[5]

Some of the prayers of this feast were incorporated from the Jewish table fellowship. It was a common practice among Jewish people to repeat blessings at the meal over a cup and the bread. Thus, it was natural for the early Christians, who were also Jewish, to change these prayers slightly for use in the Christian communal meal. Compare, for example, the following prayers over the cup and bread.[6]

JEWISH	CHRISTIAN
The blessing over the cup: Blessed art Thou, O Lord our God, King Eternal, who createst the fruit of the vine. The words said over the bread: Blessed art Thou, O Lord our God, King Eternal, who bringest forth the bread from the earth.	We thank Thee, our Father, for the Holy Vine of David, Thy servant which Thou hast made known to us through Jesus Christ, thy Servant; to Thee be glory forever. We thank Thee our Father, for the life and knowledge which Thou hast made known to use through Jesus Thy Servant: to Thee be glory forever.

The table prayers are beautiful in content, expressive of the theology of creation, the church, and the return of Christ. An important feature of these prayers, including the prayers at the end of the meal, is that they give us an early insight into the structure of the Eucharistic prayer.

Justin Martyr

The next document, *The First Apology*, comes to us from the middle of the second century. It was written by the apologist Justin[7] to the Emperor Antoninus Pius. This work provides a considerable amount of information about the structure and meaning of Christian worship. Here is Justin's most important statement regarding the structure of Christian worship:

> And on the day called Sunday there is a meeting in one place of those who live in cities or the country, and the memoirs of the apostles or the writings of the prophets are read as long as time permits. When the reader has finished, the president in a discourse urges and invites [us] to the imitation of these noble things. Then we all stand up together and offer prayers. And, as said before, when we have finished the prayer, bread is brought, and wine and water, and the president similarly sends up prayers and thanksgivings to the best of his ability, and the congregation assents, saying the Amen: the distribution, and reception of the consecrated [elements] by each one, takes place and they are sent to the absent by the deacons.[8]

An important feature of this worship service is the two-part structure of the Word and the Lord's Supper. By including information about worship from other sources along with Justin's writings, the following outline appears to be the normative structure of early Christian worship:

THE SERVICE OF THE WORD

Readings from the memoirs of the apostles and the prophets
Sermon by the President
Prayers by all the people, said standing

THE SERVICE OF THE LORD'S SUPPER

The kiss of peace (mentioned elsewhere)
Presentation of bread and a cup of wine and water to the President
The Eucharistic Prayer (prayers of praise and thanksgiving offered by the President in an extempore manner)
Response (the people say "Amen")

Reception (the bread and wine is distributed and taken by the deacons to
the absent)
Collection (alms are received and distributed to the needy)

These descriptions of worship provide insight into the accepted structure
and content of Christian worship by the middle of the second century. We are
now in a position to trace worship patterns that developed into this normative
two-part structure.

THE NEW TESTAMENT ORIGINS OF THE TWO-PART STRUCTURE OF CHRISTIAN WORSHIP

The concern of this section is to discuss the origins of the two-part structure of Christian worship. Two lines of development informed and shaped early
Christian worship. They grew out of the practices of the synagogue with its emphasis on the Word and out of the Last Supper. Although these two institutions
can be traced separately, it is significant that they have a common basis in the earliest worship experience of the church. It is to this experience that we turn first.

Earliest Christian Worship

The earliest description of Christian worship is found in Acts 2:42, "They
devoted themselves to the apostles' teaching and to the fellowship, to the breaking of bread and to prayer." Some scholars have argued for a twofold sequence
of Word and sacrament in this text.[9] But there is no universal agreement on this
matter, and the text itself can stand as no better than a probable twofold sequence. However, the sequence of Word and sacrament is more firmly based on
1 Corinthians 16:20–24. The conclusions about this passage reached by John A.
T. Robinson and the suggestions of Hans Lietzmann and Günther Bornkamm
are now generally accepted. They are (1) that in 1 Corinthians 16:20–24 the
language is "not merely of epistolary convention, but of one worshiping community to another, the converse of the saints assembled for the Eucharist," and
(2) that in this pericope there can be traced "the remains of the earliest Christian
liturgical sequence which we possess, and which is pre-Pauline in origin."[10] The
basic structure of worship from the New Testament church appears to be a
twofold emphasis on the Word and the Lord's Supper, attended by prayer and
praise. First Corinthians likely was to be read in the service of the Word, and immediately after that the service of the Lord's Supper was to be celebrated, as indicated by the allusions in 1 Corinthians 16:20–24.[11]

This twofold sequence of the Word and the Lord's Supper is rooted in both
a theological and a historical context. Theologically, the sequence of Christian
worship is grounded in the structure of the biblical covenant, discussed in
Chapter Two. In granting the covenant on Mount Sinai, God proclaimed his

commandments, which were to govern this relationship. He described the behavior that pleases him, through which his people were to demonstrate their faithfulness and obedience. As a response, the people and their leaders pledged themselves in a series of acts of commitment. First they made a verbal confession: "Everything the Lord has said we will do." Then they offered a sacrifice, with the blood of the slain animal being sprinkled on the people. Finally, they ate a sacred meal in the presence of the Lord (Ex. 24:3–11). When Jesus instituted the Lord's Supper, he specifically called it "the new covenant in my blood" (Luke 22:20). We can fully appreciate the meaning of the Lord's Supper, and understand its position in the twofold sequence of Christian worship, only when we see it as a response of commitment to the relationship of the covenant that God offers through the proclamation of the gospel of Christ in his Word.[12]

Historically, the twofold sequence of worship seems to be related to the synagogue-style worship, which combined Scripture reading, prayer, and blessing with the distinctively Christian ceremony of "breaking bread" together in obedience to the command of Jesus himself. We can draw connecting lines between the rudimentary sequence of worship in the New Testament and that expressed by Justin in 150. By tracing both the influence of the synagogue on early worship and the development of the Lord's Supper, the relationship will become apparent.

The Influence of the Synagogue

It was Paul's practice to go to the synagogue to preach Christ (Acts 14:1; 17:2). Those who became Christians remained in the synagogue at first and gradually formed worshiping communities of their own.[13] At the death of Paul in the mid-sixties, Christianity was still a Jewish sect, but by the middle of the second century it had attained a separate identity. Thus, the break between the two groups took place within that period of time. Contributing factors to this break included the differing opinions over the literal observance of the law and the Christian view of Jesus as the Messiah.[14]

In spite of the antagonism between Jews and Christians at the end of the first century, there is considerable evidence that the relationship that existed between them before their break was of sufficient duration to influence Christian worship significantly. The evidence suggests that the first part of Christian worship, the liturgy of the Word, was directly influenced by the synagogue.

First, Christian worship, like that of the synagogue, held to *the centrality of the Scriptures*. It was the Jewish custom to read and comment on the Scriptures.[15] Portions from the Pentateuch and the prophets were read regularly. Likewise, the Christian practice of reading and expounding upon Scripture was attested to by Luke, who described Paul as one who "reasoned with them from the Scriptures, explaining and proving that the Christ had to suffer and rise from the dead" (Acts 17:2–3). Soon the writings of the apostles were read in worship along with the Old Testament. Early evidence of this practice is found in Colossians 4:16: "After this letter has been read to you, see that it is also read in the church of the Laodiceans and that you in turn read the letter from Laodicea" (see also 2 Peter 3:16). The earliest noncanonical evidence of the reading of Scripture is found in *the First Apology* of Justin (quoted earlier): "The memoirs of the apostles or the writings of the prophets are read as long as time permits. When the reader has finished, the president in a discourse urges and invites [us] to the imitation of these noble things." The dependence here on the form of the synagogue is hardly coincidental.[16]

Second, the church, like the synagogue (which followed temple practice), emphasized *prayer*.[17] There is a correspondence in the time of prayer. The first Christians observed the daily hours of prayer practiced in the synagogue: the third hour (Acts 2:15), the sixth hour (Acts 10:9), and the ninth hour (Acts 3:1). These times of prayer were continued in the early church as evidenced by Tertullian and Hippolythus in the early third century. There also seems to be a correspondence in the use of the *shemoneh 'esreh* (the Eighteen Benedictions) and of the Lord's Prayer. In the synagogues the *shemoneh 'esreh* was read at each of the services (it is the prayer *par excellence* of the synagogue).[18] Likewise, according to the *Didache*, the Lord's Prayer was said three times daily.[19]

More striking, however, is the correspondence between the language and the content of the prayers. The matters of concern articulated in the *shemoneh 'esreh* appear to have had a strong influence on the prayers of the early church, which bear a striking resemblance to the Jewish benedictions. A comparison with an early Christian prayer found in the letter of Clement to the Corinthians bears this out.

SHEMONEH 'ESREH	CLEMENT
(Grant us) to hope in Thy Name, the first source of all creation; open the eyes of our heart to know Thee, that Thou alone are the Highest among the highest, and remainest Holy amongst the holy ones.	Thou art holy, and holy is Thy Name; and holy ones praise Thee every day. Blessed art Thou, O Lord, the Holy God.[20]

Clement's prayer, which is much longer than the above quotation, strongly influenced the development of Christian prayer in the early church. The central emphasis on the holiness of God and the praise given him by the highest is frequently found in the liturgical prayers of the early church.

Other traces of the *shemoneh 'esreh* can be found in early Christian prayer. Examples of such prayers include prayers for spiritual enlightment, the *agape* prayer over the bread, prayers regarding the creation, intercessory prayers, prayers of confession, prayers for the forgiveness of sin, and the doxology. Such other aspects as the central emphasis on redemption, the sanctification of the Name ("Holy, holy, holy is the LORD Almighty; the whole earth is full of his glory," Isa. 6:3), the saying of the Amen, the use of the Psalms in recitation and singing, the confession of faith, the reading of the Decalogue, and using the Lord's Prayer are all traceable to the influence of the synagogue. Even the inclusion of extempore prayers as indicated by Justin has its roots in the prayer life of the synagogue.[21]

Because Christian liturgy was in the process of development, we cannot expect to find exact nor complete parallels between the *shemoneh 'esreh* and Christian prayer. Nevertheless, the sheer number of parallelisms and the similarity of the language offer weight to the argument that the entire liturgy of the Word in the early church owes its structural origin to the practices that developed in the synagogue. The practices of the synagogue served as the matrix out of which the early Christian's experience of worship was initially formed.

However, students of worship should keep in mind the more skeptical conclusions of recent scholarship, particularly those of Paul Bradshaw in his work *The Search for the Origins of Christian Worship*. While Bradshaw recognizes the impact of the synagogue on Christian worship, he does not share the certainty of the scholarship of the previous generation regarding the impact of the synagogue on Christian worship. He cautions his readers: "A revolution in Jewish liturgical studies has taken place, a revolution which has almost completely changed our perception of how sources should be used to reconstruct the forms of worship of early Judaism. This has resulted in the need to be much more cautious about affirming what would have been the liturgical practices with which Jesus and His followers were familiar."[22]

The Development of the Lord's Supper

The origin of the Lord's Supper stems from the night before the crucifixion.[23] The earliest written mention of the Lord's Supper was in Paul's first letter to the Corinthians (11:17–34). This has raised some questions about the origin and development of the Lord's Supper. These questions focus in part on the interpretation of "the breaking of bread" mentioned in Acts 2:42, 46; 20:7. Are we to assume that this term refers to the Lord's Supper?

We have already noticed that the worship of the early church recorded in Acts 2:42 occurs in the context of a meal. The question is this: Was "the breaking of the bread" part of the common meal itself (as in a Jewish meal) or does it designate an act apart from the meal, though in the context of the meal? If the breaking of the bread was a self-contained act, then a case can be made that this expression is an early reference to the Lord's Supper. Because the act of breaking bread is structurally separated from fellowship, and the term *breaking bread* was used for Jewish meals, one could suggest that Christians used the term to refer to the Holy Bread of Christian Communion. Although this argument is not indisputable, two other considerations also favor this interpretation.

First, in the postresurrection appearances of Jesus, the disciples often *ate* with him as they had done at the Last Supper (see Luke 24:30, 41–43; John 21:12–13). In the Emmaus road account, Jesus went through the same fourfold action as at the Last Supper. He "took bread, gave thanks, broke it and began to give it to them" (Luke 24:30; compare Matt. 26:26). When the disciples returned to Jerusalem to tell the other disciples what had happened, they told "how Jesus was recognized by them when he broke the bread" (Luke 24:35). On the shore of the Sea of Galilee they "knew it was the Lord" and "Jesus came, took the bread and gave it to them" (John 21:12–13). The breaking of the bread in the early Christian community may have been a means of recalling the presence of Jesus, who was made known in the breaking of the bread.

Second, it should be noted that the breaking of the bread was always in the context of a meal. Not only does the breaking of the bread evoke the memory of Christ, but the meal also serves the same purpose. For the meal goes back to that last meal and is a reminder of the promise of future meals (Matt. 26:29). Both the meal and the breaking of the bread of the early Christian community stem from the Last Supper and the meals of the postresurrection appearances. Now, in this new meal of Communion, the resurrected and ascended Christ is made especially present in the meal and in the breaking of the bread. For this reason the worship of the early church was characterized by a tremendous sense of joy and gladness (Acts 2:46–47).

The relationship between the meal and the Lord's Supper is seen in Paul's letter to the Corinthians (1 Cor. 11:17–34). Here it is unquestionable that the Corinthians "really connected the holy celebration with a great banquet."[24] It is equally clear that certain abuses had crept into this resurrection celebration, at least in Corinth. Paul chastised the Christians for their poor conduct.

> When you come together, it is not the Lord's Supper you eat, for as you eat, each of you goes ahead without waiting for anybody else. One remains hungry, another gets drunk. Don't you have homes to eat and drink in? Or do you despise the church of God and humiliate those who have nothing? What shall I say to you? Shall I praise you for this? Certainly not!
>
> 1 Corinthians 11:20–22

It appears that the banqueting aspect of the communal meal had gotten out of hand. Because of the overemphasis on the party aspect of the Corinthian meal, Paul emphasized the death of Christ by reminding the Corinthians of Jesus' words at the Last Supper. That he was not introducing a *new* element is evident in the words, "I received from the Lord what I also passed on to you" (1 Cor. 11:23). The words of institution were known in the tradition of the church and had been passed down in the practice of the church.[25] Apparently the practice was to have the meal first, followed by the Lord's Supper.[26] The Corinthians had so perverted the purpose of the meal by being drunk and not taking the Lord's Supper seriously. Consequently, Paul urged them to eat at home. "If anyone is hungry, he should eat at home, so that when you meet together it may not result in judgment" (1 Cor. 11:34).

Paul's emphasis on the Lord's Supper as a remembrance of Christ's death and his admonition for the hungry to eat at home provide evidence of a separation between the Lord's Supper and the meal.[27] By the middle of the second century the meal had been dropped from the service of worship. It was replaced by the ritual of bread and wine, which remained the essential feature of the second half of the liturgy.

No documents available from this period provide clear insight into the reasons why the meal was separated from the Lord's Supper. The earliest explanation is the account provided by Paul in 1 Corinthians. Here the reason is clear. The Corinthians were violating the spirit of the meal. The letter of Pliny and the *Didache* seem to assume a separation between the meal and the Lord's Supper. In the time of Pliny the meal was omitted because of persecution. In other cases the meal may have been omitted for practical reasons. It may have become burdensome for the growing church to accommodate increasing numbers of people at the common meal. Consequently, the many tables were replaced by one—the table of the Lord on which the bread and wine were placed. In this way the concept of the meal and the Lord's Supper were fused into the single ritual action that we find by 150 A.D. in the description provided by Justin.

BAPTISM IN THE EARLY CHURCH

While baptism is not a part of every worship experience, the study of baptism should not be neglected. In the early church, baptism was the worship ritual that brought a person into the fellowship, the worship, and the Eucharist of the early church. In the New Testament the theological significance of baptism is that it is the worship ritual that expresses an identification with the death and resurrection of the Lord, which worship on the Lord's Day repeatedly remembers and celebrates. How can people remember and celebrate an experience with which they have not identified?

On the day of Pentecost those who were "cut to the heart" responded by saying "Brothers, what shall we do?" (Acts 2:37). The forthright answer of Peter was "repent and be baptized, every one of you, in the name of Jesus Christ for the forgiveness of your sins. And you will receive the gift of the Holy Spirit" (Acts 2:38).

There is a clear progression here: Repentance, baptism, forgiveness, and the reception of the Holy Spirit. Here we have the skeleton of the rites of initiation. They include an inward disposition, outward marks, and specific results.

Through baptism a person identifies with the death and resurrection of Jesus and enters into the worship life of the church (Rom. 6:1–4; Col. 2:11–12). Baptism is a life-changing rite through which the person is born anew (Mark 16:16; John 3:5). This ritual is so important to the Christian life that Paul refers to it as "the washing of rebirth and renewal by the Holy Spirit" (Titus 3:5) and associates baptism with entry into the church: "For we were all baptized by one Spirit into one body" (1 Cor. 12:13). The eschatological nature of baptism, like the eschatological nature of the work of Christ and of worship itself, is also stressed by Paul (Titus 3:5–7).

The church of the second century continued to see baptism in the New Testament tradition. Far from being an option, baptism was a central ritual of worship that identified a person with the death and resurrection of Christ and with the ultimate overthrow of the powers of evil. Consequently, those who sought to be baptized and worship in the church did so to have the power of Jesus, who overthrew the powers of evil, active in their lives.

In the *Didache* those being baptized were required to receive "public instruction." The instruction refers to the presentation of the "two ways," the way of death and the way of life.[28] The "two ways" teaching bears striking similarity to the New Testament admonitions to put to death the nature of sin and to receive the life of the new person, an image patterned after the death and resurrection of Christ.

Later in the second century, Justin confirmed the importance of baptism. "Those who are persuaded and believe that the things we teach and say are true, and promise that they can live accordingly, are instructed to pray and beseech God with fasting for the remission of their past sins, while we pray and fast along with them. Then they are brought by us where there is water, and are reborn by the same manner of rebirth by which we ourselves are reborn."[29] While Justin did not give any specifics about the "things we teach," he certainly made it clear that new believers were to come to baptism with an understanding of its meaning. Given its short removal from the New Testament era, we can be confident that this teaching focused on the meaning of dying to sin and being raised to a new way of life in Jesus Christ.

Baptism in the early church was not an incidental matter, but a sign-act that lay at the heart of the worshiping community.

CONCLUSION

Both the Old and New Testaments contributed to the worship patterns of the early church. The normative pattern that emerged included the following essential features of Christian worship:

1)   The *content* of Christian worship was Jesus Christ—his fulfillment of the Old Testament, birth, life, death, resurrection, ascension, and return.

2)   The *structure* of Christian worship was Word and sacrament, including prayers, hymns, doxologies, benedictions, and responses.

3)   The *context* in which worship took place was the Christian church, called by God to worship, where each member played his or her part and where God spoke and the worshiper responded. This worship was highlighted by sign-acts (baptism and Eucharist). In content, structure, and context, we are able to discern a continuity with Jewish worship, and particularly with the biblical themes surrounding the twofold action of God initiating worship and the people responding in faith through remembrance, anticipation, and celebration.

---

1. Joachim Jeremias, *The Eucharistic Words of Jesus* (Philadelphia: Fortress, 1977), 132ff.

2. See Henry Bettenson, *Documents of the Christian Church*, 2d ed. (New York: Oxford Univ. Press, 1963), 5–6.

3. Joseph Jungmann, *The Mass of the Roman Rite*, trans. Francis A. Brunner and Rev. Charles K. Riepe (New York: Benzinger Brothers, 1959), 4.

4. Jungman, *Mass of the Roman Rite*, 10–11.

5. *The Didache*, 9, in *Ancient Christian Writers*, vol. 6, trans. J. A. Kleist (Westminster, Md.: Newman, 1948), 20–21.

6. See Jeremias, *The Eucharistic Words of Jesus*, 110.

7. See L. W. Bernard, *Justin Martyr: His Life and Thought* (Cambridge: Cambridge Univ. Press, 1967).

8. Justin Martyr, *First Apology*, chap. 67, in Cyril Richardson, ed., *Early Christian Fathers* (Philadelphia: Westminster, 1953), 287–88.

9. See Jeremias, *The Eucharistic Words of Jesus*, 119.

10. Quoted by Ralph Martin, "Approaches to New Testament Exegesis," in Howard Marshall, ed., *New Testament Interpretation* (Grand Rapids: Eerdmans, 1977), 231.

11. See also Oscar Cullmann, *Early Christian Worship* (London: SCM, 1973), 12–20.

12. Richard C. Leonard, "Worship of Christ and the Biblical Covenant," *Reformation and Revival Journal*, 2, no. 2 (Spring, 1993), 116.

13. Older discussions of the relationship between the synagogue and the church are

found in the following books: W. O. E. Oesterley, *The Jewish Background of the Christian Liturgy* (Gloucester: Peter Smith, 1965); C. W. Dugmore, *The Influence of the Synagogue Upon the Divine Office* (Westminster: Faith, 1964); Eric Werner, *The Sacred Bridge: Liturgical Parallels in Synagogue and Early Church* (New York: Schocken, 1970). More recent discussions of the relationship between Jewish and Christian worship are found in Paul F. Bradshaw, *The Search for the Origins of Christian Worship* (New York: Oxford Univ. Press, 1992); Paul F. Bradshaw and Lawrence A. Hoffman, eds., *The Making of Jewish and Christian Worship* (Notre Dame: Univ. of Notre Dame Press, 1991); Carmine Di Sante, *Jewish Prayer: The Origins of Christian Liturgy* (New York: Paulist, 1985); and Eugene J. Fisher, ed., *The Jewish Roots of Christian History* (New York: Paulist, 1990).

14. Dugmore, *Influence of the Synagogue*, 2.

15. Dugmore, *Influence of the Synagogue*, 13–14.

16. See Oesterley, *Jewish Background*, 5.

17. See Werner, *Sacred Bridge*, 8.

18. See Oesterley, *Jewish Background*, 54, 125.

19. *The Didache*, 8.

20. Oesterley, *Jewish Background*, 127.

21. Oesterley, *Jewish Background*, 129–50.

22. Bradshaw, *Search for the Origins*, 1.

23. There are numerous discussions of the origins and development of the Lord's Supper. Older works include Hans Lietzmann, *Mass and the Lord's Supper*, trans. Dorthea H. G. Reeve (Leiden: Brill, n.d.); A. J. B. Higgins, *The Lord's Supper in the New Testament* (Chicago: Regnery, 1952); Max Thurian, *The Eucharistic Memorial*, 2 parts (Richmond: John Knox, 1963). New works include William R. Crockett, *Eucharist: Symbol of Transformation* (Collegeville, Minn.: Liturgical, 1989), chap. 1; Dennis C. Smolarski, *Eucharistia* (New York: Paulist, 1982), chap. 2–3; Kenneth Stevenson, *Eucharist and Offering* (New York: Pueblo, 1986), chap. 2.

24. Jungmann, *The Mass of the Roman Rite*, 8.

25. See Jeremias, *The Eucharistic Words of Jesus*, 103–5.

26. Jeremias, *The Eucharistic Words of Jesus*, 121.

27. Jeremias, *The Eucharistic Words of Jesus*, 117–19.

28. *Didache*, 7.

29. Justin Martyr, *First Apology*, 61.

PART II

A Biblical Theology of Worship

The theologian's task is to think about the biblical narrative and teachings and then to systematize these materials into a coherent whole. In this sense theology is a reflective discipline.

For example, the ancient church approached theology from the adage *lex orandi, lex credenti*, which means that the rule of prayer is the rule of faith. Theology is a reflection on worship whereby the mind contemplates what the church does in its experience of worship. Consequently, when theology is divorced from the liturgy, theology becomes abstracted from the life of faith, thereby losing its life. That's because worship, not theology, is the most basic way of communicating the life and spirit of God. For this reason it is most appropriate to think theologically of *worship as the Gospel in motion.*

In the next three chapters we will explore the idea that worship is the Gospel in motion. And we will see how the faith of the worshiper is not only expressed in worship but nurtured and strengthened. In this we will be doing theology, that is, thinking about worship.

Chapter 6

Worship Is the Gospel in Motion

We saw in chapter 2 that the epicenter from which biblical worship flows is an event. In this chapter we will reflect on how the life, death, resurrection, and return of Jesus Christ are central to the experience of Christian worship.[1]

Worship is not a mere memory or a matter of looking back to a historic event (that is an Enlightenment notion). Rather, worship is the action that brings the Christ event into the experience of the community gathered in the name of Jesus. Three implications to this understanding of worship are: (1) worship recapitulates the Christ event, (2) worship actualizes the church, and (3) worship anticipates the kingdom.

RECAPITULATION OF THE CHRIST EVENT IN WORSHIP

The word *recapitulate* simply means to "sum up" or to "repeat." In worship there is a summing up of those events in history that constitute the source of the church's salvation.[2] In worship we rehearse the Gospel story. We rehearse the Creation, Fall, Incarnation, death and resurrection of Christ, and the consummation of all things. Therefore, our worship, whether baptism, preaching, or Eucharist, proclaims Jesus Christ and his saving reality again and again. In this action a recapitulation takes place on three levels: in heaven, on earth, and in our hearts.

The recapitulation that takes place in heaven occurs in the everlasting worship of the Father because of the work of the Son. Jesus served the Father by destroying the works of the devil (1 John 3:8) and thus reconciled the Creator and his creation through his death (Rom. 5:10). Since Jesus offered himself to save humanity, he has returned to God the glory of all his works. This offering is his "one sacrifice" in which "he has made perfect forever those who are being made holy" (Heb. 10:14).

For this reason the heavens ring with worship. Both Isaiah and John attest to this heavenly worship (Isa. 6; Rev. 4–5). The description in the Apocalypse seems to suggest that the entire creation of God (angels, archangels, apostles, martyrs, and the entire communion of saints, material and immaterial) offers unceasing praise to God. And here, in this heavenly worship, the central focus is on the "Lamb," who stands at the "center of the throne." All gather around him in worship and song (Rev. 5:6–9).

Some scholars believe that the structure of the book of Revelation was based on early Christian worship.[3] Whether it was or not, it at least appears that John recognized the need to pattern earthly worship after the heavenly (Rev. 4–5). Our worship is like heavenly worship in that it centers around Jesus and his work. In worship we "sum up" or "recapitulate" the work of Christ. That one unrepeatable event in history is made real again and again through the power of proclamation (by the Holy Spirit) that confronts us with the reality of new life in Jesus Christ.

This is not, as late medieval theology suggested, a resacrifice of Christ. It is instead the continual recognition of the once-for-all offering of Jesus Christ. In worship we recall the Christ event that accomplished our redemption, and we offer our praise and adoration to the Father through the accomplished work of the Son. Thus, the character of Christian worship is informed and shaped by the retelling of the Christ event.

The third aspect of recapitulation is concerned with making certain that what happens in heaven and on earth happens in the heart. The relationship between the eternal and the internal must never be neglected in worship. What we do externally should signify what is happening internally. In worship we offer ourselves as Paul admonished: "Offer your bodies as living sacrifices, holy and pleasing to God—this is your spiritual act of worship" (Rom. 12:1).

The experience of worship as a recapitulation of the Christ event brings heaven, earth, and the believer together in a single whole. The church joins in that great chorus of voices to offer praise to the Father through the Son by the Spirit, and in this action the church is actualized.

ACTUALIZATION OF THE CHURCH IN WORSHIP

The image that best describes what happens when the church comes together for worship is taken from the congregation of Israel at Mount Sinai. Here Israel through the covenant became the people of God. The technical term used to describe these people is the *qehal Yahweh*. They are the assembly saved from Egypt; thus they become as this term implies "the assembly of God." The special characteristic of this assembly is worship. Thus, the five elements of worship discussed in chapter 3—divine initiative, the structure of responsibility, the proclamation of the Word, the assent of the people, and the act of ratification—characterized this assembly. These elements define the nature of the gathering in which Israel as God's special people become actualized.

Similarly, the church is an assembly gathered for worship. The church constitutes the people of God on earth, assembled in the name of Jesus. Like the nature of the people of Israel, the nature of this assembly is defined by an event. In this sense the church may be defined as the "people of the Christ event." Thus, when believers come together, the church, as the people of the Christ event, becomes a reality. One can say, "Here is the church," or, "Here are the people who belong to God" as a result of the Christ event. In this way the church is actualized.

The view that worship actualizes the church rests on two arguments. First, all the physical signs of Christ's presence in the church are evident. Second, these signs represent a spiritual reality.

First, the physical signs of Christ are evident in the variety of gifts and workings within the body. Each member of the body has his or her own gift (Rom. 12:6; 1 Cor. 7:7). No one person fills all the offices or possesses all the gifts, but worship brings believers together and arranges them according to their functions. These people have the Word of God, through which God speaks to them. They also have the sacraments, baptism and Communion, which remind them of the purpose for which they have gathered. The point is that in these signs—people, offices, gifts, Word, sacraments—the church is present and visible.

Second, these signs communicate the spiritual reality they represent. God has made his material world in such a way that it could be the vehicle through which spiritual realities are realized. We see one thing, but we apprehend another. The offices and gifts are expressed through people, but through them we also see the ministry of Jesus Christ, who oversees the church, pastors the flock, and serves the church. In the Word we hear the voice of God. In baptism and the Eucharist we apprehend the cleansing of our sin and are nurtured in Christ.

In this way worship actualizes the church and becomes the means through which Christ, the head of the church, becomes present to his body. We dare not deny this physical side of spiritual communication where through the action of worship the triumphant presence of the risen Lord is actualized and the anticipation of his bodily return is celebrated.

ANTICIPATION OF THE KINGDOM IN WORSHIP

Because worship has to do with the Christ event, the eschatological hope for the consummation of the work of Christ cannot be neglected.[4] Thus, worship expresses the tension between Christ's resurrection and his return. Although we celebrate the triumph of Jesus over the powers of sin and death, we acknowledge that the powers have not yet been put under the feet of Jesus completely. Therefore, in worship we raise a prophetic voice against the powers and express our hope in the future completion of Jesus' triumph over sin and death. This anticipatory note of worship is expressed in Word and sacrament.

In the Word, the kingdom is announced and proclaimed in the preaching of Christ. The earliest preaching included the insistence that Christ would come again as Judge and Savior. This same anticipation is expressed in the prayer Jesus taught his disciples: "Your kingdom come, your will be done on earth as it is in heaven" (Matt. 6:10). The same theme is found in the institution of the Lord's Supper. Paul told the Corinthian church, "Whenever you eat this bread and drink this cup, you proclaim the Lord's death *until he comes*" (1 Cor. 11:26). In the Eucharist the church prefigures the new creation. Here common elements—bread and wine—become the symbols of a new world. The partaking of the bread and wine by the people symbolizes the messianic banquet—the celebration of the new heavens and the new earth. Thus, worship transports the church from the earthly sphere to the heavens to join in that everlasting worship described by John (Rev. 4–5). In this way the church at worship displays its relationship to the age to come and derives from worship the power to live in this world now—in the tension between the Resurrection and the Second Coming, between promise and fulfillment.

CONCLUSION

In this chapter we have seen that the focus and meaning of worship is rooted in the work of Christ. Thus, our worship to the Father is offered in and through Jesus Christ, who has accomplished redemption for the sake of and glory of the Father. Therefore, worship recapitulates the work of Christ by proclaiming it through Word and sacrament. In this action, the church (the body of Jesus) is actualized. That is, it comes together and can be seen and experienced in a visible and concrete manner. But the work of Jesus is not yet complete, so the church in worship acknowledges that it anticipates that final triumphant destruction of sin and death that will take place when Christ returns to consummate all things.

In this way the church experiences worship as the Gospel in motion. Worship renewal cannot occur without the recovery of this primary principle in the mind, heart, and actions of the worshiping community.

---

1. For theology of worship see James Empereur, *Models of Liturgical Theology* (Bramcote, Nottingham: Grove, 1987); Aidan Kavanaugh, *On Liturgical Theology* (New York: Pueblo, 1984); David N. Power, *Unsearchable Riches: The Symbolic Nature of Liturgy* (New York: Pueblo, 1984); and Geoffrey Wainwright, *Doxology: The Praise of God in*

Worship, Doctrine, and Life (New York: Oxford Univ. Press, 1980).

2. For a detailed discussion of this point see Jean-Jacques von Allmen, *Worship: Its Theology and Practice* (New York: Oxford Univ. Press, 1965), 21.

3. See Massey H. Shepherd, *The Paschal Liturgy and the Apocalypse* (Richmond: John Knox , 1960).

4. Shepherd, *Paschal Liturgy,* 57ff., and Wainwright, *Eucharist and Eschatology,* 110ff.

Chapter 7

Worship Is the Gospel Enacted

Worship is a dramatic enactment of the relationship that we have with God, a relationship that stems from historical events. Enactment may be done by means of recitation and drama. Recitation (creeds, hymns, and preaching) and drama (or ritual) have their basis in the Old Testament and the New Testament, particularly in the Passover and Eucharist. In worship we enact or act out the Gospel.

DEFINING ENACTMENT

The principle of acting out in worship is similar to what we do in other areas of our lives. For example, we act out greetings, birthdays, weddings, and national holidays such as Thanksgiving and Independence Day through organized ritual and symbolic gestures that communicate the meaning of the event. Thus, a handshake or a nod, a cake and candles, a turkey with all the trimmings, and fireworks all signify the meaning of the specific event.[1]

In baptism, preaching, and the Eucharist we act out a story. The story has to do with what God has done for us and our response to God's work. It is an enactment of the event that gives meaning and purpose to life. It aligns the believer with the Christ event and with the community of the faithful throughout history. Therefore, when worship is acted out in faith, the believer experiences again the refreshment of his or her relationship to God and he or she spontaneously experiences the joy of salvation.

The principle of enactment is rooted in the Scriptures. An examination of worship in both the Old and New Testaments demonstrates that worship is not thrown together in a haphazard way. Instead, worship is carefully designed to bring the worshiper through a well-ordered experience. In this sense the organization of worship is simply the means through which the meeting between God and human beings takes place in a vital, dynamic, and living way.[2]

Because worship is the enactment of an event, the organization of worship is not left to the whim of creative people or community consensus. Rather, it is rooted in the historic meeting that has already taken place between God and his people. This meeting, enacted by God's people, is the organizing principle of worship. Therefore, the overriding feature of biblical enactment is the representation of history.

A cursory examination of biblical worship makes the *historical orientation* of enactment abundantly clear. All the events around which Israel's worship was organized were the actions of God in history. For example, it is significant that the major institutions of worship in Israel derived foundationally from the Exodus event: The institution of public worship at Mount Sinai celebrated the covenant that God established with Israel; the elaborate worship of the tabernacle and the temple were a commentary on the relationship between God and Israel; the synagogue accented the giving of the law; the festivals, especially the Passover, which was the central feast of Israel, commemorated the redemption from bondage.

Historical orientation also underlies New Testament worship. Christian worship derives from the death and resurrection of Christ. In preaching we retell the story; in the Eucharist we dramatize the event. Even worship on Sunday has significance in terms of enactment, for that is the day of the Resurrection. Furthermore, the special emphasis we place on Christmas and Easter is for the purpose of making the meaning of those historic days come alive in our experience.

The significance of the historical orientation of biblical worship is this: *Worship re-creates and thus re-presents the historical event.* In this way worship proclaims the meaning of the original event and confronts worshipers with the claim of God over their lives.[3]

Therefore, the overriding concern of worship is not simply the reenactment of the event, but a personal meeting with God. On one side, the emphasis is on God who has acted; on the other side, the emphasis is on humans responding. In this way *something happens* in worship: God and his people meet. Worship is not simply going through the motions of ceremony. It becomes the visible and tangible meeting of God through the signs and symbols of his presence.

In worship the order is set forth in such a way that the worshiper is able to enter vicariously into the original event. This enactment of past events occurs through recitation and drama.

ENACTMENT THROUGH RECITATION

An examination of both Old and New Testament worship shows how enactment occurs through recitation in at least three ways: creeds, hymns, and preaching.

Creeds

The purpose of a creed is to compress historical events into a summary statement. For example, study the historical dimension and the theological breadth contained in this brief Old Testament recital:

> Then you shall declare before the LORD your God: "My father was a wandering Aramean, and he went down into Egypt with a few people and lived there and became a great nation, powerful and numerous. But the Egyptians mistreated us and made us suffer, putting us to hard labor. Then we cried out to the LORD, the God of our fathers, and the LORD heard our voice and saw our misery, toil and oppression. So the LORD brought us out of Egypt with a mighty hand and an outstretched arm, with great terror and with miraculous signs and wonders. He brought us to this place and gave us this land, a land flowing with milk and honey."
>
> Deuteronomy 26:5–9

The emphasis of this statement is historical—in a few words the most formative period of Israel is summarized. The sojourn, the harsh treatment, God's remembrance, the redemption, and the Promised Land are mentioned swiftly and succinctly. But equally important to this recitation is the meaning that stands behind it. It is not simply the recalling of a number of events, but specifically those events that had to do with the covenant. In and through these events a special relationship was established between God and Israel. Thus, the recitation of these events in faith renews the relationship of the covenant that they represent.

Similar creedal statements are found in the New Testament.[4] Consider, for example, the compression of events and the meaning suggested in the following:

> Christ died for our sins according to the Scriptures,
> . . . that he was buried,
> . . . that he was raised on the third day according to the Scriptures.
>
> 1 Corinthians 15:3–4

> He appeared in a body,
> was vindicated by the Spirit,
> was seen by angels,
> was preached among the nations,

was believed on in the world,
was taken up in glory.

1 Timothy 3:16

Examples are also later found in Christian worship. By the fourth century, creedal affirmations were a vital part of worship. Through creedal recitation the believer witnessed in brief form the significant events of the Christian faith. Consider the vast amount of Christian teaching compressed in the brief recitation of the Apostle's Creed.

> I believe in God, the Father almighty,
> creator of heaven and earth.

> I believe in Jesus Christ, his only Son, our Lord.
> who was conceived by the holy Spirit
> born of the Virgin Mary,
> suffered under Pontius Pilate,
> was crucified, dead and buried.
> He descended into hell.
> On the third day he rose again from the dead,
> ascended into heaven,
> sits at the right hand of God the Father almighty.
> Thence he will come to judge the living and the dead.

> I believe in the Holy Spirit,
> the holy catholic Church, the communion of saints,
> the forgiveness of sins,
> the resurrection of the body,
> and the life everlasting. Amen.

(Textus Receptus, ca. 700)

Here, in a matter of a few sentences, the entire framework of Christian truth is recited. The believer confesses the triune God; his or her personal faith in the Father as creator; in Jesus Christ incarnate, dead, buried, ascended, and coming again in judgment; and in the Holy Spirit, who creates the church, establishes community, applies the work of Christ for forgiveness, raises the body from the dead, and confirms our eternal destiny. The important feature of reciting these events is to act out the meaning that results from these events. In this confession the believer enacts a worldview. The members of the congregation tell the story that brings them together, and they express their faith in the triune God, who has acted in history for their salvation.

Hymns

Historical truth is also recited through the use of many of the psalms used in the worship of Israel and the church. While they may refer to the experience of Israel as a nation or that of a single person, the effect of using psalms in worship is to re-create the experience of the psalmist for the worshiper. For example, to proclaim God as king (see Pss. 93; 96; 97; 99) is to experience God as king in the activity of worship and to allow life to be lived in the meaning of that experience. Historical recitation also occurs through the recitation of the penitential psalms or psalms of praise (see Ps. 136).

There are similar examples in the hymns of the New Testament.[5] These hymns recount the events that give shape to the Christian faith. A good example is the hymn from Philippians 2.

> Who, being in very nature God,
>   did not consider equality with God something to be grasped,
> but made himself nothing,
>   taking the very nature of a servant, being made in human likeness.
> And being found in appearance as a man,
>   he humbled himself and became obedient to death—
>   even death on a cross!
> Therefore God exalted him to the highest place
>   and gave him the name that is above every name,
> that at the name of Jesus every knee should bow,
>   in heaven and on earth and under the earth,
> and every tongue confess that Jesus Christ is Lord,
>   to the glory of God the Father.
>
>   Philippians 2:6–11

The nonbiblical hymns we sing in our churches today are also intended to tell a story, to enact an event, and to make that event contemporaneous in our experience. This is the purpose of familiar hymns like "When I Survey the Wondrous Cross," "O Sacred Head Now Wounded," and countless other hymns of the church.

Preaching

The concept of recitation laid the groundwork for the development of preaching. Preaching at its best is a form of recitation because it re-creates the past and applies the past to the present.[6] The entire book of Deuteronomy is a good example of Old Testament preaching. Consider, for example, the beginning of this sermon. It sets the tone for the entire message, a retelling of God's actions in history on behalf of the people of Israel (see Deut. 1:5–8).

The sermons of the early church are excellent examples of recitation through preaching. In each instance the preacher tells the story of God's work in history right up to the coming of Jesus and offers an interpretation of the meaning of this history. Here, for example, is a section of Peter's sermon on the day of Pentecost:

> Men of Israel, listen to this: Jesus of Nazareth was a man accredited by God to you by miracles, wonders and signs, which God did among you through him, as you yourselves know. This man was handed over to you by God's set purpose and foreknowledge; and you, with the help of wicked men, put him to death by nailing him to the cross. But God raised him from the dead, freeing him from the agony of death, because it was impossible for death to keep its hold on him. . . .
>
> Therefore let all Israel be assured of this: God has made this Jesus, whom you crucified, both Lord and Christ.

Acts 2:22–24, 36

These illustrations point out the important role of recitation in biblical worship. The implication for contemporary worship is clear: We must be concerned to recover the place and meaning of enactment through recitation in our worship.

ENACTMENT THROUGH DRAMA

While recitation compresses and conveys a historical event through the medium of language, drama reenacts and thus conveys a historical event through visual, tangible, and concrete symbols. It thus acts out a historical event in order to re-create that event and proclaim its meaning to the worshiper.[7]

Old Testament Enactment Through Dramatic Representation

The temple rituals were re-presentations through drama that symbolized the relationship between God and the worshiper, as in the act of ratification at Mount Sinai. They also looked forward to the definitive sacrifice of Christ, when the ultimate and eternal drama of salvation would reach its climax.

An excellent example of temple ritual may be taken from the enactment on the Day of Atonement. Here, after the high priest had conducted an elaborate ritual in the sanctuary and in the Holy of Holies to make atonement for the people of Israel, the high priest visually demonstrated forgiveness of sin by laying his hands on the head of a live goat (which transmitted the sins of the Israelites to the goat) and sending it off into the desert (see Lev. 16:20–22).

The most striking example of re-presentation through drama in the Old Testament is the Passover. The purpose of the Passover *seder* (ritual meal) was to retell the historical events in which Israel's redemption was secured and from which Israel's spiritual life developed (see Deut. 6:20–23).

The dramatic re-presentation of the flight from Egypt was a highly complicated service that was first passed on by memory and later written down and preserved in the *haggadah* (body of interpretations of Jewish law). The haggadah contains specific instructions for every detail of this event. The home preparations were elaborate and time consuming, requiring the involvement of the entire family.

Today the seder is based on three pedagogical principles. The first is the biblical injunction that all Jews are bound to tell their children about the redemption of their ancestors from Egypt (see Ex. 12:26–27). The parent is admonished not to be hasty but to tell the story in depth so that it is understood and grasped. For this reason the second and third principles have to do with the method of teaching.

The second principle calls for the child to be placed in the center of the seder ritual. The child then asks about the meaning of the unleavened bread, the parsley that was dipped in salt water, and the bitter herbs. The answer to these questions is fulfilled in an elaboration of the story of the Exodus. The children, having dramatically replayed the original situation, are in a strategic position to hear and understand the meaning of the actions they have repeated.

The third principle is that all participants must consider themselves personally redeemed from Egypt. This personal dimension of the original event is carried out through a series of gestures and the eating of particular foods to memorialize and identify with the Exodus event.[8]

Not only is the order of the service intended to reenact the historic event, but even the elements of the meal are to re-create the exact event. Consequently, each portion of the meal has meaning. The matzo represents the "double portion" (Ex. 16:22) and the "bread of affliction" (Deut. 16:3); the shank-bone of lamb represents the paschal lamb; the roasted egg commemorates the festival offering; the horseradish reminds one of the bitterness of Egypt; and the *haroseth* (fruits, nuts, cinnamon, and wine) symbolizes the clay in Egypt.

The meaning of this enactment for those who celebrate it is captured by the Old Testament liturgical scholar Abraham Idelsohn in his work *Jewish Liturgy*.

> This memorable celebration has retained its value for our days as in the days of old, and has exercised a great pedagogical influence upon the children for which purpose it was chiefly instituted. It was introduced so that the father could teach his child the religio-ethical doctrines deduced from that [the Passover] event and from its underlying lofty ideals that the child may be permeated with them and draw strength from them to carry on the fight for justice and righteousness and spiritual liberty with firm belief of the ultimate success.

The story tells of suffering, of sorrow and pain, of struggle with the iron yoke of slavery, of afflictions which penetrate the very core of life; it also speaks of hope for deliverance and of idealistic devotion to the cause of humanity as evinced by the illustrious leader, Moses, who created a free people out of slaves and gave them laws of the highest ethical value.

On the occasion of this celebration every Jewish home receives the atmosphere of a sanctuary in which each member of the family is a priest and the house-master—the high priest—a sanctuary to serve the purest human ideals and the living God.[9]

New Testament Enactment Through Dramatic Representation

One can clearly see the elements of dramatic enactment in the Eucharist, or the Lord's Supper.[10] The Lord's Supper was initiated within the context of the Passover. The suggestion that Christ's sacrifice was the Christian Passover (1 Cor. 5:7) put the celebration of the Eucharist in the larger context that it shared with the drama of the Passover. This sense of enacting the drama of the Last Supper was carried into the early church and down through history.

The sense of dramatic enactment is first expressed in the meaning of the word remembrance (*anamnesis*). Jesus said, "Do this in remembrance of me" (Luke 22:19). The ancient meaning of *anamnesis* is not "mere memory of the mind" as we have interpreted it in our Enlightenment-conscious world. Rather, in the ancient world it carried a more active connotation. In the anamnesis, Christ is proclaimed in word and deed.[11]

The fact that the early Christians had a sense of dramatically playing out the meaning of the Last Supper in the Eucharist is suggested by the careful representation of the meaning of Christ in the earliest liturgies of the church. The emphasis is on dramatically portraying Christ in a kind of visual language, a language that is to "image" him or make him present through the imagination. In this action Jesus is visibly dramatized. This dramatic element, simple at first, became more elaborate in the fourth and fifth centuries and practically lost its meaning in the medieval period when the drama took the nature of an epiphany. Unfortunately, the Protestants reacted too strongly and lost the sense of drama, allowing the Eucharist to lose its special quality of enactment.

The Nature of Worship as Dramatic Enactment

Worship is not drama in the technical sense. Nevertheless, worship is characterized by dramatic elements and has many parallels with drama. For example, the dramatic element can be clearly seen in the worship experience of bringing the ark of the covenant to the new temple built by Solomon.

The priests then withdrew from the Holy Place. All the priests who were there had consecrated themselves, regardless of their divisions. All the Levites who were musicians—Asaph, Heman, Jeduthun and their sons and relatives—stood on the east side of the altar, dressed in fine linen and playing cymbals, harps and lyres. They were accompanied by 120 priests sounding trumpets. The trumpeters and singers joined in unison, as with one voice, to give praise and thanks to the LORD and sang: "He is good; his love endures forever."

Then the temple of the LORD was filled with a cloud, and the priests could not perform their service because of the cloud, for the glory of the LORD filled the temple of God.

2 Chronicles 5:11–14

Worship contains all the *external elements* of drama—a script, a director and players, words, sound, actions, a time to meet, and the use of space.[12]

Since worship means to enact the Christ event, there can be only one script. The notion that there should be a new and creative worship service week after week is unnecessary. There is a basic sameness to worship because the script cannot depart from the historic event of Jesus. However, the Scripture readings, the hymns, and the prayers may vary from week to week (especially if the church year is followed) and thus address different needs.

Because worship contains the dramatic element of a director (pastor) and players (worshipers), it ought to be seen as the dramatic action of the congregation. This viewpoint escapes the false performer-audience dichotomy. In worship *everyone is part of the play*; there is no audience! The pivotal persons, of course, are the worship leaders. If they do not have a sense of the dramatic and do not understand the play (enacting the Christ event), there is little hope that the people who are worshiping can fulfill their own role adequately.

It is imperative that the worship leader or celebrants understand the meaning of the words, sound, and actions that make up the play. They must direct worship in such a way that the actions and sounds complement the words. To do this, they must understand the meaning of every part of the drama. They must lose themselves in the action so that they play their part and lead the other players into a union with the entire enactment.

For this reason the time of meeting (the sense of Sunday resurrection and the particular emphasis of the week, whether Advent, Epiphany, Lent, Easter, or Pentecost) and the use of space (the placing of the players as well as the symbols or props of the play such as the pulpit and table) are significant. They relate to the sense of what is happening, to the feeling of what is being played out.

This leads to the second element of drama in worship, namely the notion that worship contains all the *internal elements* of drama. It has to do with tempo, emotions, and the senses.

In drama the tempo is always important. When the tempo lags, the entire play is affected. The same is true in worship. In evangelical churches a serious distraction that utterly destroys the tempo of worship is the constant interruption of announcements. The need to announce every hymn and to make remarks here and there throughout the service interrupts the flow and destroys the sense of enacting the drama of the Christ event.

Careful attention must also be given to emotion in worship. The use of appropriate emotion is normal and good. The drama of worship calls for joy and excitement as well as quietness, sobriety, and sorrow. It is important that the emotion fit the words and the actions (no one likes to hear about the love of God when the emotion of the preacher, reader, or singer is anger).

Furthermore, the senses ought also to be engaged in worship. In drama we see, hear, smell, and even taste. So it is in worship. God has given us all our senses, and he does not deny our use of them in any aspect of life, especially worship. If what we see, hear, smell, and taste in worship is unpleasant to the senses, then the act of worship will be disturbing and unfulfilling.

The external and internal elements of worship must be assembled properly to give worship a sense of movement and a dynamic quality. Because the entire congregation constitutes the players in the drama of worship, it is important that all of the members know their parts, understand the meaning of what is being done, and participate purposefully. For this reason it is important to remember that worship is a *group activity* and that the meaning of worship must be *learned*.

CONCLUSION

In this chapter we have been concerned with the method of worship. What do we do when we come together to meet God through Jesus Christ by the Spirit? Worship is a dramatic enactment of a meeting with God. God and his people encounter each other as the story of God's work in Jesus Christ is retold through recitation of the Word, the dramatization of his death, and the response of his people. In these actions the Gospel is enacted again and again, and the people experience anew the good news, which nourishes and encourages them in their faith.

---

1. See Thomas Howard, "Imagination, Rites and Mystery," *Reformed Journal* 29 (March, 1979): 15–19; see also "The Order of Worship" in Jean-Jacques von Allmen *Worship: Its Theology and Practice* (New York: Oxford Univ. Press, 1965), 283–311.

2. See "The Church as a Cult Community," in A. Verheul and H. Winstone, *Introduction to the Liturgy* (Collegeville, Minn.: Liturgical, 1968), 75ff.

3. See Donald L. Williams, "The Israelite Cult and Christian Worship" in James M. Efird, ed., *The Use of the Old Testament in the New and Other Essays* (Durham: Duke

Univ. Press, 1972), 110ff.

4. See "The Pattern of Sound Words—Early Creeds and Confessions of Faith," in Ralph P. Martin, *Worship in the Early Church* (Grand Rapids: Eerdmans, 1974), 53–65.

5. See "Hymns and Spiritual Songs," in Martin, *Worship in the Early Church*, 39–52; "Early Christian Hymns," in James D.G. Dunn, *Unity and Diversity in the New Testament* (Philadelphia: Westminster, 1977), 132ff; "Psalmody and Hymnody," in Hughes Oliphant Old, *The Patristic Roots of Reformed Worship* (Zurich: Theolgoischer Verlag Zurich, 1975), 251ff.

6. See "The Ministry of the Word" in Martin, *Worship in the Early Church*, 66–76; and "The Decline of Preaching," in Abraham Millgram, *Jewish Worship* (Philadelphia: The Jewish Publication Society, 1971), 530ff.

7. See Douglas Shand Tucci, "The High Mass as Sacred Dance," *Theology Today* 34 (April, 1972); 58–72.

8. Abraham Idelsohn, *Jewish Litrugy and Its Development* (New York: Schocken, 1960), 177.

9. Idelsohn, *Jewish Liturgy and Its Development*, 173.

10. See James F. White, *Introduction to Christian Worship* (Nashville: Abingdon, 1980), 145ff.

11. See "ἀνάμνησις," Gerhard Kittel, ed., *Theological Dictionary of the New Testament*, trans. Geoffrey Bromiley (Grand Rapids: Eerdmans, 1964), 1:348–49.

12. See Robert Howard Clausen, "Using Drama in Worship," *Concordia Journal* (November, 1977): 246–54.

Chapter 8

Worship Is the Gospel Enacted Through Forms and Signs

Because worship is something done by way of enactment, it necessarily involves certain forms. Forms are not mere externals but signs and symbols of a spiritual reality. Even as God who is immaterial met with humans in the material form of a human person (Jesus), so Christians meet God in worship in the context of visible and tangible forms. These forms, however rudimentary and basic, are signs and symbols of a relationship with God.[1] We will first consider the theological basis of form—creation, revelation, and incarnation—and then discuss the kinds of signs and symbols that have been found appropriate for enacting the Christ event.

A THEOLOGY OF FORM

The theological basis of form is found in the doctrines of creation, revelation, and incarnation.[2]

Creation

Christianity affirms the goodness of creation as the product of God's imagination and action, a creative work that reflects the Creator. Therefore, to reject creation is to reject the Creator.[3]

The doctrinal implications of creation became clear in the second-century conflict between Christianity and Gnosticism. The Gnostics rejected creation, insisting that it was the result of the creative act of an evil god. For Gnostics there were two gods, one good and one evil. The good god was spirit and immaterial;

the evil god was fleshly and material. For the Gnostics true spirituality denied the material (flesh) in order that the immaterial (spirit) could eventually return to the pure spirit god from which it came.

The outcome of the Gnostic view of creation was to deny that a spiritual reality could be made known through a material expression. The most serious implication of this viewpoint is the denial of the Incarnation. For Gnostics, Jesus was not God in the flesh. Rather, Jesus was a spirit, an apparition. They reasoned that the god of spirit could not become enfleshed in the creation of the evil god without becoming the prisoner of evil. Thus a denial of the physical stood at the center of the Gnostic faith. This necessitated a rejection of all material signs of spiritual reality.

Such rejection had significant implications for church practice. For example, in Scripture, water is the symbol of God's creativity and a sign, therefore, of passing from one stage to another: The people of Israel were brought through the waters of the Red Sea to Mount Sinai and passed through the waters of the Jordan to the Promised Land. In the early church, water was part of a passage rite into the church. Consequently, when Christians were baptized into Jesus through water, this represented a spiritual passage from one condition to another. Salvation was not without faith. Early Christians believed in the inner experience and the outer sign. Baptism was the sign of an inner reality. In the case of adults, the inner reality preceded the outer sign of water. The Gnostics' rejection of visible forms as signs of spiritual reality led them to regard water baptism as unnecessary. Tertullian, a late second-century theologian, wrote a treatise against their viewpoint, concluding, "It is not to be doubted that God has made the material substance which governs terrestrial life act as agent likewise in the celestial."[4] Tertullian's principle, expressing the general consensus of the early church, was based on the biblical view that God had created the physical and that he could be known in and through it.

A second example of the Gnostic rejection of the material is found in the Gnostic view of the Eucharist. Since Gnostics denied that Jesus had come in the flesh, it was logical for them to deny the value of material bread and wine as a sign of Jesus' presence in the worshiping community. Ignatius, the early second-century bishop of Antioch, warned the Smyrnaeans against the Gnostic viewpoint in these words: "They hold aloof from the Eucharist and from the services of prayer, because they refuse to admit that the Eucharist is the flesh of our Savior Jesus Christ, which suffered for our sins and which, in his goodness, the Father raised (from the dead)."[5] It is not clear whether the Gnostics abandoned the Eucharist altogether. What is clear is that their rejection of Jesus as a physical person led them to reject the view that Jesus was signified in the forms of bread and wine.

Revelation

The second theological basis for the use of material form as a means of communicating spiritual truth is found in the doctrine of revelation. First, God communicates himself through the natural creation. The psalmist testifies that "the heavens *declare* the glory of God; the skies *proclaim* the work of his hands" (Ps. 19:1; see also Rom. 1:19–20; italics added). Second, God communicates knowledge of himself through historical events. He is a God of action. Through this action he makes himself known to his people. The central action in the Old Testament is the Exodus, and the central action in the New Testament is the Cross. These principal actions of God are replete with symbolic references.

Third, God reveals himself through the institutions of worship. Patterns of worship in the tabernacle and later the temple are laden with symbolic language. The exact architectural floor plan, the use of gold and other precious metals, the colors, the rituals of sacrifice, the presence and organization of the priests, the sacred days and hours—all of these were physical signs of a spiritual reality.[6]

The writer to the Hebrews interpreted all of these forms as "a shadow of the good things that are coming" (Heb. 10:1; see also Heb. 7–10). He recognized, as did the early church, that all of the earthly regulations of the Old Testament were fulfilled in Jesus Christ. Consequently, the Old Testament regulations were no longer needed. However, the early Christians did not reject the principle that the earthly forms were signs of eternal realities. New forms were established in the New Testament (e.g., water baptism, the Lord's Supper, laying on of hands in ministry, the twofold structure of Word and sacrament), recognized in the church, and developed in the Christian community to bespeak heavenly realities. Therefore, what was abolished by the New Testament was the particular Old Testament forms, not the principle that earthly forms may communicate eternal truths.[7]

Incarnation

The doctrine of the Incarnation is the focal point for a theology of form. In the Incarnation the eternal Word was enfleshed in a human person; as John said, "The Word became flesh and made his dwelling among us" (John 1:14). This fact of history forever affirms the principle that spiritual reality may be known through earthly form. God used creation (the body of his Son) as the instrument of salvation. Therefore, the physical creation (including the body as well) has a place in worship.

Through the proper use of creation, mortal creatures may signify eternal realities. As we saw in chapter 7, the entire experience of worship is a symbolic meeting with God in which the eternal covenant established by Jesus Christ is reaffirmed in the physical action of worship. Here Christians proclaim by word and rite Christ's death and resurrection, and they respond in faith with praise and thanksgiving. For this reason worship necessitates forms and signs. Because humans wear a body and live in a physical world and communicate through language and symbol, there can be no such thing as bodiless, orderless, signless worship. Nevertheless, worship acted out in the body, according to form and by sign, is a spiritual worship because it signifies the eternal truth that is its ultimate point of reference. Just as in the Incarnation the immaterial Word was made present in material form, so in worship the material form is the means through which the church makes its spiritual worship present to God the Father.

The form of worship is determined by three considerations. First, because worship is a meeting between God and human beings, it is bound by the rules of order. It must contain a beginning and an ending and follow a sequence of events. It is natural, therefore, that worship should begin with acts of entrance (going to something) and end with acts of dismissal (leaving the meeting). Since it is a meeting with God, the people should first come before God with appropriate actions and in departing receive a benediction from God.

Second, because the meeting is an enactment of the gospel story, it is appropriate that it should follow the sequence of God's work in history. For this reason the Scripture readings and the sermon act as a sign of God's speaking to his people and precede the Eucharist—a sign of God's coming to his people.

Third, because worship demands response, it is appropriate that God's people praise him in doxologies, hymns, prayers, confessions, creeds, and offerings. These responses may be placed throughout the ordering of the service that sequentially sets forth the gospel story. The details of the historic order of worship will be discussed more fully in the chapters 14–16.

A THEOLOGY OF SIGN

Signs may be defined as language that communicates more than what is seen by the eye.[8] In a sign we see one thing and understand another. For example, one may see a cross but understand the death and resurrection of Christ. In this way a sign is an *action*—it reveals something by putting us into contact with an invisible reality and by the power of the Spirit creates within us a longing for that which cannot be seen.

It is generally recognized that there are three kinds of language.[9] First, there is the *language of everyday speech*. In this, we utilize words to convey meaning, to elicit thoughts, and to establish feeling. Words are, of course, the most common form of communication and are basic to all peoples. Second, there is the *language of science*. This language utilizes concepts that have empirical reference and are capable of being tested by experiment. Third, there is the *language of poetry* in which we utilize symbols to elicit thoughts, feelings, and intuitions. All of these kinds of language belong to the Christian religion and are employed in worship.

Protestants are the weakest in the third area of communication, the language of symbols. We have capitulated to the Enlightenment penchant for scientific objectivity, for observation and proof, for cerebral communication. This has resulted in a loss of our ability to express feelings and intuition symbolically.

If we are to restore symbolism, we must distinguish between dominical and ecclesiastical symbols. The former are symbols especially designated by Jesus, while the latter are those long established by usage and tradition in the church. For example, dominical symbols include the water of baptism and the bread and wine of the Eucharist. Ecclesiastical symbols include acts and rituals surrounding confirmation, reconciliation, marriage, holy orders, and unction. These are limited in number. On the other hand, the symbols of the tradition are many and varied. They include universally accepted symbols such as the Bible, the pulpit, the table, the baptismal font or pool, and the cross. Still other symbols are more local and reflect the cultural bearing of a particular congregation. These include the use of icons, vestments, candles, colors, the sign of the cross, and other bodily gestures such as kneeling, bowing, genuflecting, raising hands, and the like. The ancient church (and later Roman Catholic and Orthodox Christians) was accustomed to a broader and more complete use of symbols than are evangelicals. These symbols allow the whole person (body, mind, feelings, and the senses) to be engaged in the worship of God. The misuse of symbolic communication by the late medieval church led the Reformers, and especially the leaders after them, to opt for what they thought was a more spiritual (less physical) approach to worship. Unfortunately, this led to a loss of the use of the body as well as of other legitimate physical and material signs of worship.[10]

It is particularly important to recognize the objective and subjective significance of symbols. A symbol is not an end in itself. It is a medium that relates to the object to which it refers and serves the subject who beholds it. A symbol in Christian worship signifies supernatural reality. Thus, a cross represents the event of Jesus in history. Gestures, such as bowing or raising the hand, signify the worthiness or greatness of God. The importance of the symbol is found, therefore, in that which it signifies. On the other hand, a symbol has significance for the person whose imagination and heart attitude are triggered by the sight of the symbol. So a cross may evoke praise, and a gesture may signify humility in the presence of God. Thus, subjectively symbols and symbolic representations deal with the language of the unconscious. They elicit an emotion, a feeling, and an intuition—all of which belong to worship.[11]

All symbols have external, internal, and spiritual qualities. The external quality is the physical entity, such as a cross or an appropriate gesture. The internal quality is the interpretation given to a symbol by the group (in this case the church). The spiritual quality is the spiritual energy released by the individual or congregation in relation to the external symbol and the internal meaning. Consequently, symbols demand faith if they are to become a means of worship. For an unbeliever a cross represents little more than a historic event, but to a believer a cross evokes the energy of faith in Jesus as Savior.

Therefore, the purpose of a symbol is to function like a parable. It both reveals and conceals. It reveals its meaning to the believer but conceals its meaning to the unbeliever. Because worship is for the believer, it is important to teach the believer the meaning of the action, so that the work of worship will be done out of faith as it is directed to the glory of God.[12]

For this reason Christian congregations must learn certain premises about symbols in order to enter into a full worship of God. First, the worshiper must concentrate on the supernatural meaning of the symbol. There must be an intent to worship, a purposeful desire to offer praise from the heart. Second, the worshiper must allow himself or herself to meditate on the ultimate meaning of the symbol. This leads to the incarnation of the meaning of the symbol so that "the thing intended" by the symbol becomes a reality in the person's life.

Our worship is incarnated and enacted by the proper use of space, time, and sound. Such proper use, when accompanied by faith, incites the worshiper and the worshiping community to offer praise to the Father through the Son by the Holy Spirit.

CONCLUSION

There are a number of implications to the theology of form and sign. The principle to keep in mind is that forms and signs constitute the tangible context in which intentional worship takes place. They are not ends in themselves; rather, they are the tangible meeting points between human beings and God in which spiritual worship takes place. This is true of the order of worship, which is a sign-act just like baptism and the Eucharist.

---

1. See Everett M. Stowe, *Communicating Reality Through Symbols* (Philadelphia: Westminster, 1966).

2. See Robert Webber, *God Still Speaks* (Nashville: Nelson, 1980), esp. chaps. 4–6, 9.

3. See Langdon Gilkey, *Maker of Heaven and Earth: A Study of the Christian Doctrine of Creation* (Garden City, N.J: Doubleday, 1959).

4. Tertullian, *On Baptism*, 11.

5. Ignatius, *To the Smyrnaeans*, 7:1.

6. See William Dyrness, *Themes in Old Testament Theology* (Downers Grove: InterVarsity, 1979), 146–60.

7. The misunderstanding of this point by evangelicals has produced a negative attitude toward symbolic communication. See, for example, Paul E. Engle, *Discovering the*

Fullness of Worship (Philadelphia: Great Commission, 1978), esp. 20, 31, 65–73.

8. See James F. White, *Introduction to Christian Worship* (Nashville: Abingdon, 1980), 145ff.

9. See Peter Roche de Coppens, *The Nature and Use of Ritual* (Washington, D.C.: Univ. Press of America, 1979), 137ff.

10. See James Hasting Nichols, *Corporate Worship in the Reformed Tradition* (Philadelphia: Westminster, 1968), esp. chaps. 5–7.

11. See "Gesture," J. G. Davies, e.d., *Westminster Dictionary of Worship* (Philadelphia: Westminster, 1972), 185ff.

12. See Geoffrey Wainwright, *Doxology: The Praise of God in Worship, Doctrine, and Life* (New York: Oxford Univ. Press, 1980), 119–22.

PART III

A Brief History of Worship

O ne of the most significant problems of Protestantism, and particularly North American Protestantism, is its lack of interest in history, which grows out of the relative youthfulness of the North American culture and its rugged individualism. Among Protestant Christians the frequent movements to go back to Scripture alone without an appropriate appreciation of traditions based on Scripture also contribute to this problem.

From a theological point of view, the lack of interest in history grows out of the mistaken notion that the history of God's involvement in the faith of his people is exclusively relegated to the biblical time period. To be sure, the biblical time period is of paramount importance and constitutes the source of all our theological thinking. But to neglect the ongoing activity of the Holy Spirit in the life of the church is at worst heresy and at best spiritual arrogance.

God is the God not only of biblical history, but of all history, and particularly the history of the church. In the history of the church we see that God continually initiates a relationship with his people. And the people, just as in biblical history, continue the pattern of responding to God and then falling away from him.

In this sense, the pattern of church history is not vastly different than the pattern of the children of Israel. However, in reading the Old Testament, we do not begin with this or that renewal movement in Israel. Instead, we see the whole and interpret the part from the whole.

The same principle needs to be applied to the history of the church and its worship. It is not appropriate to leap from the pages of Scripture to the Reformation or to the evangelical awakenings of the nineteenth century or to one of the many renewal movements of the twentieth century, as though each renewal is a new beginning that stands alone. Instead, we need to envision the whole of history with all of its up periods and down periods, recognizing that all of that history is God's history and our history.

By accepting our connectedness with all of history and with all of God's worshiping communities, our own faith experience and our own worship experience are bound to be enriched. For in that history we will find rich treasuries of resources given to the church not only in a particular time and place, but for us to adapt and use in our own cultural setting. On the other hand, we discover the mistakes of our historical parents, learn from them, and discern when our own worship seems to be taking an unfruitful path.

It is in this spirit that we approach a brief history of Christian worship from the third century to the present.

Chapter 9

Ancient and Medieval Worship

W orship in the church of the third century is best understood against the background of a hostile culture. Christians continued to worship in homes and, like second-century worshipers, continued the practice of both hearing the Word and celebrating at the table. Worship remained relatively simple in an intimate context.[1]

The conversion of Constantine in the early part of the fourth century resulted in a significant worldview shift in the Roman Empire. A political world previously at enmity with the church was now courting the favor of the church and in the late fourth century decreed the church to be the only legitimate religion of the Roman world. This worldview shift put the church into a friendly environment where, with gifts of buildings in which to worship, the worship of the church shifted from intimacy to theater.

Because of the subsequent fall of Rome and the continuation of the Empire of Constantinople, two major histories of worship emerge: in the East (Byzantine) and the west (Roman). This chapter surveys the worship of the church in these different political and geographical settings.

THIRD-CENTURY WORSHIP

The third-century sources of worship are few in number, the most important being *The Apostolic Tradition* of Hippolytus of Rome (ca. 220) and the *Didascalia* of the apostles (from northern Syria in the first half of the third century). Information is also given in the writings of Clement of Alexandria (d. 220) and Origen (d. 251). These sources provide a smattering of information from the three major centers of Christianity.[2] A worship service dating from the end of the third century may have looked something like the following liturgies.[3]

95

THE LITURGY OF THE WORD

Lections: Law, Prophets, Epistles, Acts, Gospels, Letters from bishops
Psalms sung by cantors between the lections
Alleluias
Sermon or Sermons
Deacon's litany for catechumens and penitents
Dismissal of all but the faithful

THE LITURGY OF THE UPPER ROOM

Deacon's litany for the faithful, with diptychs (lists of names) of living and
dead
Kiss of peace
Offertory: Collection of alms
Presentation of elements
Preparation of elements and admixture of water to wine
    Sursum corda [Lift up your hearts]
    Consecration Prayer:
    Preface: Thanksgiving and adoration for creation, holiness of God,
    etc.
    Sanctus [Holy, Holy, Holy]
    Thanksgiving for redemption [a prayer]
    Words of Institution
    Anamnesis [remembrance]
    Epiclesis [invocation of the Holy Spirit]
    Great intercession for living and dead
    Lord's Prayer
    Fraction [breaking of the bread]
    Elevation—"Holy things to the holy"—and Delivery
    Communion of all in both kinds, each communicant replying
    "Amen"; during reception
Psalms 43 and 34 were sung by cantors.
    Post-communion thanksgiving
    Deacon's litany and celebrant's brief intercession
    Reservation of bread only, for sick and absent
    Dismissal

A comparison of the above service of worship with that provided by Justin
100 years earlier shows no essential change in the structure of Word or sacrament,
in the Christ-centered nature of worship, or in the sense of enactment. However,
some ceremonial additions had also been made. Let us look at these.

Salutation

Minister: The Lord be with you.
> *or*, Peace be with you.
> *or*, The grace of the Lord Jesus Christ, the love of God and the
> communion of the Holy Ghost be with you all.

People: And with thy spirit.

The salutation had its origin in ancient Israel as a greeting exchanged between people. For example, when Boaz arrived from Bethlehem, he greeted the harvesters with "The LORD be with you," and they called back, "The LORD bless you" (Ruth 2:4). This same kind of greeting, which was common among Christians, soon became the greeting that signaled the beginning of Christian worship and preceded the prayers of the church. Its usage in the third-century liturgies testifies to its common acceptance in the church by the end of the second century, although the actual origin of its usage is unknown.

Sursum Corda

Minister: Lift up your hearts.
People: We lift them up to the Lord.
Minister: Let us give thanks to the Lord.
People: It is meet and right to do so.

Hippolytus is the first to give us evidence of the use of the *Sursum corda*, though the exact origin of it is not known. It was developed, however, as a preface to the Lord's Supper to accent the spirit of thanksgiving. It is found everywhere in all the liturgies after Cyprian.

Sanctus

Holy, Holy, Holy, Lord God Almighty,
Heaven and earth are full of thy glory;
Glory be to thee, O Lord.

The biblical origin for the use of the *Sanctus* in worship is found in the heavenly visions of Isaiah (6:3) and John (Rev. 4:8). The first allusion to its use in Christian worship is made by Clement (A.D. 96) in his letter to the Corinthians. Although it is not possible to trace its development, it was in wide usage by the third century. It was used during the Lord's Supper and marks the beginning of the special prayer of thanksgiving (the eucharistic prayer).

Ancient sources also mention the use of the *Kyrie eleison* (Lord, have mercy) as well as the "thanks be to God" after Scripture readings and the "Amen" after prayers. The Lord's Prayer was also frequently used after the prayer of consecration (of the bread and wine).[4]

Prayers were probably said while people stood with their arms stretched heavenward or folded on the breast as in ancient Jewish worship. The Scriptures were read from a rostrum. It was the custom to stand during the reading of the

Gospels to accentuate the fact that these books are the most precious of the New Testament because they speak directly of the Savior. Gradually signs of respect accompanied the reading of the Gospel and the bringing forth of the elements of bread and wine. These two acts were among the most significant actions of the worshiping community because they were the chief points of proclamation.

The chief officiant of worship was either the bishop or the minister (or ministers), depending on the size of the congregation. The deacons were also highly involved in worship. They directed the people, read the Scriptures, led in prayer, guarded the doors, maintained order, presented the elements, and helped to distribute them. The people were also involved. They assisted in the readings and played their part in the drama with responses, prayers, and alms.[5]

It is generally recognized that while certain parts of the service were fixed (e.g., the use of the Scripture, prayers, salutation, *Sursum corda* and *Sanctus*), there was nevertheless a great deal of freedom. The prayers were not yet fixed and the liturgy was not so completely structured that free worship could not be contained within the generally accepted order. The statement that Justin had written, "The president similarly sends up prayers and thanksgiving to the best of his ability," appears to have been true in the third century as well. Nevertheless, the increasingly strict attention given to the content of the eucharistic prayer in the third century is evidenced by Hippolytus's *The Apostolic Tradition*.

FOURTH- AND FIFTH-CENTURY WORSHIP

In the fourth and fifth centuries the status of the church changed dramatically following the conversion of Constantine. In this favored context the church grew rapidly, formulated its theology in various creeds, and developed a more fixed form in its worship. This era is known as the period of classical Christianity, the golden age of the Fathers, and the most creative and formative time in the history of the church. While there is warrant for criticism of worship in this era, it still remains the most important historical period for the thoughtful working out of the rituals that have characterized Christian worship through the centuries. Therefore, an understanding of this period is highly important if we are to know how to worship today.[6]

One important factor was the emergence of ecclesiastical centers in the influential cities of the Roman Empire. These centers gradually developed a particular style that was reflected in theology and worship. Each area assumed, as it were, a special stamp. In basic structure all the liturgies are the same, retaining the two foci of Word and sacrament. The difference arises in the ceremony and style that reflect the local culture.

The Eastern Liturgy

Worship in the fourth century began to reflect local culture. This is particularly true of Eastern Christian worship. The Eastern worldview was informed by the Hellenistic love for the aesthetic. The great contributions of this culture were poetry, literature, art, and philosophy. All of these interests aided the development of a poetic mind and a sense of imagery and artistic expression. That worship was shaped by the Hellenistic imagination is evident in the extensive use of ceremonial signs and symbols in Eastern worship. Byzantine worship was highly ceremonial, gloriously beautiful, and deeply mystical.[7]

Ceremony in the St. John Chrysostom liturgy is most clearly seen in the Little Entrance and the Great Entrance. The Little Entrance centers around the reading of the Gospel and intends to accent the significance of the Word of God. In a rich ceremony intending to invoke awe and reverence for the Word of God, the book is carried by a deacon accompanied by a procession of ministers and acolytes, who bear crosses, candles, and incense. They proceed through the north door of the iconostasis screen, a screen on which the icons are arranged, dividing the altar area from the sanctuary. They walk down the center aisle of the church where the gospel book is ceremonially blessed and kissed. They then return through the royal door to the holy table where the gospel lesson is sung or read.

The Great Entrance centers around the bread and wine and intends to accent the death and resurrection of Jesus Christ. It is even richer in ceremony than the Little Entrance to emphasize its importance in the work of redemption. This procession includes all the ministers, with the acolytes carrying lights, the thurifers swinging the incense, and others carrying signs of the Passion such as the cross, the spear, the scourge, and the thorns. They pass through the north door of the iconostasis, returning again through the royal door. The celebrant bears the cup, and the deacon carries the paten on his head so all can see the veiled symbols of bread and wine. The doors are shut while the ministers receive the elements and then are flung open for the people to come and communicate.[8]

These rich ceremonies are carried out in settings of glorious beauty. The Eastern church has been strongly influenced by the images of heavenly worship described by the apostle John in Revelation 4–5. The opening lines of John's vision provide a glimpse of this beauty: "I was in the Spirit, and there before me was a throne in heaven with someone sitting on it. And the one who sat there had the appearance of jasper and carnelian. A rainbow, resembling an emerald, encircled the throne" (Rev. 4:2–3). This vision combined with the natural Hellenistic propensity toward beauty has given shape to the rich colors of the fresco painted walls, the simple beauty of the icons, and the colorful vestments of the clergy. The concern of Eastern worship is to bring heaven down to earth and transport earth to heaven. It is born of the conviction that we earthlings join in that heavenly assembly. No beauty can surpass the beauty of God on his throne encircled by his creation while his creatures worship him.

A story in the *Russian Primary Chronicle* relates how Vladimir, the Prince of Kiev, chose to adopt the Orthodox form of Christianity. He sent emissaries to search for the true religion. They visited the Muslim Bulgars of the Volga, the German and the Roman Christians, and finally traveled to Constantinople where they found the true religion as a result of attending the liturgy of the church of the Holy Wisdom. In their report to Vladimir, they wrote: "We knew not whether we were in heaven or on earth, for there is no such splendor or beauty anywhere upon earth. We cannot describe it to you; only this we know, that God dwells there among men, and that their service surpasses the worship of all other places. For we cannot forget that beauty."[9]

The rich ceremony combined with this glorious beauty intends to convey the sense of the mystical. Since earthly worship joins heavenly worship, God is present. For this reason care is taken to communicate the mystical presence of God in the ceremony and beauty of the liturgy. This sense of the mystical is communicated especially in the development of the sanctuary screen. Behind the screen the great mystery of Christ's death and resurrection is enacted in the drama of the Eucharist.[10]

The Western Liturgy

The information about the development of the Western liturgy is scant and late by comparison with the sources available from the East. Early sources are found in Justin Martyr and Hippolytus, but between 220 and 500 we have no adequate sources of information regarding the Western liturgy.[11]

After 500, two rites (the Gallican and the Roman) appear to exist side by side in the West. The Roman rite was used principally in Rome, whereas the Gallican rite was used throughout Europe and varied considerably according to local custom. There is evidence that both of these rites influenced each other until the ninth century when the Gallican rites were suppressed under Pepin and Charlemagne. Thereafter, the Roman rite was the standard approach to worship in the West. From the tenth to the sixteenth centuries the Roman rite underwent numerous minor changes in ceremony and emphasis until 1570 when it became fixed in form.

The Gallican rite, originating from the primitive worship of the early church, reflects customs that are more colorful, sensuous, symbolic, and dramatic than does the Roman liturgy. It is longer and more flexible than the Roman rite as well.[12]

The origins of the Roman rite are equally unclear. The earliest liturgies, in Greek, were gradually translated into Latin in the fourth century. The only document of importance from this period is the *de Sacramentis*, which provides insight into the developing customs of worship. More helpful are the *Gelasian*

Sacramentary from Pope Gelasius (492-496), and the *Gregorian Sacramentary*, named after Gregory the Great, pope from 590 to 604. The texts between the ninth and fifteenth centuries, contained in *Ordines Romani*, are more helpful because they give detailed descriptions of the Mass.

Like the Eastern church, the Western church also reflected the local culture. The Roman mindset was considerably different from that of the Greek East. The Romans were characterized by a spirit of pragmatism. This is evident in their buildings and in the development of Roman laws. This spirit is reflected in early Roman worship. It is not ostentatious or highly ceremonial, but sober and simple.

The tendency toward simplicity is obvious in both the order and symbols of worship. A brief comparison of the Roman rite with the Byzantine rite clearly indicates the uncluttered nature of Roman worship. It moved simply without much ceremony from part to part. It had not developed much beyond the simple movement of a third-century liturgy. The character of simplicity was equally true in Roman ceremony. Ceremonies included the elevation of the host, the ringing of bells, and the use of lights. In the Roman rite, censing and genuflections did not come into use until much later. There was great beauty, a sense of God's presence, and a feeling of awe and reverence provoked by the simple majesty of the Roman rite.[13]

BAPTISM IN THE ANCIENT CHURCH

One of the most fruitful areas of worship scholarship in recent years is the study of the rites of initiation in the early church. These rites, which flowered in the third and fourth centuries in particular, carried the person coming for baptism through seven steps, four of which were periods of development and three of which were passage rites laden with rich symbolism. The entire process, which took up to three years in some places, presupposed the theme of Christ as victor over the powers of evil, the baptismal candidate as the recipient of Christ's power over sin through an identification with his death and resurrection, the church as the mothering and nurturing community, and public worship (the candidate went to the service of the Word for instruction but was not allowed to celebrate the Eucharist until after baptism) as the context for instruction and character formation. The seven steps are as follows:

1) Inquiry: A presentation of the faith to the seeker with an affirmative response.
2) Rite of Welcome: Welcome into the church as a new catechumenate. Rituals included the rite of the renunciation of false worship and signing with the cross as a symbol of belonging to Christ.
3) The catechumenate: A two or three year period of instruction and personal character formation.

4)   The Rite of Election: The catechumenate affirms a personal relation with Christ by writing his or her name in the book of life. This ritual is also known as the enrollment of names.

5)   Period of Purification and Enlightenment: In the spirit of Ephesians 6:12, the soon-to-be baptized person receives a daily exorcism for personal purity of life and faith.

6)   The Rite of Initiation: Baptism is usually held on an Easter Sunday morning after the all-night Paschal vigil. The rite of baptism is accompanied by numerous signs and symbols such as the removal of clothing and the donning of a new white gown, the renunciation of the devil, the washing in oil as a symbol of the reception of the Holy Spirit, the passing of the peace, and the first Eucharist.

7)   Mystagogue: During this period of time the newly baptized Christian learns more about the mysteries of faith (Eucharist) and is taught to be mindful of the needs of other.

During the medieval era this highly symbolic and deeply moving process fell into disuse primarily because of the rise and spread of infant baptism along with the shift from living in a hostile culture to the now post-Constantinian culture friendly to the Christian church.

There are other developments during this period that we will examine in part 4. They include the emergence of church buildings, the development of the church year, and the development of church music.

MEDIEVAL WORSHIP

The medieval period witnessed a shift in the meaning of worship. We can trace the beginning of this change from the fourth and fifth centuries to the early medieval period, the time when two distinct lines of development become discernible. The established church increasingly emphasized worship as a mystery, while the monastic movement stressed the devotional character of worship.

Worship as Mystery

The idea of worship as mystery has its origin in the mistaken use of ceremonial forms. Forms in and of themselves are not wrong. They are the means through which worship is conducted, the signs and symbols of the reality they bear. However, when ceremonial forms become an end rather than a means, they assume a cultic character and tend to replace the message they bear.[14]

The change that occurred in medieval worship was not in the form of worship but in the understanding, the meaning, and the experience of forms. The ceremonial form (hereafter referred to as the cult) became more and more a sacred action in itself, a mystery performed for the sanctification of those participating. This is most noticeable in the evolution of the external organization of the cult: in the gradually increasing separation of clergy (who "perform the mystery") from the people; in the emphasis by means of ceremony on the mysterious, dreadful and sacred character of the celebrant; in the stress which is laid henceforth on ritual purity, the state of untouchableness, the "sacred" versus the "profane."[15]

There are a number of reasons why this change of understanding occurred. First, during the Constantinian era the church converted many pagan festivals and customs and invested them with Christian meaning. This missiological strategy had its definite advantages in Christianizing the Empire but also suffered the disadvantage of an unhealthy influence from the mystery cults (although scholars now believe that the influence was much less than previously assumed). The mystery cults regarded cultic action as an end in itself. This notion influenced the church, making the action of worship a mystery.[16]

The idea that the church's worship was a mystery was augmented by several other developments. The change in language, for example, was a factor. Although the church spread into remote areas, far from Rome, it retained Latin as the language of the Mass. This surrounded the Mass and the clergy with an aura of mystery since most of the people did not understand what was happening. Furthermore, the church distanced itself from the people even more as it increasingly viewed itself as a hierarchical institution rather than a body. The church dispensed salvation. The liturgy, especially the Eucharist, became the means of receiving this salvation. This view of the church was enhanced by the developments in eucharistic theology. In the ninth century, Paschasius Radbertus proposed a view of the presence of Jesus in the Mass by virtue of the miraculous change that occurred in the bread and wine. The view laid the groundwork for the doctrine of transubstantiation that became dogma at the Fourth Lateran Council in 1215.[17]

A major result of the mystical view of worship is that the Mass became an epiphany of God. An overemphasis on the *action of God* in the Mass tended to overshadow the corporate action of the people in worship. The Mass assumed the character of a sacred drama that was played out by the clergy while the people watched. Furthermore, the Mass itself assumed an allegorical character. This sacred drama of the life, death, and resurrection of Jesus was perceptible to the eye. Each part of the liturgy, the vestments, the liturgical utensils, and the motions of the clergy were invested with meaning from the life of Christ. A typical example of this approach is found in the ninth-century writings of Amalor.

The *introit* alludes to the choir of the Prophets (who announced the advent of Christ just as the singers announce the advent of the bishop); . . . the *Kyrie eleison* alludes to the Prophets at the time of Christ's coming, Zachary and his son John among them; the *Gloria in excelsis Deo* points to the throng of angels who proclaimed to the shepherds the joyous tidings of our Lord's birth (and indeed in this manner, the first one spoke and the others joined in, just as in the Mass the bishop intones and the whole church joins in); the *first collect* refers to what our Lord did in His twelfth year; . . . the Epistle alludes to the preaching of John; the *responsorium* to the readiness of the Apostles when our Lord called them and they followed Him; the Alleluia to their joy of heart when they heard His promises or saw the miracles He wrought; . . . the Gospel to His preaching. . . . The rest of what happens in the Mass refers to the time from Sunday on, when the disciples drew close to Him (along with the multitude—making their gift-offerings), up to His Ascension or to Pentecost. The prayer which the priest says from the *secreta* to the *Nobis quoque peccatoribus* signifies the prayer of Jesus on Mount Olivet. What occurs later signifies the time during which Christ lay in the grave. When the bread is immersed in the wine, this means the return of Christ's soul to His body. The next action signifies the greetings offered by Christ to His Apostles. And the breaking of the offerings signifies the breaking of bread performed by the Lord before the two at Emmaus.[18]

Another example of the mysteriological view of worship is the notion that the Mass is a sacrifice offered to God for the benefit of the living and the dead. This resulted in an extreme reverence for the handling of the host (no layperson's hand was to touch it) and outlandish claims for the efficacy of the Mass. For example, it was argued that food tastes better after hearing a Mass, that one will not die a sudden death during a Mass, and that the souls in purgatory will not suffer while a Mass is being said for them. This view led to a multiplicity of masses and the practice of "saying mass" for the benefit of someone (living or dead) for a stipend. More altars were needed for this purpose (a requirement that affected architecture in the medieval period), and the Mass became more firmly entrenched as something belonging to the clergy. In many instances the mystery was turned into a superstition and the real meaning of worship was lost to both clergy and the people alike.[19]

Worship as Devotion

The second strand of development in the medieval period occurred within the monastic movement. Originally the monastics began as a protest against the growing worldliness of the church, but gradually they became a formative and influential movement within the church, though they maintained a prophetic stance.

At first the worship of the monastic orders was no different than that of the church. They celebrated the Eucharist on Saturday and Sunday even though they had to walk long distances to do so. However, the monastics developed their own approach to prayer. Prayer had always been important in the Christian tradition, but the new attitude saw prayer as the sole content of life. The difference was not that the monks did not work (though some did spend their entire time in prayer), but that everything in life became subordinated to prayer. Prayer became the chief work of the monks.[20]

This attitude of monasticism came into sharp contrast with the growing institutionalism and worldliness of the medieval church. The emphasis of the established church shifted from the eschatological kingdom of God to the kingdom of God on earth. The church became, therefore, the protector and sanctifier of the world. Monasticism, as it continued to emphasize the coming kingdom, reacted against the secularization of the church and continued to emphasize the other-worldly character of the Christian faith.

The continued eschatological concern of monasticism was reflected in an approach to worship that became increasingly pietistic or devotional. For example, the Eucharist became an instrument of piety. Participation in the Eucharist was a means of becoming holier, a means of sanctification and growth in Christ. The early church's emphasis on the Eucharist as the actualization of the church and an anticipation of the future feast of the kingdom was not denied. The newer view considered Communion as an act of spiritual benefit, a means of receiving spiritual nourishment.

A similar case may be made for the emergence of the rules of prayer, the devotional manuals developed for the various times of daily prayer. These times of prayer remained consistent with the times set aside in the church, and the devotions retained the same content of Psalms, prayer, Scripture, and chants. In addition, a private rule of prayer developed among the monks, having a strong emphasis on personal prayer and the Psalms. Originally, the church's prayers were offered because of their content, and the set times were intended to demonstrate that all time from morning to night belonged to God. Those prayers were a proclamation of the meaning of time and life and, though devotional, did not have as their prime intent the development of personal piety. In the medieval period, however, the personal pietistic concern of the monastic life of prayer influenced the prayer of the church toward a personal devotional meaning. As a result prayer became a means to increase piety.

CONCLUSION

In this chapter we have seen an outline of the development of worship from the third century to the dawn of the Reformation. Although space has not permitted a detailed discussion of this development, the lines along which worship was passed down were clear.

In brief, the norm of Christian worship is both Word and sacrament that proclaim the death and resurrection of Jesus Christ for the salvation of the world. Around these two foci are gathered the prayers of the church and words of acclamation and praise. In these actions the church, as the people of God, is actualized and the kingdom is anticipated.

Gradually, however, beginning with the Constantinian era, worship changed by the increasing addition of ceremony and the subtle influence of the mystery religions. These new emphases became more extreme in the medieval period. Although the basic structure and content of worship remained continuous with the past, the meaning of worship for both the clergy and the laity underwent some major changes. Worship became a "mystery" in which God was made present (an epiphany). This was accomplished through an allegorical view of the Mass and the doctrine of the bodily presence of Jesus in the bread and wine. In this way the Mass assumed the character of a sacrifice and was celebrated for the benefit of both the living and the dead (creating a multiplicity of masses and other abuses).

Thus, the principle to keep in mind in constructing a worship philosophy for today is that we ought not allow worship to be accommodated to current cultural norms to such an extent that worship loses its meaning.

---

1. A great deal of historical material is contained in Cheslyn Jones, Geoffrey Wainwright, and Edward Yarnold, eds., *The Study of Liturgy* (New York: Oxford Univ. Press, 1978); and Joseph Jungmann, *The Mass of the Roman Rite*, trans. Francis A. Brunner and Rev. Charles K. Riepe (New York: Benzinger Brothers, 1959). Two shorter but highly valuable works are Theodor Klauser, *A Short History of the Western Liturgy*, 2d ed. (New York: Oxford Univ. Press, 1979), and William Maxwell, *An Outline of Christian Worship* (London: Oxford Univ. Press, 1939). For primary sources of liturgy see Bard Thompson, *Liturgies of the Western Church* (New York: New American Library, 1974). Recent surveys include James F. White, *A Brief History of Christian Worship* (Nashville: Abingdon, 1993); Robert Webber, ed., *The Twenty Centuries of Worship* (Nashville: Abbott Martyn, 1994), and Edward Foley, *From Age to Age* (Chicago: Liturgical Training Publications, 1991).

2. See Lucien Deiss, *Early Sources of the Liturgy*, trans. Benet Weatherhead (Collegeville, Minn.: Liturgical, 1975), and Willy Rordorf, et al., *The Eucharist of the Early Christians* (New York: Pueblo, 1978).

3. Maxwell, *An Outline of Christian Worship*, 17.

4. For evidence of the widespread usage of these forms in the early liturgies of the church

see R. C. D. Jasper and G. C. Cumings, eds., *Prayers of the Eucharist: Early and Reformed*, 2d ed. (New York: Oxford Univ. Press, 1980); see also Maxwell, *An Outline of Christian Worship*, 15–16.

5. For a good description of congregational action in early worship see Gregory Dix, *The Shape of the Liturgy* (London: Dacre, 1975), chap. 2.

6. An excellent interpretation of this era is provided by Alexander Schmemann, *Introduction to Liturgical Theology* (Bangor, Maine: American Orthodox, 1967), chap. 3.

7. See Nikolaus Liesel and Tibor Makula, *The Eucharistic Liturgies of the Eastern Church* (Collegeville, Minn.: Liturgical, 1963). This work contains the text, together with pictures, of the Coptic, Ethiopic, Syrian, Malankarese, Maronite, Greek, Melkite, Russian, Ruthenian, Chaldean, Malabarese, and Armenian rites.

8. Maxwell, *An Outline of Christian Worship*, 40–41.

9. See Timothy Ware, *The Orthodox Church* (Baltimore: Penguin, 1963), 269.

10. For an interpretation of the Orthodox liturgy see Alexander Schmemann, *For the Life of the World* (Crestwood, N.Y.: St. Vladimir's Press, 1973). And *The Eucharist* (Crestwood, N.Y.: St. Vladimir's Pess, 1988).

11. See Jungmann, *The Mass of the Roman Rite*, 37ff.

12. See Jasper and Cumings, *Prayers of the Eucharist*, 105ff.

13. See Thompson, *Liturgies of the Western Church*, 41–42.

14. For an excellent interpretation of this process see Schmemann, *Introduction to Liturgical Theology*, 72ff.

15. Schmemann, *Introduction to Liturgical Theology*, 98.

16. For an evaluation of the influence of mystery cults on ancient Christian worship, see Joseph Jungmann, *The Early Liturgy to the Time of Gregory the Great* (Notre Dame, Ind.: Univ. of Notre Dame Press, 1959), 122ff.

17. See Thompson, *Liturgies of the Western Church*, 42.

18. Quoted by Jungmann, *The Mass of the Roman Rite*, 67–68.

19. Jungmann, *The Mass of the Roman Rite*, 97ff.

20. See Schmemann, *Introduction to Liturgical Theology*, 105ff.

Chapter 10

Reformation and Free Church Worship

T he sixteenth century was a time of great upheaval in the world and in the church. The old medieval synthesis of church and state achieved in the thirteenth century had cracked and fallen apart by the beginning of the sixteenth century. The rise of nation states, the shift toward a money economy, the rise of learning connected with the Renaissance, and the emergence of a worldly humanism resulted in a new way of seeing the world.

In this context, a great religious upheaval took place known as the Reformation. Leaders like Martin Luther and John Calvin wanted to strip the church of unnecessary traditions and return it to the purity of the early church, both in doctrine and in worship.

In the period beyond the Reformation (1700–1900), the Western world continued to undergo vast changes. The most significant of these changes was the rise of the Enlightenment, the Age of Reason. The desire to prove Christianity, to gather evidence for its truthfulness (Conservatives), and the desire to reinterpret Christianity in a nonsupernatural way (Liberals) moved the Christian conversation and dialogue in radical new directions.

In addition, the rise of individualism, tolerance, pluralism, and the American experiment altered the face of the church toward the rise of a new movement known as the free church tradition.[1] In the midst of all these changes, worship underwent vast changes of its own and emerged in a form quite different from the past. In this chapter we will survey those changes.

109

CLASSICAL PROTESTANT WORSHIP

Although the Reformation was principally a reform of theology, it was inevitable that a reform of worship should also result. How worship was conceived at the beginning of the Reformation is aptly summarized in the following words of William D. Maxwell:

> We have seen that, at the beginning of the sixteenth century, the celebration of the Lord's Supper in the Western Church had become a dramatic spectacle, culminating not in communion but in the miracle of transubstantiation, and marked by adoration, not unmixed with superstition, at the elevation. Said inaudibly in an unknown tongue, and surrounded with ornate ceremonial and, if a sung mass, with elaborate musical accompaniment, the rite presented only meager opportunity for popular participation. The people were not encouraged to communicate more often than once a year. The sermon had fallen into a grave decline, most parish priests being too illiterate to preach; and the place of the Scripture lections had been usurped on a great many days by passages from the lives and legends of the saints. The Scriptures were not fully accessible in the vernacular, and paid masses and indulgences were a source of simoniacal exploitation. Reformation was an urgent necessity.[2]

In spite of the similarities among reforming groups, the reform of worship was not uniform. Some groups retained continuity with the past, while others completely broke with tradition to forge new styles of worship. In order to understand these trends, we will look at the common concerns of Reformation worship and the differences between Reformers that accounted for the various styles of worship in the Reformation churches.

Common Concerns of the Reformers

First, Protestants rejected the Mass because of the medieval view of it as a repetition of the sacrifice of Christ. Luther, in "The Babylonian Captivity of the Church," called the Mass an "abuse" that brought

> an endless host of others in its train, so that the faith of this sacrament has become utterly extinct and the holy sacrament has been turned into a veritable fair, tavern, and place of merchandise. Hence participants, brotherhoods, intercessions, merits, anniversaries, memorial days, and the like wares are bought and sold, traded and bartered in the church, and from this priests and monks derive their whole living.[3]

Luther's most direct criticisms were aimed at the Roman prayers of the eucharistic canon. The Mass, Luther charged, had lost its original focus as a *thanksgiving* and had become a propitiation to please God. For Luther, this notion was incompatible with the Scriptures. It stood against the gospel and had, therefore, to be excised from worship. Furthermore, the theology of sacrifice in the Mass created a host of other problems. People expected all sorts of benefits and advantages from hearing Mass, including healings, the release of souls from purgatory, and other magical results. The Mass had even lost the idea of communion, because people did not have to be present at the Mass—it could be said on their behalf. Consequently, the priest *saying* the Mass took the place of worship by the people and became a legalistic means of buying salvation. For the Reformers these late medieval practices struck at the heart of the Christian message and perverted the essential nature of the Christian faith as a religion of *grace*. The overthrow of the Mass as a sacrifice was necessary. In this all the Protestants concurred.

The Reformers rejected the doctrine of transubstantiation. Underlying transubstantiation was the Roman notion of *opus operatum*, the belief that the mere performance of the Mass effected the presence of Christ automatically. In this view the performance of the rite imparted a blessing without the faith of the recipient, even without the elements of the Mass being distributed to the congregation. Transubstantiation explained the means by which Christ became present in the sacrifice. The *substance* of the bread and wine changed into the body and blood of Christ and was offered to the Father as a sacrifice for salvation. The connection between the Mass as a sacrifice and transubstantiation naturally led the Reformers, who rejected the one, to reject the other as well.

Next, the Reformers insisted on the restoration of the Word to its ancient and proper place in worship. The imbalance between Word and sacrament that led to the falling away of preaching and teaching was regarded as a one-sided approach to worship. In the spring of 1523 Luther issued instructions in a pamphlet entitled *Concerning the Ordering of Divine Worship in the Congregation* in which he concluded with these words:

> This is the sum of the matter: that everything shall be done so that the Word prevails. . . . We can spare everything except the Word. We profit by nothing so much as by the Word. For the whole Scripture shows that the Word should have free course among Christians. And in Luke 10, Christ himself says: "One thing is needful"—that Mary sit at the feet of Christ and daily hear his Word. . . ."[4]

Ulrich Zwingli, a Swiss Reformer, went even farther than Luther in insisting that the people were to give ear to the Word of God alone. He abolished organs as well as other music, vestments, pictures, and anything else that would detract from the centrality of the Word.

Finally, the Reformers also agreed that worship should be in the vernacular and that the twofold structure of Word and sacrament be maintained. Zwingli was the only Reformer who disagreed with the desire to return to the ancient structure of Word and sacrament. His emphasis was on the Word only. Zwingli's position remained the most influential in the circles of Calvinism, and, to the distress of John Calvin, quarterly communion, rather than weekly communion, became standard in the churches most influenced by Calvinism. This influence extended through the English Puritans to the Baptists, Presbyterians, Congregationalists, and independents and spread through them to most of American Protestant Christianity.

Differences Among the Reformers

In spite of the unity on the above matters, differences regarding worship existed among the Reformers. The fundamental disagreement occurred over continuity with the Roman Catholic heritage. The Lutheran and Anglican traditions retained much of ancient worship; the Zwinglian and Anabaptist traditions made a radical break with the past; and the Reformed church maintained a middle position.[5] For example, the Lutheran Augsburg Confession states:

> Our churches are falsely accused of abolishing the mass. Actually, the mass is retained among us and is celebrated with the greatest reverence. *Almost all the customary ceremonies are also retained.*. . . . The mass among us is supported by the example of the church as seen from the scriptures and the fathers.[6] (emphasis added)

The Anglicans also retained much of the past. After the break with Rome, the Mass remained essentially the same throughout the reign of Henry VIII. Not until the reign of Edward VI were strong Protestant notions asserted in the Mass. These were contained in Cranmer's *Order of the Communion* and included such things as the deletion of the word *mass*, the abolishing of vestments, and the replacement of altars by communion tables. Other changes were made in the order of worship including the deletion of the *introit*, the *Glory be to thee, O Lord* at the Gospel reading, and the prayers for the dead. These changes, however, were short lived because of the accession of the Roman Catholic Mary to the throne. Her short reign was followed by the lengthy reign of Elizabeth, under whom the *Book of Common Prayer* (as revised in 1559) was established by law. In the *Book of Common Prayer* and in the tract entitled *Of Ceremonies* the Anglican church reaffirmed continuity with the ancient rite with few changes.[7]

A more drastic approach was taken by Zwingli and the Anabaptists. Zwingli repudiated all ceremonies as pagan and commenced to rid the church of traditions and many worship rubrics regardless of their possible value to the church. He was convinced that faith came through the Holy Spirit alone apart from physical channels or external means.

The Anabaptists not only rejected ceremonies in worship but the necessity of formal public worship as well. It was their conviction that the true church was an obedient and suffering people whose daily walk with God was of utmost importance. This walk climaxed in the gathering of Christians together for prayer, Bible reading, admonition, and the Lord's Supper in the informal atmosphere of the home. They thus refused to attend the worship of the state church and met in secret at various times in an unscheduled and impromptu manner. The time and place of other scheduled meetings were communicated by word of mouth to those who belonged to the closely knit community.[8]

The Reformed community forged out a middle-of-the-road approach to worship. John Calvin's major source was the work of Martin Bucer of Strasbourg, who combined a Zwinglian emphasis with Lutheranism and developed *The Strasbourg Liturgy*.[9] Before Bucer, the worship at Strasbourg retained ceremonial aspects such as vestments, elevation, washing of the celebrant's hands, and genuflection but omitted all indications of a doctrine of sacrifice. Bucer reduced the worship to its simplest forms. Most of the versicles and responses disappeared with the resulting loss of the antiphonal character of worship. Proses such as the *Gloria in excelsis Deo* and the *Kyries* were replaced by metrical psalms and hymns. Even the *Sursum corda* and the prefaces such as the *Sanctus* and the *Benedictus* disappeared, being substituted by a general prayer of thanksgiving for Christ's work. The lections also disappeared, allowing the minister to "pick his text," and sermons became an hour in length. In general, it may be said that the historic substance of worship was replaced by forms less aesthetic and graceful. A more rational approach to worship had taken root and would flower among the Protestants.[10]

Calvin came to Strasbourg and ministered to a small group of French exiles between 1538 and 1541. It was here that his views on worship, influenced by Bucer and the *Strasbourg Liturgy*, began to take shape. His standard was the corporate worship of the early church, which he thought was best represented in the rites of Strasbourg. His writing on worship, *The Form of Prayers and Manner of Ministering the Sacraments According to the Use of the Ancient Church*, shows where his sympathies lie. Calvin made some changes in the *Strasbourg Liturgy* in the variants, the confession, the Lord's Prayer, the reading of the Decalogue, and the singing of psalms. But none of this changed the Zwinglian approach to worship. Calvin's liturgy, following Bucer's synthesis, became the major approach to worship in the Reformed churches.[11]

One further matter should be noted about Calvin. It was his intent, in keeping with his appreciation of the worship of the early church, to maintain the ancient structure of worship proclaiming Christ's death, resurrection, and return in *both Word and sacrament*. The fact that most Reformed churches today follow the Zwinglian practice of quarterly communion is no fault of Calvin. The magistrates who were influenced by Zwingli in this matter did not allow Calvin to celebrate Holy Communion weekly as he wished. This attitude is seen in a letter Calvin wrote to the magistrates of Berne in 1555.

There is another matter, though not a new one [to which I would call your attention], namely, that we celebrate the Lord's Supper four times a year, and you three times. Please God, gentlemen, that both you and we may establish a more frequent usage. For it is evident from St. Luke in the Book of Acts that communion was much more frequently celebrated in the primitive Church; and that continued for a long time in the ancient Church, until this abomination of the mass was set up by Satan, who so caused it that people received communion only once or twice a year. Wherefore, we must acknowledge that it is a defect in us that we do not follow the example of the Apostles.[12]

The pattern of Lutheran and Reformed worship, or what is sometimes called "state church" worship, did not change significantly into the twentieth century.[13] where change in worship style is particularly seen is in the development of free church worship, or worship anticipated by the Anabaptists of the sixteenth century who refused to allow the church to be in relationship with the state.

FREE CHURCH WORSHIP

The most distinct feature of the free church movement was in its understanding of how salvation is received. In the past centuries salvation had always been connected with baptism. But now the shift emphasized personal appropriation through understanding or experience. Baptism was less God's action and more a sign of faith and acceptance by the believer. The shift toward experience devalued not only baptism but other sign-acts such as the Eucharist and the liturgical calendar. Faith in Jesus Christ and the worship of God were to happen in the mind or in the heart. Consequently, signs, symbols, bodily postures and gestures, and the forms and ceremonies that accompanied traditional worship rituals were feared as idols and images that turned the heart away from God. Worship was to be spiritual and only spiritual. Examples of these new convictions can be seen in the antiliturgical movement, the rise of pedagogical worship in the seventeenth and eighteenth centuries, and the rise of an evangelistic approach to worship in the nineteenth century.[14]

The Antiliturgical Movement

The antiliturgical movement originated with the Puritans in England.[15] The emphasis shifted away from the use of a prayer book to "spiritual" worship. Three examples from the early Baptists, the Congregationalists, and the Quakers will suffice to illustrate the point.

John Smyth, an early Baptist, wrote:

We hold that the worship of the New Testament properly so called is spiritual proceeding originally from the heart; and that reading out of a book (though it is a lawful ecclesiastical action) is no part of spiritual worship, but rather the invention of the man of sin, it being substituted for the part of spiritual worship.

We hold that seeing prophesying is a part of spiritual worship: therefore in time of prophesying it is unlawful to have the book [i.e., the Bible] as a help before the eye.

We hold that seeing singing a psalm is a part of spiritual worship: therefore it is unlawful to have the book before the eye in time of singing a psalm.[16]

The Congregationalists rejected the use of written prayers, insisting that prayer should be from the heart, directed by the Spirit of God. In support of this view, they set forth six arguments.

1) Written prayers deprive the person of his or her own thoughts and words.

2) Set forms could not meet the variety of needs in a particular congregation.

3) Set forms are idolatrous as they equate the liturgy with the Bible.

4) Set forms lead to overfamiliarity and lack of interest.

5) Imposing set forms is a manner of persecution. [The desire was for each congregation to be free to order its own worship.]

6) Set prayers oppose the appropriate approach to the Father.[17]

Quaker worship is characterized by its abandonment of the ordained ministry and the sacraments in favor of a personal "waiting upon the Spirit" by every member of the congregation. The central concern of Quaker worship is the simple intention of the people of God to open themselves to the presence of Christ in the meeting ("where two or three come together in my name, there am I with them") and to wait upon him to speak through the Spirit. This view rejects any dependence on external aids or rites such as the sacraments (in extreme groups the Spirit's revelation was more important than the Bible). It argues that all ceremonies and forms have been abolished by the new covenant, and that the offices of Christ as prophet, priest, and king are exercised in the worshiping community as they silently wait upon him. Worship is supremely *inward*. Water baptism is an inward spiritual reception of Jesus that has no need of an external rite.[18]

Pedagogical Worship

A second trend in free church worship stressed the need for understanding the Word of God. The primary source of this pedagogical worship comes from the Puritan influence, which affected worship among the Presbyterians, the

Congregationalists, and the independents. The majority of the time in the three to four-hour services was spent in biblical instruction. Below is a description of the kind of pedagogical worship that dominated the eighteenth and nineteenth century.

> Clergy began the service with prayers of *thanksgiving* and later led prayers of *intercession* incorporating concerns spoken out or written by laity. All continued to *stand for singing* led by laity. Often from the table, clergy read the scriptures interspersed with *exegesis* so that the word could be heard and not be a dumb reading. Then they went into the *pulpit* to give their sermons bearing the Bible on any of a wide range of issues related to God's kingdom on earth. Immediately after the sermon as the worship continued, they came down from the pulpit and sat at a table to answer the congregation's questions and hear witnessing by laity, who were free to agree or disagree with what clergy had said. And from the table, clergy gave thanks and gave the bread and wine, as often as each Sunday or at least once a month, to lay leaders who distributed communion to the people. After more singing, the people often gave their offerings at the table.[19]

These congregations developed a commentary approach to the reading of Scripture that opposed what they called "dumb reading." The reader, usually the minister or one trained in the Scripture, always made comments on the meaning and interpretation of the text as it was being read. After the "commentary reading," people from the congregation were encouraged to make prophetic statements or ask questions. The reading was followed by the sermon, which ran for two or three hours with a pause in the middle to allow the people to stretch.[20]

Presbyterians placed a strong emphasis on the use of Scripture in worship. The greatest grievance of the Puritans against the Anglican *Book of Common Prayer* was that it limited the use of Scripture. Later the *Westminster Directory* stipulated the reading of two full chapters (from both the Old and the New Testaments), along with the Psalms as responsive reading. Presbyterians also practiced "lecturing," the habit of making comments on the Scripture as it was being read, and emphasized expository preaching. The minister was encouraged to seek the illumination of God's Spirit through prayer and a humble heart. His sermon was to consist of three parts: the doctrinal content of the text, a development of the argument and reasons for the doctrine in the text, and the application of the text to the hearer. For this reason ministers were to be highly trained in the use of original languages and theology. They were cautioned, however, against using the original languages in the pulpit. Although the *Directory* recommended "frequent" communion, Presbyterians adopted the practice of quarterly communion. Thus the Scripture and its exposition became the dominant and most central factor in Presbyterian worship. Finally, Presbyterianism rejected the use of all "ceremony" in worship unless it was prescribed in the New

Testament.[21] For this reason worship remained simple and appealed to the mind alone, not to sight, smell, taste, and hearing (other than the Word of God).

Evangelistic Worship

A third trend in free church worship emphasized personal experience. This can be illustrated from Pietism, Moravianism, and Revivalism.

Pietism was a movement against dead orthodoxy. It began in Lutheranism in the seventeenth century and spread into pockets of both Protestant and Roman Catholic Christianity. Its major concern was to effect a personal reform of faith over against a mere formal doctrinal or external adherence to the Christian faith. Consequently, Pietists rebelled against established Protestant worship as too dependent on external form. Externalism, it was believed, prevented personal involvement motivated by an openness to the Spirit.[22]

Jean de Labadie of Middleburg was one who emphasized informal worship over ordered worship. Ordered worship was for the nominal Christian, but free worship was for the truly converted person. Converted Christians frequently met in homes, where they prayed from the heart and where a free exposition of Scripture by all was predominant. The key to Pietist worship is found in the stress on *conversion*. In conversion, worship centered no longer on the objective and corporate action of the church, but on the personal experience of the worshiper in worship and was followed by a rigorous ethical walk. In effect, those who were truly converted needed less structure and were less dependent on others for worship. In this way the corporate worship of the congregation and systematic order of congregational action were gradually replaced by the stress on individual experience in worship and a personal walk with the Lord.

One of the most prominent contributions of Moravianism to personal experiential worship is in hymnody. Hymn singing among the Moravians dates all the way back to their beginnings in pre-Reformation days. The special feature of Moravian hymns is the concern to create a subjective experience of the Savior's suffering. These hymns are "emotional, imaginative, sensuous, with a minimum of intellectual structure."[23] The concern of the worshiper was to feel the pain of the Savior and to cause, therefore, a turning to him in love and adoration. One such favorite hymn written by Zinzendorf is "Jesus Thy Blood and Righteousness." In time the preoccupation with "the bloody sweat, the nail prints, the side's cleft opened wide for the faithful" was replaced with less exotic symbolism.

The most famous revivalist of the eighteenth century was John Wesley. His approach to worship represented a blend of classical Protestant forms with the personal element of Pietism. He was strongly influenced by the Moravians and through them learned to stress the importance of conversion and personal experience.[24]

Like the Moravians, the revivalists made significant contributions in hymnody. Their hymns stress conversion and a personal experience of the Savior. The use of hymns in mainline Protestant worship was greeted with a great deal of skepticism. The classical Protestant and Puritan heritage prescribed only Psalms and Scripture. The notion that the church could write its own hymns of praise was an innovative suggestion met with some suspicion. It was through Wesley, however, that hymnody became a mark of Protestant worship. Many of the hymns written earlier in the century by the Congregationalist Isaac Watts stressed the personal devotional element: "When I Survey the Wondrous Cross," "Alas! And Did My Savior Bleed?", "Come, Holy Spirit, Heavenly Dove." Many of the hymns of Charles Wesley, considered to be the greatest literary achievement of the revivalist movement, also contain a strong emphasis on personal experience: "Jesus Lover of My Soul," "Soldiers of Christ, Arise."

A second significant influence of Revivalism was the shift of daily worship from the church building to the home. Because the converted layman had gifts for praying and teaching Scripture daily, morning and evening prayers were moved from the church into the home where the father became minister to his family. In this change, personal involvement and the exercising of gifts for ministering were developed in the home and then made available in the free worship of the church meeting.

A third mark of Revivalism was the introduction of field preaching. In field preaching the services were held in public places outside of the church dwelling. These services developed a unique style of praying, singing, and preaching. The main concern was evangelism—communicating the gospel of Christ to the unconverted. Consequently, the services were designed as an appeal to the unconverted. These services were the forerunner of mass revivals.

Revival worship of the nineteenth century, particularly under the influence of Charles Finney, actually swept away the pedagogical worship of the seventeenth and eighteenth centuries. It introduced an evangelistic style of worship into many churches, an approach to worship still found today in many rural churches. The following comment describes the vast change that took place in free church worship in the nineteenth century:

> It [the pedagogical model of worship] was only fully swept away in some churches by the Second Awakening of the early nineteenth century when "new means" were adopted to evangelize vast numbers of unchurched persons. Adopted for revival circumstances, the "new means" posited the preacher on a stage as the central focus in a worship service devised to convert the people in the congregation. . . .

The revivalists' major alterations in the order and conduct of the worship were made visible in the internal architectural changes that gutted meeting houses from the late 1820's until the Civil War. Removed were the communion table and places for ministers and lay leaders to sit together near the people. And the eighteenth century family box pews were replaced with slip pews so that all people faced forward to the newly erected high platform where the preacher presided throughout the worship. Often the choir and organ (if any) were moved from the back balconies onto the same front platform with the preacher to present a series of prayers, anthems, and preaching to convert individuals. . . .

The changes were even more profound than appear from the alterations in order, conduct and architecture of worship. Clearly communion and substantive lay participation in prayer and preaching declined. But while a sermon remained in the worship service, its scope narrowed. With the sermon focusing on converting individuals, a range of wider social and political concerns received less attention from the pulpit and in the people's exhortations and prayers.[25]

CONCLUSION

This brief survey of Protestant worship suggests several things. First, it shows that the Reformers desired a restoration of those biblical principles of worship that had been enunciated by the early Church Fathers and the classical liturgies. Second, the history of modern Protestant worship points to the importance of the subjective needs of the worshiper. It cannot be denied that modern Christians want to understand what they are doing when they worship and through worship desire an authentic experience of God. Thus, the urgent need to find a viable worship for the contemporary Christians must take into consideration both the objective content of worship and the personal need to understand and experience God. Lasting worship renewal will occur only through emphasis upon the substance of worship and the experience of the worshiper. One without the other will not do.

---

1. A good comparison of sixteenth-century Protestant liturgies is found in Bard Thompson, *Liturgies of the Western Church* (New York: New American Library, 1974). For liturgies from 1600–1900, see Robert E. Webber, *Twenty Centuries of Christian Worship* (Nashville: Abbot Martyn, 1994).

2. William D. Maxwell, *An Outline of Christian Worship* (London: Oxford Univ. Press, 1939), 72.

3. See "The Babylonian Captivity of the Church" in Robert Ferm, *Readings in the History of Christian Thought* (New York: Holt, Rinehart, and Winston, 1964), 500.

4. Thompson, *Liturgies of the Western Church*, 98.

5. The most thorough work on the relationship between Reformation worship and the ancient church is detailed in Hughes Oliphant Old, *The Patristic Roots of Reformed Worship* (Zurich: Theologischer Verlag Zurich, 1975).

6. Augsburg Confession, 24.

7. See Thompson, *Liturgies of the Western Church*, 231–32.

8. See Riedemann's Confession quoted in "Worship, Public," in *The Mennonite Encyclopedia* (Hillsboro, Kans.: Mennonite Brethren, 1955), 4:984–85.

9. For information about Bucer's liturgy see Thompson, *Liturgies of the Western Church*, 159–66; Old, *The Patristic Roots of Reformed Worship*, 119ff.

10. See R. C. D. Jasper and G. C. Cumings, *Prayers of the Eucharist: Early and Reformed* 2d ed., (New York: Oxford Univ. Press, 1980), 153ff.

11. For a description of Calvin's service see Maxwell, *An Outline of Christian Worship*, 115.

12. Quoted in Maxwell, *An Outline of Christian Worship*, 118.

13. For a brief history of Lutheran and Reformed worship see James F. White, *Protestant Worship* (Louisville: Westminster, John Knox Press, 1969), chaps. 3–4, 6.

14. For free church worship see White, *Protestant Worship*, chaps. 7–11.

15. See James Hastings Nichols, *Corporate Worship in the Reformed Tradition* (Philadelphia: Westminster, 1968), 90ff.

16. Quoted in "Baptist Worship," J. G. Davies, ed., *Westminster Dictionary of Worship* (Philadelphia: Westminster, 1972), 65.

17. "Congregationalist Worship," Davies, *Westminster Dictionary of Worship*, 149.

18. See "Quaker Worship," Davies, *Westminster Dictionary of Worship*, 328–29.

19. Doug Adams, *Meeting House to Camp Meeting* (Austin, Tex.: The Sharing Company, 1981), 13.

20. Nichols, *Corporate Worship*, 96.

21. See "Reformed Worship," Davies, *Westminster Dictionary of Worship*, 331ff.

22. See Nichols, *Corporate Worship*, 111ff.

23. Nichols, *Corporate Worship*, 122.

24. For further discussion see "Methodist Worship," Davies, *Westminster Dictionary of Worship*, 269ff.

25. Adams, *Meeting House to Camp Meeting*, 14–15.

Chapter 11

Worship Renewal in the Twentieth Century

The twentieth century has been one of the most turbulent centuries in modern history. In its beginning a number of Christian leaders thought it was going to be "the Christian century." But as it has turned out, the twentieth century has witnessed an increase in wars, violence, famine, and misery.

In the latter part of the twentieth century the western world has undergone a paradigm shift of enormous importance. The Newtonian worldview that saw the world in a rationalistic, mechanistic, and almost static way has been challenged by the introduction of a dynamic and expanding world. This worldview shift has challenged the closed worldview of rationalism and allowed for the rediscovery of mystery, the supernatural, and spirituality. This new atmosphere has produced the New Age movement, which has revived ancient customs of astrology and a false religion based on philosophical monism. While the New Age movement is a direct challenge to the Christian faith, the atmosphere of the supernatural and of personal spirituality has resulted in the rediscovery of Christian disciplines of spirituality from ancient and medieval Christianity.

At the same time that all these worldview changes have been taking place, worship has undergone an unprecedented revolution. Worship changes of the twentieth century began with the rise of the holiness-Pentecostal movement, which, in its rediscovery of the supernatural, is regarded by many as the first post-Enlightenment approach to worship. Next, the Roman Catholic Church, which had been locked into a rigid rubricism since the sixteenth century Council of Trent, underwent an upheaval of enormous proportion with the publication of the "Constitution on the Sacred Liturgy" in 1963. The impact of worship re-

121

newal soon affected the mainline Protestant church. Mainliners have drawn from the Catholic worship renewal and have expressed a hope for a unified worship among all Christians. This mainline dream is expressed in the landmark publication of *Baptism, Eucharist and Ministry*, published in 1982. A new form of worship was ushered in by the charismatic movement, which emerged in the 1960's and has made, with its openness to the Spirit, an undeniable impact on worship around the world. In addition, the rise of the Jesus movement in the early 1970's has resulted in the development of a new tradition of worship centering around choruses (the praise and worship movement). In recent years the insights and practices of all of these movements seem to be merging together in what some have called the convergence movement of worship. This chapter examines these trends in greater detail.

HOLINESS-PENTECOSTAL WORSHIP

Modern Pentecostalism began with the Azuza Street revival of 1906 in Los Angeles. Here the Holy Spirit fell upon a group of worshipers and gifted them with the ability to speak in tongues.

Modern Pentecostalism cannot be understood apart from its roots in the nineteenth-century Holiness movement. The Holiness movement traces its origin to John Wesley and to his conviction that a conversion experience should be followed by a second work of God's grace. Some American Methodists, on the basis of that premise, insisted that an instantaneous second work of sanctifying grace should be a part of everyone's Christian experience.

The people who sought this experience of practical holiness gathered in camp meetings to hear teaching, sing, and through agonizing prayer, break through to the second work of grace. Eventually, the Holiness movement produced new denominations such as the Church of the Nazarene, the Free Methodists, the Wesleyan Church, and the Christian and Missionary Alliance.

All of these groups were known in the nineteenth century as movements that desired an intense religious experience in worship. The camp meetings in particular were characterized by spontaneous freedom in worship accompanied by shouting when they "broke through" and experienced sanctifying grace. It was not unusual for people to weep and wail, to groan out loud, and enter a near convulsive state as they sought God. The *Beulah Christian* (May, 1897) records the following description of a camp meeting service, a description which helps us see how worship in this setting touched the emotions on a deep level:

> In the evening, Bro. R. S. Robson of Boston, sang, "When I see the blood I will pass over you." After prayer, and while the congregation were [sic] singing, "Rivers of Love," a wave of glory came upon the people, and shouts of holy triumph were heard from many who were in touch with God. Rev C. H. Bevier preached a sermon full of holy in-

spiration, from Ezekiel's vision of the river. On invitation at the close, a large number were at the altar, who gave evidence of finding real victory in God.[1]

When Pentecostalism emerged in the early part of the twentieth century, it drew heavily on the convictions and experience of the Holiness movement. Pentecostals drew their music lyrics and forms from songs that had emerged among the Holiness movement. They reinterpreted some of the words and phrases to accentuate the Pentecostal experience of the baptism in the Holy Spirit.

Worship among Pentecostals like that of their Holiness predecessors, was characterized by freedom, spontaneity, individual expression, and joy. In its beginning, worship was not corporate as much as it was a corporate gathering for the purpose of simultaneous individual praise and worship. This gave the worship of Pentecostalism, in the minds of some, a veneer of disorder and chaos.

One strong characteristic of early Pentecostal worship was its singing and music. From the beginning it has used the musical idiom of popular culture to present the Gospel. These songs tell stories of how people came to faith and received Jesus: "I Came to Jesus Weary, Worn and Sad; He Took My Sins Away." Pentecostals have also written many choruses that are seen as "given" by the Holy Spirit to a particular person. Some of these choruses have found a place in the repertoire of churches across the country and even around the world, while others are particular possessions of a local church. Pentecostalism has also broken with the pipe organ tradition of Christian music and introduced a wide variety of musical instruments into its worship including the guitar, drums, and the synthesizer. Many Pentecostal churches have a full orchestra that accompanies soloists, supports congregational singing, and performs sacred music.

Another feature of Pentecostal worship is praying and singing in the Spirit. This kind of prayer is more than Spirit-directed prayer, it is an actual Spirit-given language known as tongues. Tongues may occur in two different forms. First, in some cases, a message may be given in tongues. During this time a hush falls over the congregation and everyone listens to the message in tongues. This tongue is followed by an interpretation through which the message given by God in another language is communicated in the language of the people. A second form of tongues is manifested when everyone is praying out loud, many in a prayer language that is understood only by God. In these times of prayer directed by the worship leader or occurring spontaneously after a song, no interpretation is made, for tongues in this instance is not a message from God, but a personal "prayer language." Prophecies are also a unique feature of Pentecostal worship. A prophecy is a short message given by a person for the purpose of strengthening, encouraging, or comforting the worshiper (see 1 Cor. 14:3).[2]

LITURGICAL REFORM IN
THE ROMAN CATHOLIC CHURCH

The liturgy of the Roman Catholic Church had been set in the sixteenth century by the reforms of the Council of Trent. Between the sixteenth century and the promulgation of the *Constitution on the Sacred Liturgy* by Vatican II in 1963, almost no change had been made in Catholic worship.

Early in the twentieth century, Pope Pius X attempted to make changes in the liturgical calendar by purging it of many of the saints days so that the primacy of Sunday worship and the cycle of the Christian year were made more prominent. These changes were largely unsuccessful. Again in 1947, Pope Pius XII issued an encyclical on worship, *Mediator Dei et Hominium.* This work presented an exposition on the liturgy and called for more lay participation. *Mediator* was followed by a special commission set up in 1948 to study and implement liturgical reform. This commission continued its work until its fulfillment in the promulgation of the *Constitution on the Sacred Liturgy* in 1963.

The *Constitution on the Sacred Liturgy* views worship as the central activity of the church. Through the celebration of the liturgy, Christ's work of redemption is made real. What is meant by this is that worship is primarily an action from above and secondarily a response from below. When the church worships, God becomes present to give to the church the salvation that comes from Jesus Christ. As the church responds in faith, the church is built into the holy temple of the Lord.

Catholic worship is defended through theological principles set forth in the section of the *Constitution* entitled "the Nature of the Liturgy and its Importance in the Church's Life." Below is a summary of these principles:

1) God sent his Son Jesus Christ to bring salvation to the world. Therefore, "the perfect achievement of our reconciliation came forth and the fullness of divine worship was given to us."

2) On the day of Pentecost the church was called into being. The church continues to celebrate the death and resurrection of Christ and his triumph over evil in its worship. People are baptized into the death and resurrection. The Word proclaims the death and resurrection, and the Eucharist celebrates the death and resurrection.

3) The risen Christ continues to be present in his church so that all the liturgical actions of the church are Christ's actions. It is Christ who baptizes, Christ who preaches, Christ who celebrates the Eucharist.

4) In the earthly liturgy we take part in the heavenly liturgy. We join the angels, archangels, and the heavenly host in praise of God.

5) Before people are able to worship, they must be called to faith and to conversion. Therefore, the liturgy proclaims the good news of salva-

tion to those who do not believe and calls believers to continual repentance and obedience.

6) Liturgy is the summit toward which the activity of the church is directed. At the same time it is the fount from which all the church's
power flows.

7) In order that the liturgy may possess its full effectiveness, it is necessary that the faithful come to it with proper dispositions, that their
minds be attuned to their voices, and that they cooperate with divine grace, lest they receive it in vain.[3]

These basic guidelines to worship underscore the gospel nature of worship
reform in the Catholic Church. What worship proclaims, enacts, and celebrates
is the life, death, and resurrection of Jesus Christ and his victory over sin, death,
and the powers of evil.

These reforms have resulted in vast changes in the Catholic Church such
as new texts of worship, the restoration of preaching, new music and songs, worship in the language of the people, worship returned to the people through increased participation in singing, praying, saying of responses, and a greater in-
tegration of the liturgy with contemporary culture. As a result, Catholic worship
has lost its rigid uniformity and, while the order of worship is fixed, the liturgy
has been opened to a greater degree of flexibility and spontaneity. This is particularly true in those Catholic Churches that have incorporated the musical
style of the contemporary culture and worked toward a more informal liturgy.

WORSHIP RENEWAL AMONG MAINLINE
PROTESTANT CHURCHES

The revolution introduced by the Catholic Church was soon felt in
Protestant circles. Most mainline Protestant churches had paid very little attention to their worship since the time of the Reformation. Slight changes had been
made, of course, as the church passed through history and new Protestant movements had developed different styles of worship (e.g., the free church and
Holiness-Pentecostal movements). But for the most part, churches that traced
their roots to the Reformation had never undergone a thorough revolution in
their worship.

As Catholic reform in worship was studied by Protestants, new denomi-
national worship commissions were founded to study worship. Eventually the
Episcopal Church produced a new *Book of Common Prayer* in 1979, the Lutheran
Church produced a new combined hymn book and service book (the *Lutheran
Book of Worship*), the Presbyterians produced a whole new series of worship re-
sources that culminated in *The Book of Services* in 1993, and the United
Methodists produced numerous resources and published a new combination
hymn book and worship book called *The United Methodist Worship Book*. Nearly

every major denomination in the world has produced new worship materials, including a new hymn book, since 1980.

The essence of worship renewal in the mainline churches is captured best in James F. White's "A Protestant Worship Manifesto." He calls upon the mainline church to accomplish twelve reforms. Here is a summary of those reforms that have been accomplished in varying degrees among mainline denominations and local congregations.

1) *Worship should be shaped in the light of understanding it as the church's unique contribution to the struggle for justice.* The weekly reiteration of the death and resurrection of Christ should shape the attitudes and values of people in such a way that their behavior results in an obedience to God expressed in acts of justice.

2) *The paschal nature of Christian worship should resound throughout all services.* Worship is grounded in God's work for us in Jesus Christ. In all worship we should experience anew the events of salvation in our own lives.

3) *The centrality of the Bible in Protestant worship must be recovered.* Scripture functions in the worship of many Protestant churches only as a means of reinforcing what the preacher wants to say. This makes the use of the Bible optional rather than the source of Christian worship.

4) *The importance of time as a major structure in Christian worship must be rediscovered.* Because the church and its worship are rooted in the saving events of Christ, the church needs to rediscover the events of salvation and mark time by the celebration of these events—Advent, Christmas, Epiphany, Lent, Holy Week, Easter, and Pentecost.

5) *All reforms in worship must be shaped ecumenically.* Much that is happening in worship renewal is the result of churches borrowing from all other churches. Every church from Orthodox to Quaker brings something to the discussion of worship. Our worship will be enriched as we listen to each other and draw from each other's resources.

6) *Drastic changes are needed in the process of Christian initiation.* Initiation into the church should be seen as a process of evangelization. There is a need to rethink how worship evangelizes and nurtures persons into the faith.

7) *High on the list of reforms is the need to recover the Eucharist as the chief Sunday service.* The prayer of thanksgiving must be rediscovered as a proclamation of the gospel, and people must be physically engaged in walking forward, standing, or kneeling to receive the bread and wine as opposed to sitting in the pew.

8) *Recovery of the sense of God's action in our "commonly called sacraments" is essential.* The church needs to institute additional services such as

9) *Music must be seen in its pastoral context as fundamentally an enabler of fuller congregational participation.* Music must serve the text of worship rather than function as an interruption or an interlude. Recovery of psalm singing in worship is an encouraging sign.

10) *The space and furnishings for worship need substantial change in most churches.* If the quality of worship celebration is to be improved, attention must be paid to the space in which the celebration takes place. One must acknowledge people's visual, aural, and kinetic senses.

11) *No reform of worship will progress far until much more effort is invested in teaching seminarians and clergy to think through the functions of Christian worship.* Worship understanding and training in worship leadership must find its rightful place in the seminary curriculum.

12) *Liturgical renewal is not just a changing of worship but is part of a reshaping of American Christianity, root and branch.* Worship renewal relates to and affects every part of the church's life.[4]

THE CHARISMATIC RENEWAL OF WORSHIP

Throughout history there have been groups of people who claim to have been especially touched by the Holy Spirit and empowered to minister in the name of the Spirit.

Initially the response of the established church toward the charismatic movement of this century was quite negative. However, in the passage of time the charismatic movement has been recognized by the Catholic Church and by most Protestant churches as a true moving of the Holy Spirit. Consequently, aspects of charismatic worship and ministry have penetrated into nearly every circle of the church.

During the 1960s and 1970s the charismatic movement was primarily a prayer movement, having as one of its central characteristics a spirit directed worship. Although the charismatic movement spread into the Catholic Church and many mainline churches, it gradually spread beyond the borders of the established churches as independent charismatic churches were started all over the world. Some of these churches have joined into new charismatic fellowships and denominations, but thousands of those churches remain independent from any denominational connection.

Charismatic leader Gerritt Gustafson identifies four principles of Charismatic worship. "(1) Charismatic worship is based on the activation of the priesthood of all believers. (2) Charismatic worship involves the whole person—spirit, soul and body. (3) Charismatics experience the real presence of Christ in worship. (4) In worship charismatics experience God's power."[5]

In the actual practice of worship, D. L. Alford points out that charismatic liturgy is associated with "freedom in worship, joyful singing, both vocal and physical, expressions of praise, instrumental accompaniment of singing, and acceptance of a wide variety of music styles." It is not unusual he says "to find charismatic worshipers singing, shouting, clapping hands, leaping and even dancing before the Lord as they offer him sincere praise and thanksgiving." Alford furthermore summarizes the characteristics of charismatic worship in six statements.

1)   Emphasis upon the singing of psalms and scripture songs.
2)   Reliance upon music and/or praise and worship in church, at conferences and festivals, in small groups, and in private.
3)   Use of musical instruments.
4)   Emphasis upon congregational singing with the use of praise leaders.
5)   Use of dance and pageantry, both spontaneous and choreographed.
6)   Use of drama and pantomime.
7)   Emphasis upon the prophetic role of, or anointing upon, the musicians.[6]

Richard Riss writes that "other characteristics of charismatic worship include the uplifting of hands, the linking of arms, the freedom for all participants to contribute, especially in the functioning of prophetic gifts and in acts of healing and the use of music, art and other sacramental signs."[7]

These characteristics of worship, while primarily those of the charismatic movement, are finding a place among the worship of an increasing number of Catholics and Protestants as the movement continues to spread. This wide receptivity suggests that the needs of the subjective side of the human person are being met significantly by the charismatic approach to worship.

THE PRAISE AND WORSHIP MOVEMENT

A new style of worship has been spreading throughout North America and other parts of the world in the last several decades. While this approach to worship goes by a variety of names, the designation that seems to be gaining most acceptance is the praise and worship movement.

The praise and worship movement emerged from several trends in the sixties and early seventies. These trends included the perception some people had that traditional worship forms were dead. Along with that conviction went a concern for the immediacy of the Spirit, a desire for intimacy, and a persuasion that music and informality must connect with people of a post-Christian culture.

One of the earliest expressions of these trends was the rise of testimonial music through the leadership of Bill Gaither in the early 1960s. Songs such as "He Touched Me," "There's Something About That Name," "Let's Just Praise the Lord," and "Because He Lives" touched many lives and introduced people to a new genre of music. At first these were performance songs, but soon they became congregational: People sang along or at least joined in on the refrain. A second expression of these trends came in the late 1960s on the west coast (and all over the world) in the "Jesus movement." A major emphasis of this movement was the singing of praise choruses, some of which were written and sung as the congregation was at worship.

Since those early days in the 1960s and early 1970s, this form of music and style of worship has developed into a new worldwide approach to worship.

While the exact origins of the praise and worship tradition are ambiguous, the movement itself is not difficult to describe. It seeks to recapture the lost element of praise found in both Old and New Testament worship. It stands in the tradition of the Talmud, saying, "Man should always utter praises, and then pray." Praise God first and foremost, *then* move on to the other elements of worship, say the proponents of praise and worship.

A major feature of the praise and worship movement is its tendency to distinguish praise from worship. Judson Cornwall, a praise and worship leader in the movement and author of numerous books, addresses the distinction between praise and worship in his book *Let Us Worship*. Cornwall cites Psalm 95 as a good example of this distinction. In the opening verses, the psalmist invites praise.

> Come, let us sing for joy to the LORD; let us shout aloud to the Rock
> of our salvation.
> Let us come before him with thanksgiving and extol him with music
> and song. (vv. 1–2).

Only then, *after* praise has been offered, does the psalmist invite worship.

> Come, let us bow down in worship, let us kneel before the LORD our
> Maker. (v. 6)

So Cornwall concludes that "the order is praise first, worship second."[8]

"Praise," Cornwall writes, "prepares us for worship"; it is a "prelude to worship."[9] Praise is not an attempt to get something from God; it is a ministry that we offer to God. We offer praise for what God has done—for God's mighty deeds in history and his continued providential presence in our lives.

While we praise God for what he has done, we worship God for who he is. The one extols the acts of God, the other the person and character of God. Cornwall clarifies this distinction between praise and worship.

> Praise begins by applauding God's power, but it often brings us close
> enough to God that worship can respond to God's presence. While
> the energy of praise is toward what God does, the energy of worship is
> toward who God is. The first is concerned with God's performance,
> while the second is occupied with God's personage. The thrust of worship, therefore, is higher than the thrust of praise.[10]

The Temple Sequence

The order of the service, the swing from praise to worship, is patterned after the movement in the Old Testament tabernacle and temple from the outer court to the inner court and then into the Holy of Holies. All of these steps are accomplished through song. The song leader (or the worship leader, as he or she is more often called) plays a significant role in moving the congregation through the various steps that lead to worship.

The leader begins with choruses of personal experience or testimony, such as "This Is the Day the Lord Has Made" or "We Bring Sacrifices of Praise into the House of the Lord." These songs center on praise, are all upbeat in tempo, and relate to the personal experience of the believer. They are songs that often mention "I," "me," or "we." In the tabernacle typology, during this first step the people are still outside the fence that surrounds the tabernacle. They cannot worship until they come through the gates into the tabernacle court.

This movement by way of song prepares us for what takes place in the second step: The mood and the content of the music shift to express the action of entering the gates and coming into the courts. Here the worship leader leads people in songs that express the transition from praise to worship. These are songs of thanksgiving, such as the Scripture song from Psalm 100. "I will enter his gates with thanksgiving in my heart, I will enter his courts with praise" or "Come let us worship and bow down, let us kneel before the LORD our God, our Maker."

According to Cornwall:

> It is a matter of bringing them from a consciousness of what has been done in them and for them (testimony) to who did it in and for them (thanksgiving). The procession through the eastern gate into the outer court should be a joyful march, for thanks should never be expressed mournfully or negatively. While the people are singing choruses of thanksgiving, they will be thinking both of themselves and of their God, but by putting the emphasis upon the giving of thanks, the majority of the thought patterns should be on their God. Singing at this level will often be a beginning level of praise, but it will not produce worship, for the singers are not yet close enough to God's presence to express a worship response.[11]

The third step, into the Holy of Holies, brings believers away from themselves and into a full conscious worship of God alone. No longer is the worshiper thinking about what God has done, but rather of who God is in person and character. A quiet devotion hovers over the congregation as they sing songs such as "Father, I Adore You," "I Love You, Lord," and "You Are Worthy." In these moments of worship clapping will likely be replaced with devotional responses of upturned faces, raised hands, tears, and even a subtle change in the timbre of the voices. For when there is an "awareness that we have come into the presence of God, we step out of lightness with sobriety."[12]

The third phase of the sequence is often described as an experience of "the manifest presence of God." This experience does not differ greatly from the liturgical experience of the presence of Christ at the Lord's table. In this atmosphere the *charismata* (spiritual gifts) are released, and just as men and women throughout the history of the church have experienced physical and spiritual healing while partaking of the table of Christ, so many today are tasting of special manifestations of the Holy Spirit in worship renewal as he inhabits the praises of his people (Ps. 22:3).

Variations

While the tabernacle-temple order of worship is quite prominent in praise and worship churches, it is not the only order or sequence of song. For example, the Vineyard Church in Anaheim, California, is a church that fits into the broader category of the praise and worship tradition of worship. Worship here has a slightly different variation of the progression that brings a worshiper into God's presence.

Vineyard Church worship begins with an *invitation phase*, which is like a call to worship. Songs of invitation such as "I Just Came to Praise the Lord" may be sung with clapping, swinging the body, and looking at other worshipers, smiling and acknowledging their presence.

In the next movement, the *engagement phase*, the people are brought closer to God, and their songs are addressed to him, not to one another. A good example may be "Humble Yourself in the Sight of the Lord."

The song leader then moves the people into the *adoration phase*. In this stage of worship the broad range of pitch and melody that characterized the previous phases is exchanged for the smaller range of music and the more subdued tone of songs such as "Jesus, Jesus, There's Something About That Name" or "Father, I Adore You."

Next, the congregation is led into the *intimacy phase*, which is the quietest and most personal part of the worship. Songs such as "O Lord, You're Beautiful" and "Great Are You, Lord" are personal statements of an intimate relationship directed from the believer to the Lord. As these songs are sung, people may become highly intense and lose themselves in the ecstasy of the moment. During this phase of the worship service that I attended at the Vineyard Church, people stood with heads and hands turned upward and eyes closed as they sang these songs of, as John Wimber calls them, "lovemaking to God." Some people, especially in the front rows, were kneeling or even prostrate on the floor during this "quiet time." The final phase of the Vineyard worship progression is a *closeout* song, a song that helps the people move out of the experience of being transfixed on God to prepare for the next segment of the service, the time of teaching.[13]

Praise, Worship, Teaching, Prayer, and Ministry

It is common in the praise and worship tradition to distinguish between the various acts of a typical service. The most significant distinction is that of praise from worship, as described above. Other acts in the service include the time for teaching, the time for intercessory prayer, and the time for ministry.

Because most praise and worship churches are informal, the various acts of the service are done in an informal way. For example, while teaching is fairly straightforward, it may end with a time of brief feedback or discussion (depending on the size of the congregation). Intercessory prayer may also be informal. The idea of the traditional pastoral prayer may be replaced by a prayer circle. After prayer, many churches enter a time of ministry. People are sent into various rooms where those gifted with ministry for particular needs lay hands on them and pray. What is experienced in this setting can be very meaningful, ministering in a powerful way to the people of God.

Response to Praise and Worship

Broadly speaking, traditional churches have responded to the spread of praise and worship in three ways.

First are those churches that have not responded at all—perhaps because they are not consciously aware of the praise and worship tradition. These congregations may have heard one or two of the movement's songs and be vaguely aware of the existence of such a style of worship in nontraditional churches, but for the most part they are ignorant of the movement.

Second are those congregations who are more aware of the praise and worship traditions but are indifferent to them or who actively dismiss them, arguing that they are "too superficial" or "too charismatic."

The third set of traditional churches are not only aware of praise and worship and its relevancy to a post-Enlightenment culture but also seek to integrate this new approach to worship into the local church.[14]

THE CONVERGENCE OF WORSHIP TRADITIONS

In the 1980s and 1990s a movement that converges the liturgical and the contemporary forms and experiences of worship has emerged. The antecedents of this movement are clearly found in the twentieth century liturgical renewal and in both the charismatic and praise and worship movements.

However, the convergence movement also draws from the evangelical and reformed movements as well, clearly making it eclectic. Below is a summary of the emphasis of the three streams that feed into the convergence movement.

LITURGICAL/ SACRAMENTAL	EVANGELICAL/ REFORMED	CHARISMATIC
• Theology • Orthodoxy • Universality • Historic connection • Liturgical worship • Social action • Incarnational understanding of the church (based on theology, history, and sacrament)	• Biblical foundation • Personal conversion • Evangelism and mission • Pulpit-centered worship • Personal holiness • Biblical and reformational understanding of the church (pragmatic and rational)	• Five-fold ministry and government • Power of the Spirit • Spiritual gifts • Charismatic worship • Kingdom • Spiritual, organic, and functional understanding of the church (dynamic and informal)[15]

Randy Sly and Wayne Boosahda have summarized the common concerns of the convergence movement as follows:

> Those who are being drawn into this convergence of streams can be characterized by several common elements. While these are not exhaustive or in any order of importance, they form the basis for the focus and direction of the convergence movement. (1) A restored commitment to the sacraments, especially the Lord's Table. (2) An increased motivation to know more about the early church. (3) A love for the whole church and a desire to see the church as one. (4) The blending in the practice of all three streams is evident, yet each church approaches convergence from a unique point of view. (5) An interest in integrating structure with spontaneity in worship. (6) A greater involvement of sign and symbol in worship. (7) A continuing commitment to personal salvation, biblical teaching, and the work and ministry of the Holy Spirit.[16]

CONCLUSION

Having addressed the renewal movements of the twentieth century and noting that the most recent trend is toward a convergence of worship, we are left wondering about the future of Christian worship.

One thing seems certain, and that is that we are not likely to see uniformity of worship throughout the church, nor even the uniformity of worship among specific denominations.

Convergence worship itself does not propose uniformity. It suggests that denominations and local churches learn from and borrow from churches of other traditions. We can be fairly certain that this appreciation of each other's worship will continue into the future as the church continues to be blessed with a variety of worship styles.

1. See Brad Estep, "A Holiness Model of Worship," *The Twenty Centuries of Worship* (Nashville: Abbott Martyn, 1994), 253.

2. See Gary S. Liddle, "A Holiness-Pentecostal Theology of Worship," *The Twenty Centuries of Worship* (Nashville: Abbott Martyn, 1994).

3. For the historical background to the Constitution and the sacred liturgy see Frederick R. McManus "Liturgical Reform of Vatican II," Peter Fink, ed. *The New Dictionary of Sacramental Worship* (Collegeville, Minn.: Liturgical, 1990), 1081–97. For the full text of the "Constitution on the Sacred Liturgy," see Mary Ann Simcoe, ed., *The Liturgy Documents* (Chicago: Liturgy Training, 1985), chap. 1. For a good introduction to Catholic worship see Jean Lebon, *How to Understand the Liturgy* (New York: Crossroad, 1988).

4. James F. White, "A Protestant Worship Manifesto," *The Christian Century*. For a general introduction to worship renewal in the mainline church read James F. White, *Introduction to Christian Worship* (Nashville: Abingdon, 1990).

5. See Robert E. Webber, *Twenty Centuries of Christian Worship* (Nashville: Abbott Martyn, 1994), forthcoming.

6. D. L. Alford, "Pentecostal and Charismatic Music" *Dictionary of Pentecostal and Charismatic Movements* (Grand Rapids: Zondervan, 1988), 693–94.

7. Richard Riss, "The Charismatic Renewal," *Twenty Centuries of Worship* (Nashville: Abbott Martyn, 1994), 121–25.

8. Judson Cornwall, *Let Us Worship* (Plainfield, N.J.: Bridge Publishing, 1983), 143.

9. Cornwall, *Let Us Worship*, 166.

10. Cornwall, *Let Us Worship*, 146.

11. Cornwall, *Let Us Worship*, 156.

12. Cornwall, *Let Us Worship*, 157.

13. See Barry Liesch, *People in the Presence of God: Models and Directions for Worship* (Grand Rapids: Zondervan, 1988), 92–93.

14. Robert Webber, "The Praise and Worship Renewal," *Twenty Centuries of Christian Worship* (Nashville: Abbott Martyn), 131–34.

15. From Randy Sly and Wayne Boosahda, "The Convergence Movement," *The Twenty Centuries of Worship* (Nashville: Abbott Martyn, 1994), 134–40.

16. Sly and Boosahda, "The Convergence Movement," 137–39.

PART IV

The Practice of Worship

The practice of worship in the contemporary church should be based on the solid foundation of biblical, historical, and theological studies. Knowledge of the material of the preceding sections is therefore indispensable to the task of renewing worship in the local church.

But the question remains: How does the biblical, theological, and historical material relate to the contemporary church? How does the church that dares to be rooted in the past form a worship that is relevant for the present?

Part 4 addresses this all important question. First, it speaks to the setting of worship, then to the matter of content, structure, and style of worship. Next, the four acts of Sunday worship are addressed: the act of assembling, the hearing of God's Word, the table of the Lord, and the Dismissal. Next, we examine important matters such as the role of music, the role of the arts, the services of the Christian year, the sacred actions of worship (baptism and the Lord's Supper), and the relationship of worship to the other ministries of the church. In these chapters we address all the aspects of the church's worship from the viewpoint of the contemporary worshiping church. By studying these chapters and this material, the leaders of worship in the local church will find ample suggestions and direction to develop a worship that is rooted in biblical sources and aware of historical developments. Finally, this section ends with a challenge to evangelical renewalists to lead the church in a worship characterized by depth and relevance.

Chapter 12

The Environmental Setting of Worship

Throughout the history of the Christian church, believers have worshiped in a variety of places. Fields, catacombs, riverbanks, homes, prisons, ships, and planes have provided the setting for worship. Yet, it has been normal for Christians to have a *place* of worship.[1] Consequently, churches, cathedrals, and auditoriums have become particular houses of worship. Because a worship building (like everything else) is not neutral, the space of worship communicates something about the convictions of the people who worship there. Thus, the church has long acknowledged that what we do in worship ought to be expressed in the way we use space.[2]

It is appropriate that this section on the practice of worship should begin with a discussion on the setting of worship. Meetings (and worship is a meeting) always takes place within a setting. We do business or enact public ceremonies within a particular space. In these situations we normally approach the arrangement of space with an eye on its function. Does it meet the needs of the group? Does it allow for a maximum sense of communication? Does it fit the mood or the tone of the meeting? These same questions need to be asked as we approach the setting of worship.

This chapter considers the theological basis for the use of space in worship, surveys the ways space has been used for Christian worship in the past, and probes the contemporary use of space in worship.

THE THEOLOGICAL BASIS FOR THE USE OF SPACE

The Redemptive Understanding of Space

We have already seen that worship celebrates the victory of Christ over evil. Therefore, Christian worship expresses hope in the final deliverance of creation from evil and the restoration of all things in the new heavens and the new earth (Rom. 8:18–25; Rev. 20–22). Because the redemption extends to the entire created order, space is a vehicle through which the Christian view of redemption may be expressed. More specifically, in worship, space becomes the stage on which the redemption of the world is acted out. This truth is expressed in the signs of redemption such as the table, the pulpit, and the baptismal font, as well as in the arrangement of space for the people, the choir, the celebrant, and others who enact the Gospel.

Biblical Support for the Spiritual Understanding of Space

In the Old Testament there are abundant references to a particular place or object regarded as sacred space (Bethel, Mount Sinai, the burning bush, the ark of the covenant, the Holy of Holies). This spiritual significance of space is emphasized particularly by the elaborate instructions given for the building of the tabernacle (and later the temple) and by the acts of consecration.

In the instructions for the building of the tabernacle as well as the directions given for worship (see Ex. 25–40), three points about space are made. First, the elaborate materials demonstrate that material things belong to the Lord and may be used to communicate truth about God. Second, the repeated emphasis that God will dwell there (25:8; 29:45) substantiates the notion that God's presence in the world may be communicated symbolically. Third, the recognition that "the glory of the LORD filled the tabernacle" (40:34–35) acknowledges God's presence in a particular space.

The act of consecration also emphasizes the importance attached to a place.[3] Solomon's dedication of the temple (1 Kings 8) provides the model for the consecration of space in the Scriptures. This act is not to be regarded as an exercise associated with magic, but as an act that sets apart a particular place for the community to publicly meet God. The Christian church has continued to use the practice of consecration and recognized that the place where people gather to worship is special.[4]

The Stewardship of Space in Worship

It is obvious that whenever a group of people gather to worship, whether in the woods or in a building, they are using space. We must determine whether the space in which we worship helps us or hinders us. We can determine this when we recognize the vital relationship between the internal and the external. The important feature of Christian worship is that the internal experience of salvation in Jesus Christ, combined with immediate external expressions of this experience, has stamped the use of space in Christian worship with a particular character. Spatial arrangements differ as a result of varying emphases on table fellowship, preaching, baptism, the orders of ministry and gifts, and the sense of body ministry.

Furthermore, thoughtful reflection by the church on the meaning of the Christian experience has found artistic expression in architecture. Unfortunately, this means that the church has also expressed theological error in its use of space as well as theological indifference.[5]

THE USE OF SPACE IN THE HISTORY OF CHRISTIAN WORSHIP

The principle that space is a vehicle through which the meaning of worship is expressed can be demonstrated from examples of worship and space in history.

THE SYNAGOGUE

Although the synagogue predated Christianity, it had a significant impact upon the formation of Christian worship. The idea that the material creation communicated eternal truth was carried over from the temple into the synagogue. Figure 1 provides a model of an early synagogue in which the theological arrangement of space is evident.[6] The orientation of the building toward Jerusalem symbolized Israel's hope that in Jerusalem all the promises of God to Israel were to be fulfilled.

SYNAGOGUE

JERUSALEM

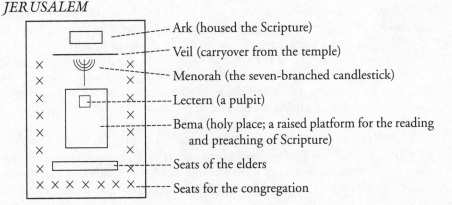

- Ark (housed the Scripture)
- Veil (carryover from the temple)
- Menorah (the seven-branched candlestick)
- Lectern (a pulpit)
- Bema (holy place; a raised platform for the reading and preaching of Scripture)
- Seats of the elders
- Seats for the congregation

The theological character of space in this synagogue can be noted in the location of the congregation and the furniture. The congregation gathered *around* those material symbols that signify the means through which God had made himself known in its history. For example, the meaning of "the seat of Moses" in the midst of the synagogue is captured by the liturgist Louis Bouyer in the following words: "The assembly of the People of God could meet as such only because there was always among them someone held as the authentic depository of the living Tradition of God's Word, first given to Moses, and able to communicate it always anew, although always substantially the same."[7]

From this vantage point both the scribes and the congregation were able to *see* the symbols that communicated the meaning of their gathering. The central symbol was the ark, which was the holiest object of ancient Israel and the only object allowed in the Holy of Holies. The people viewed the ark as a throne where God (an invisible spirit) was present. Inside the ark, which was similar to a wooden casket, were the scrolls, the testimony to God's communication to Israel. The ark and the scrolls were protected by the veil, and in front of that burned the seven-branched candlestick. All these material objects pointed beyond themselves to the presence of God in the history of Israel and his continued presence with his people.

Another feature of the synagogue was the bema, the raised platform on which the lectern stood. It was from here that the Scriptures were proclaimed and prayers were offered. The bema symbolized the place of the Word of God in the midst of the people, and the people gathered around the Word to hear God speak and to speak to God.

This simple arrangement of the major symbols of Israel's faith allowed the worship of Israel to reenact God's action in history and his promise for the future, not only in the words that were said but in the signs and symbols that accompanied those words.

An Ancient Syrian church

A second example may be taken from an ancient Syrian church (see Figure 2). This building appears to be a Christianized version of a Jewish synagogue.[8]

Here, as in the synagogue, the congregation gathered around the symbols of worship. The presence of the symbols (ark, veil, and candlestick) that were specifically Jewish expressed the continuity between the peoples of God. The bishop and the presbyters were in the seat of Moses and continued to communicate the presence of a living tradition in the ordained ministry of expounding the Word.

There were, however, two significant and noteworthy changes. First, the apse, the central focus of the congregation, contained a table. Here the bishop went to celebrate the Eucharist (the supreme symbol of God's presence in the world), which constituted the climax of Christian worship. Second, the church no longer faced Jerusalem, but pointed toward the east. This symbolized the return of Christ in the east to gather his elect from the four corners of the world.

Here again the experience of the Christian community gave shape to the use of space. God's action in history as revealed in the Scripture and incarnated in Jesus Christ was expressed through the use of space, the arrangement of the people, and the symbols of God's presence.

SYRIAN CHURCH

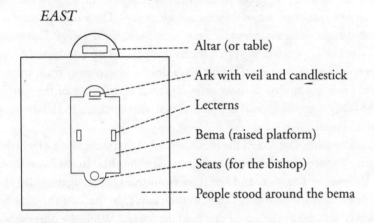

EAST

- - - - - - - - - - - - - - Altar (or table)

- - - - Ark with veil and candlestick

- - Lecterns

- - Bema (raised platform)

- - Seats (for the bishop)

- - - - - - - People stood around the bema

A Roman Basilica

A third example may be drawn from the Constantinian era (see Figure 3). During this time numerous Roman basilicas were given to the church and converted into places of worship. The alteration of space to accommodate the crowds and to facilitate the growing sense of hierarchy resulted in some significant changes, not only in the use of space but in the concept of worship.[9]

The most striking change in the use of space is the movement of the seat of the bishop from the congregation to a point behind the altar. The seat of the bishop gradually became a throne, a seat of honor and power, as the church became more institutional, hierarchical, and powerful.

In this movement the initial stages of triumphalism are seen. The church is now an institution of power. The bishop gradually assumed more power as the people raised him to a status far beyond that of a servant of the church. Gradually the bishop became an authority outside of the collective body of the people, lost his link with the people, and became a lord over them. This movement took some time to be completed, but it slowly reshaped Christian worship. What was once the collective work of the people gradually became the privilege of the clergy, and the use of space symbolized that shift.

A second spatial change is found in the modification of the bema. The ark was omitted, the raised platform removed, and the ends were opened so that the procession could walk through it to the altar. In addition, the bema became the place where the ministers of the lower ranks, together with readers and singers, stood. Pulpits were added on both sides and the seven-branched candlestick was replaced by a single large candle.

This spatial change signaled a shift in worship. The bishop and the clergy were separated from the congregation, and the ministers, the singers, and the readers became a congregation within the congregation. The worship was gradually removed from the people and became a function of the clergy. Eventually the role of the worshipers was to watch the drama of worship conducted before them as an epiphany of the Gospel. This was a dramatic step away from the earlier and more biblical approach to worship regarded as the work of the congregation. The biblical approach had demanded that all participate in the drama of enacting the Gospel.

A final alteration that sealed the move toward the clericalization of worship was to change the structure of the apse that housed the altar. In the West it was separated by rows of columns and set away from the people, against the wall where the priest said Mass with his back to the people. In the East the altar became hidden by an iconastasis screen that held the icons.[10] While the purpose was to accent the mystery of the Gospel, the effect was to remove the action from the people, to clericalize the Eucharist, and to create a church within the church. The Eucharist became remote and awesome, a matter to be feared and held at a distance, no longer to be taken by the people, except once or twice a year.[11]

ROMAN BASILICA

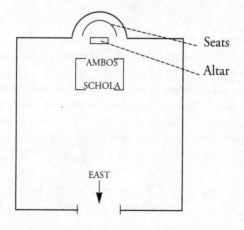

LATER MEDIEVAL CHURCHES

The movement toward the clericalization of worship in the early medieval period became solidified in the later medieval period, as the theology of worship continued to change. Of particular interest is the Roman tendency to fill a church with altars (see Figure 4).[12]

MEDIEVAL CHURCH

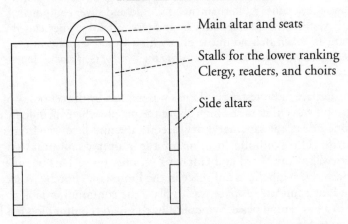

Main altar and seats

Stalls for the lower ranking Clergy, readers, and choirs

Side altars

The existence of the side altars resulted from the growing conviction that the Mass was a sacrifice offered for the benefit of the living *and the dead.* Liturgical historian William D. Maxwell puts it this way:

> As each mass was held to have value as an act of merit, it was now seriously computed how many were required to bring a soul through purgatory to paradise, and to what extent a mass could alleviate the pangs of a soul condemned to eternal punishment. There were masses for success in temporal affairs: for one going on a journey, for recovery from sickness, for the capture of thieves and the return of stolen goods, for rain or fair weather, for the release of captives; and here again the number required to achieve the object was solemnly determined. Masses were said even to bring about the death of persons; these were condemned and forbidden by the Synod of Toledo in 694. Private masses became, as Heiler says, a cancer feeding upon the soul of the Church.[13]

Again, the relationship between theology and space in worship was evident. By the sixteenth century the time for reform was ripe.

The Protestant Church

Protestants continued to worship in the cathedrals and churches that had belonged to the Roman church. Therefore, their first impulse toward changing the use of space in worship was limited to the alteration of the building in which they worshipped. Here is an example of the actions taken by the Swiss Reformer Ulrich Zwingli:

> In the summer of 1524, the "cleansing" of the churches began. Zwingli and his colleagues, accompanied by all manner of craftsmen, entered the churches and set to work. They disposed of the relics, raised their ladders against the walls and whitewashed the paintings and decorations, carted away the statues and ornaments, the gold and silver equipment, the costly vestments, and splendidly bound service-books. They closed the organs in token that no music of any kind would resound in the churches again: *the people were to give ear to the Word of God alone.*[14] [emphasis added]

The use of space in Protestant buildings was marked by the centrality of the pulpit. The pulpit was either raised high above the people where it could be easily seen (on one side of the sanctuary) or placed in the middle of the front on a raised platform. The symbolic location of the pulpit communicated the Protestant renewal of the Word and emphasis on preaching. This became the single most powerful symbolic use of space in the Protestant church.[15] A second feature of the Protestant use of space was to place the communion table under the pulpit or in a less central place. Symbolically, this made communion less important than preaching.[16]

These alterations were both an expression of the changed view of worship, and a vehicle through which the changed view of worship became more solidified. Today, many American Protestants are offended by a centralized, raised communion table. Unfortunately, the emphasis on the Word has led Protestants to a one-sided and clergy-centered worship. The mistake of the medieval period was that the congregation *watched* worship. In the modern Protestant church the mistake is that the congregation tends to *listen* to worship. There is a desperate need to return to worship that is the work of the congregation and to a use of space that permits and encourages the people to *do* worship.[17]

THE SETTING OF WORSHIP IN CONTEMPORARY CHURCHES

New shifts are taking place in worship today that call for a reconfiguration of the worship space. Underneath all these shifts is the recovery of the biblical understanding of worship as the congregational celebration of God's mighty deeds of salvation. Worship is no longer something to be watched or listened to, but something to be done by the people.

The first of these shifts is from a preacher-dominated worship to a people-centered worship. Protestant worship in particular has been a preacher-dominated worship. Consequently, the people have been arranged in rows directed toward the platform, which is directed toward the audience. In this space the preacher is often seen as the "program director" or the "teacher," while the people are there for the "instruction" or for the "show," as the case may be.

Next, the return of worship to the people (liturgy [*leitourgia*] literally means "work of the people") changes worship, which in turn creates the need to restructure worship space. For example, worship is experiencing a shift in music from an organ-dominated sound to the sound of a variety of musical instruments including strings, basses, synthesizers, pianos, guitars, and drums. Whereas church architecture once assumed the need for organ and pipe space in the front, side, or back, spatial considerations now need to take into account the need for band space, and in some cases, space for a full orchestra.

The shifting role of the choir demands a reconsideration of worship space. The choir, once playing the role of performer, is now moving into the role of cantor and musical leader for the entire congregation (the new choir). While many churches have retired the choir, most worship renewal churches continue the choir in the new role of cantor. Consequently, adequate space is needed for choir, processions, and seating. In the new worship space, seating is more frequently to the side rather than in the front of the congregation because side seating facilitates involvement with the congregation, whereas front seating implies performance.

The change in the function of the choir in worship is often accompanied by the restoration of the arts, particularly dance procession or dance that assists the text of songs through movement interpretation. Space is needed for processions and movement interpretation not only in the aisle but also in the chancel. Thoughtful space planners are widening the aisles and allowing for larger chancel space to permit greater movement for artistic interpretation of songs, Scripture readings, prayer, sermons, and other acts of worship.

Another shift taking place in worship is the increased celebration of the sacraments in Sunday worship. The move in many churches toward a weekly Eucharist, toward the celebration of baptism in morning worship, and toward the anointing of oil for healing necessitates a new consideration of spatial arrangement. Appropriate space is needed so that these actions may be done meaningfully.

Finally, many churches have introduced a time of ministry in worship that necessitates new spatial considerations. Churches that invite people to come forward for prayer, for the laying on of hands, and for other kinds of ministry need adequate space for these functions of worship ministry.

The kind of space that seems to be the most adequate for these functions and for the new participatory approach to worship is a centralized space rather than the longitudinal space. Centralized space brings the people into the action of worship and allows their worship to be considerably more participatory than longitudinal space.[18]

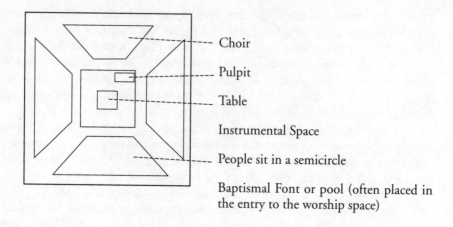

Choir

Pulpit

Table

Instrumental Space

People sit in a semicircle

Baptismal Font or pool (often placed in the entry to the worship space)

CONCLUSION

In this section we have begun with the setting of worship to emphasize how space shapes our experience of worship.

Space, it has been argued, needs to be redemptive space. It needs to reflect the work of salvation, which we celebrate. Therefore, adequate space for gathering, for the hearing of the Word, for the celebration of the Eucharist, and for music and the arts that accompany these acts is a priority. The major shift that has taken place in worship space is the shift from longitudinal space to a more centralized space, a space in which the worshipers become participants.

---

1. See "Architectural Setting," J. T. G. Davies, ed., *Westminster Dictionary of Worship* (Philadelphia: Westminster, 1972), 21ff; "The Place of Worship," in Jean-Jacques von Allmen, *Worship: Its Theology and Practice* (New York: Oxford Univ. Press, 1965), 240–82.

2. See "The Language of Space," James F. White, *Introduction to Christian Worship* (Nashville: Abingdon, 1980), 76ff.

3. See "Dedication," Davies, *Westminster Dictionary of Worship,* 162.

4. See "Means by Which the Numinous Is Expressed in Art," Rudolf Otto, *The Idea of the Holy* (New York: Oxford Univ. Press, 1977), 65ff.

5. In medieval architecture the error of the Mass as a sacrifice is expressed in the plurality of altars. Some evangelicals have made the Grecian urn and colonial architecture into the symbol of conservatism.

6. See Louis Bouyer, *Liturgy and Architecture* (Notre Dame, Ind.: Univ. of Notre Dame

Press, 1967), 8–24.

7. Bouyer, *Liturgy and Architecture*, 11.

8. Bouyer, *Liturgy and Architecture*, 24–39.

9. Bouyer, *Liturgy and Architecture*, 39–60.

10. See "Iconostasis," Davies, *Westminster Dictionary of Worship*, 196.

11. For an excellent critique of liturgical developments in the East see Alexander Schmemann, *Introduction to Liturgical Theology* (Bangor, Maine: American Orthodox, 1966).

12. See Bouyer, *Liturgy and Architecture*, 70–86.

13. William Maxwell, *An Outline of Christian Worship* (London: Oxford Univ. Press, 1939), 68.

14. Bard Thompson, *Liturgies of the Western Church* (New York: New American Library, 1974), 142.

15. See "Pulpit," Davies, *Westminster Dictionary of Worship*, 326.

16. See "Communion Table," Davies *Westminster Dictionary of Worship*, 144.

17. The following contain helpful suggestions in guiding a congregation to a renewed understanding and use of space: Edward A. Sovik, *Architecture for Worship* (Minneapolis: Augsburg, 1973); Peter G. Cobb, "The Architectural Setting of the Liturgy," Cheslyn Jones, Geoffrey Wainwright, and Edward Yarnold, eds., *The Study of Liturgy* (New York: Oxford Univ. Press, 1978), 473–87; *Environment and Art in Christian Worship* (Chicago: Liturgy Training, 1986); Marchita Mauck, *Shaping a House for the Church* (Chicago: Liturgy Training, 1990); James F. White and Susan J. White, *Church Architecture: Building and Renovating for Christian Worship* (Nashville: Abingdon Press, 1988).

18. See particularly Mauck, *Shaping a House for the Church*, and White and White, *Church Architecture*.

Chapter 13

Content, Structure, and Style

A study in the history of Christian worship or a comparative study of the contemporary church will lead the student into a bewildering variety of worshiping styles. In the face of these many approaches to worship, it is reasonable to ask which one is right. This or that church may think "we do it right here," and along with that conviction there is usually an unspoken assertion "they do it wrong over there." In this brief chapter, we will look at the deeper and more fundamental issue of content, structure, and style.

CONTENT

The primary factor in worship concerns not the structure, nor the style, but the content. Judgment about a particular style of worship must be concerned chiefly with the content of the worship. Liturgical worship, charismatic worship, and every other style of worship must be judged by its content.

There is no need in this chapter to discuss the content of worship, since we dealt with that subject in earlier chapters. It is sufficient to summarize these chapters by asserting once again that the basis of worship is the biblical story of God's initiating a relationship with fallen humanity. In worship we remember the stories of Abraham, our "Father in the faith," the patriarchs, the deliverance of Israel from Egypt, the covenant at Mount Sinai, the establishment of Israel under the monarchy, and the call of the prophets to return to the covenant. Christian worship supplements these stories with the accounts of the birth, life, death, resurrection, and ascension of Jesus, the founding of the church, and the return of Jesus Christ to destroy evil and establish the new heavens and the new earth. This story line together with the interpretation given to it in Scripture is the very essence of worship. Take it away, and there is no worship. Remember to proclaim it, enact it, celebrate it, and worship happens.

It is obvious that these stories lie at the heart of every true worshiping community. One can see them in the written liturgy of every liturgical church or hear them in the singing, reading of Scripture, preaching, and praying of every free church. For worship to be biblical and Christian, the story of God's redemption and salvation must be its content. Otherwise it ceases to be Christian worship. For it is the content of worship—the Gospel—that makes worship uniquely and distinctly Christian.

STRUCTURE

A second and less important factor in worship concerns structure. How should a congregation *structure* the content of its worship? How should the story of God's saving work be ordered so that it is clearly heard and experienced?

One way of dealing with the problem of structure is to draw upon the tradition of the early church. While we do not know as much as we would like about the worship of the early church, we do know that the broad and generally accepted approach to worship included four acts. The two most central acts of Sunday worship were the service of the Word and the service of the Eucharist—the apostolic teaching and the breaking of the bread. Through Word and Eucharist the early church proclaimed, enacted, and celebrated the gospel story. Early Christian worship also included singing, baptism, creeds, benedictions, doxologies, tongues, prophecies, and ministry (see chapters 4 and 5). All these acts of worship are related to the proclamation of the gospel story.

But how should they be ordered? How do the many acts of worship fit together in a coherent whole? There is no direct biblical teaching on this question. We can only draw inferences and consult the models of the early church.[1]

What we discover is that the four basic acts of Sunday worship included assembling the people, Scripture readings and preaching, breaking bread and pouring wine along with prayers of thanksgiving, and sending the people forth. These four acts are accomplished through a sequence of songs, Scriptures, and prayers that proclaim, enact, and celebrate the Gospel, and a sequence of congregational responses that help them experience the Gospel. One can study the history of worship from the early church to the present and discover, without exception, that Sunday worship has always been characterized by these four acts. The intensity, length, or frequency of the services may vary. For example, the early church was characterized by underdeveloped acts of assembly and dismissal, the medieval church nearly lost the service of the Word, and for most Protestants the service of the Eucharist became occasional rather than normative. In spite of these variations, these four acts have remained constant throughout history.

We must ask whether the tradition of the church is of value for worship today. How much significance should we give to these four acts? Should our worship carefully plan ways to assemble the people, ways to communicate the Scripture, ways to celebrate the death and resurrection, and ways to send people forth? Do we find in these four acts the wisdom of the ages and a practical direction for the ordering of our worship? Do these four acts provide a helpful way to structure a worship that is rooted in the Scripture, aware of historical development, and relevant to the needs of contemporary culture?

Worship leaders from many different traditions are convinced that the fourfold structure of assembling, hearing God's Word, responding at the Eucharist, and being sent forth into the world is a structure of worship that is useful for every worshiping community, from liturgical to charismatic. It is already present in nearly every worshiping community but simply stands in need of identification, clarification, and modification.

STYLE

Style is the atmosphere in which the four acts are played out. In some churches the style of worship may be formal and classical in its artistic sense. In other churches the style of worship may be very informal and draw on a contemporary artistic taste that may include gospel, country, or folk music or some other relevant cultural idiom. Some churches create a style of worship that is highly intimate, encouraging people to cluster in groups for response to the sermon, for prayer, or for ministry needs. Other churches create a style of worship that is strong in theater, encouraging participation through sight, sound, taste, and smell. Each congregation must create its own style of worship, a style that is not only comfortable for the worshipers, but also expresses the character and personality of the worshiping community.

CONCLUSION

Once churches become willing to recognize the different languages of worship that relate worship to content, structure, and style, a worshiping community is in a good position to think more clearly about its own worship. First, a church may want to address the question of primary importance: Does our worship proclaim, enact, and celebrate the Gospel? Second, a congregation may want to become more aware of its own structure: Do we assemble the people, proclaim the Word, celebrate the death and resurrection of Christ, and send people forth so that they experience the rehearsal of the Gospel through the order of worship? And finally, what style allows this congregation the greatest freedom and experience of God in worship? Does our style elicit or hinder the praise of God?

In the next four chapters we will look at the four acts of assembling, hearing God speak, celebrating at the table, and being sent forth. A major concern will be to focus on the traditional, contemporary, and convergence styles of these four acts of the worshiping community.

1. For a good discussion of the order of worship in the early church see Allen Cabaniss, *Pattern in Early Christian Worship* (Macon, Ga.: Mercer Univ. Press, 1989).

Chapter 14

Assemble the People

T he first act of worship is to assemble the people. This is no mere human act lacking in theological significance. Rather, it is an act of divine initiative through which God *calls* the people to gather and in which the worshiping community is actualized.

This act of assembling is rooted in the Hebrew notion of a divine convocation. God is the "great assembler" (Jer. 23:3; 29:14), and the people are the assembly of God. In prophetic literature God was visualized as the Shepherd leading the gathered people to good pasture (Ezek. 11:17; 34:13; Mic. 2:12; 4:6). In the New Testament period Jesus became the true Shepherd calling all to a good pasture. Consequently, Jesus became the new focus of assembly by replacing the temple and cultic practices (Matt. 23:37–39).

In apostolic literature and in the early church, the assembly was interpreted as the body of Christ coming together (1 Cor. 12), becoming actualized in the act of assembling. This ecclesial understanding of the assembling of the people prompted the early church (particularly in the fourth and fifth centuries) to think more deliberately about the meaning of assembly and to plan the assembling of the people to hear the Word and celebrate the Eucharist more thoughtfully. Today, worship planners are able to benefit from the thought of the early church as they plan the acts of worship.

Worship planners should keep in mind that the assembling of the people represents the call of God and the response of the people. This underlying structure of proclamation and response already begins as the people rise from their beds, dress, eat, and travel to the worship gathering. Here, as they enter the assembly, singing and responding to God, the church, which is Christ's body, actually and truly comes into being.

Gathering is not an end in itself, but it prepares the people to hear the Word. Gathering possesses a narrative quality. It is a journey of faith, a mystery of coming together accompanied through acts that assemble. Therefore, acts of teaching and thanksgiving, which are essential to worship, are not done in the assembling.

Below are three examples of the acts of worship in the assembling of the people. These examples may be used as guidelines by worship planners and leaders. Three styles are presented: traditional, contemporary, and convergence.

TRADITIONAL ACTS OF ASSEMBLING

The recognition that assembling takes place because of God's call and involves the people's response is expressed in the worship of the *Book of Common Prayer*. Below are those acts of worship followed by a brief commentary.

A LITURGICAL ORDER OF ASSEMBLING

A hymn, psalm, or anthem may be sung.
The people standing, the Celebrant may say:
            Blessed be God: Father, Son and Holy Spirit.
People   And blessed be his kingdom, now and for ever. Amen.
In place of the above, from Easter Day through the Day of Pentecost:
Celebrant: Alleluia. Christ is risen.
People: His mercy endures for ever.
The Celebrant says   Almighty God, to you all hearts are open, all desires
            known, and from you no secrets are hid: Cleanse the
            thoughts of our hearts by the inspiration of your Holy Spirit,
            that we may perfectly love you, and worthily magnify your
            holy Name; through Christ our Lord. *Amen.*

When appointed, the following hymn or some other song of praise is sung or said, all standing:
   Glory to God in the highest,
      and peace to his people on earth.
   Lord God, heavenly King,
   almighty God and Father,
      we worship you, we give you thanks,
      we praise you for your glory.
   Lord Jesus Christ, only Son of the Father,
   Lord God, Lamb of God,
   you take away the sin of the world
      have mercy on us;
   you are seated at the right hand of the Father
      receive our prayer.

For you alone are the Holy One,
you alone are the Lord,
you alone are the Most High,
    Jesus Christ,
    with the Holy Spirit,
    in the glory of God the Father. Amen.

On other occasions the following is used:

Lord, have mercy.		*Kyrie eleison.*
Christ, have mercy.	*or*	*Christe eleison.*
Lord, have mercy.		*Kyrie eleison.*

or this:
Holy God,
Holy and Mighty,
Holy Immortal One,
Have mercy upon us.

The Collect of the Day
The Celebrant says to the people:
        The Lord be with you.
People: And also with you.
Celebrant: Let us pray.
The Celebrant says the Collect.
People: Amen.[1]

In traditional churches the people enter and prepare for worship in a time of silence. Silence has to do with awe. Our experience of silence at the beginning of worship is akin to the feeling of speechlessness we experience when we sense the vastness of the ocean at night or the awesome expanse of the Grand Canyon. The prophet Habakkuk captured this feeling of the numinous when he declared, "The LORD is in his holy temple; let all the earth be silent before him" (2:20). Feelings of transcendence evoke silence and put one in touch with the otherworldly character of reality.

Thus, silence entails meditation, preparation, and openness. Rudolf Otto in his classic work *The Idea of the Holy* recognizes the value given to silence by the Quakers. It is, he wrote, "not so much a dumbness in the presence of Deity, as an awaiting of His coming, in expectation of the Spirit and its message." In this sense silence is a "solemn religious observance of a numinous and sacramental character . . . a communion . . . an inner straining not only 'to realize the presence of God,' but to attain a degree of oneness with Him."[2] Therefore, recovering silence in worship ought to be a matter of genuine concern to pastor and people alike. For in worship one stands before God—Creator, Redeemer, and Judge of all.

Worship then generally continues with a song or hymn and a procession. A procession is a part of life. It usually symbolizes going to something. For example, worship in the Old Testament was characterized by elaborate processions with singing, loud instruments, and dancing. Although there is no evidence of processions in the primitive church, we know that the church after the fourth century made much of the procession. The procession became increasingly elaborate through the medieval period but was abandoned by the Reformers because of late medieval abuses. There are, of course, two dangers here: On the one hand, we can overemphasize the procession so it loses its meaning; on the other hand, if we totally reject the procession, we will fail to understand the meaning of entering (or proceeding) into the very presence of God.[3]

Next, there follows a greeting or an opening sentence of worship or in the case of some churches, what is called the call to worship. These acts of worship mark the end of the procession (the church has arrived at its destination) and the beginning of the formal act of the meeting between God and his people. It is appropriate, therefore, that the people who have come to worship God should be greeted in the name of the triune God.

The greeting that serves as a call to worship has its roots in the synagogue. Abraham Millgram points out that "the daily morning service began with the reader's call to worship. 'Praise ye the Lord whose is to be praised' to which the congregation responded: 'Praised be the Lord who is to be praised for ever and ever.'"[4]

The early church used the greeting "The LORD be with you" or "Peace be to you." These greetings from Ruth 2:4 and John 20:19 came into Christian use from the beginning and are found throughout the literature of the second century. They are used not only in the beginning of worship but also as salutations before prayer and before the Eucharist. The biblical character, antiquity, universality, and dignity of this greeting suggest its importance in worship. Some congregations have replaced the ancient greeting with the more common "hello" or "good morning." Although this exchange is technically proper, it lacks the dignity that enhances a spirit of worship.

The value of a greeting was recognized by the Reformers. For example, Calvin suggested worship begin with the words "Our help is in the name of the Lord, who made heaven and earth. Amen."[5] The *Westminster Directory*, although it shied away from prescribing written prayers, recognized the significance of a prefatory prayer in these words: "The Congregation being assembled; the Minister, after solemn calling them to the worshiping of the great name of God, is to begin with Prayer."[6] Later, John Wesley prepared a list of texts (similar to the Anglican *Book of Common Prayer*) from which ministers were to choose opening sentences of worship.[7]

There is, of course, no absolute and prescribed greeting that one has to follow. It may be a brief sentence of Scripture or a longer form containing responses or even a greeting written by the congregation, and it may change from week to week.

The various acts of greeting are usually followed by a prayer or invocation. In the Episcopal setting, the prayer is one that recognizes how in God's presence nothing can be hid and therefore invites God to cleanse the heart and prepare it for true worship.

The word *invoke* means to call upon or to make a plea. In Christian worship, the members of the congregation stand before God and, through the representation of the one who is presiding, call upon God to become present with them. Theologically, the invocation claims the promise of Jesus that "where two or three come together in my name, there am I with them" (Matt. 18:20). The invocation is, therefore, a recognition that Christians worship the Father through Jesus Christ by the power of the Spirit. They do not enact worship in their own power. The ability to enter into the heavens and join the heavenly throng in worship around the throne is initiated and accomplished by the triune God. The invocation, therefore, requires thoughtful and careful attention, for it is a passage into the very presence of God.

Once the congregation stands before God (by invoking his presence), it is fitting that it should recognize God for who he is. The Scripture that has given shape to the historic burst of praise for God's character in the service of the Word is Luke 2:14, "Glory to God in the highest, and on earth peace to men on whom his favor rests."

The hymn developed from this passage has had a number of titles, but is now universally known as the *Gloria in excelsis Deo*.[8] It originated in the first three centuries and was used frequently in worship until the eleventh century, when it became a fixed portion of the church's worship. The hymn has been found in a total of 341 medieval manuscripts. Among these manuscripts there are 56 different melodies by which it was sung. It is a marvelous hymn, not only for its style, but especially for its theology, which extols and magnifies the position of Jesus in the Godhead. The verse is reflective of a Hellenistic poetic style in its repetition of the clauses. The *Gloria* was dropped in some Reformation churches and replaced (for the most part) with a hymn. But in today's worship renewal within mainline denominations, the *Gloria* has experienced a remarkable recovery and is now found in nearly every new hymnbook.

When Isaiah stood before God and saw him in the majesty of holiness, his response was one of repentance—a recognition of his sinful condition before God. "Woe to me!" he cried. "I am ruined! For I am a man of unclean lips, and I live among a people of unclean lips, and my eyes have seen the King, the LORD Almighty" (Isa. 6:5). This theme of repentance was also enunciated by the tax collector who beat his breast and said, "He would not even look up to heaven, but beat his breast, and said, 'God, have mercy on me, a sinner'" (Luke 18:13).

A response called the *Kyrie eleison* (Lord, have mercy) is found in the liturgies of the fourth and fifth centuries. By the eighth century the refrain *Christe eleison* (Christ, have mercy) was added, and the refrain was put forth in a triple sequence beginning with *Kyrie eleison* sung three times, followed by *Christe eleison* sung three times, and concluded with the *Kyrie eleison* three times again. This repetition, which recognizes the sinful condition of the worshiper, also attests to the mystery of the Trinity. It has a beautiful quality, especially when sung in Greek, the language of early Christian worship.[9]

The *Kyrie eleison* was dropped by the Reformers in favor of a hymn or a psalm that would convey the same sense of repentance. Although the use of the *Kyrie* is a matter of taste, it does seem that the recognition of our sinful condition in the presence of God is a matter of theology. How that is expressed may vary among Christian groups, though the *Kyrie* does have antiquity on its side as well as biblical roots and appropriateness. Like the *Gloria*, the *Kyrie* has experienced a remarkable recovery in twentieth-century worship, particularly in the worship of mainline churches.

The assembling of the people then ends with a collect, a prayer of the day, which collects the prayers of the people and offers them to God. The traditional collects also serve as a means to point the congregation to the theme of the day, which will be expressed in the scripture readings and the sermon.

CONTEMPORARY ORDERING OF THE ASSEMBLY

In recent years many contemporary churches, most of which have been birthed out of the rise of the praise and worship tradition, or influenced by the charismatic tradition, have introduced a whole new approach to the assembling of people for worship. The strength of this new movement is in its emphasis on singing for the first twenty or thirty minutes of worship. The weakness of this movement is that it defines worship time in terms of its music and singing and fails to adequately recognize the Word, the Eucharist, and the dismissal as acts of worship. For example, while the first thirty minutes are referred to as worship time, and the service of the Word is called teaching time, there is a great deal of uncertainty about the place of the Eucharist. The dismissal is reduced to a closing prayer. Nevertheless, as more knowledge about worship is spreading, more and more of the praise and worship churches are beginning to pay greater attention to the fullness of worship.

These churches are characterized not only by contemporary music but by contemporary instruments such as a "full drum set, synthesizers, electric pianos, electric guitar, bass guitar, a number of vocal mikes, and some other percussion instruments."[10]

Often the worship leader is dressed in a casual shirt and jeans and will lead worship with a guitar. The songs that are sung by the congregation are projected on the wall or on a screen. The music is almost always contemporary, and the songs are choruses that have gained a wide acceptance or those written by members of the local church. Singing interlaced with Scriptural comments and prayers usually leads the congregation through a journey into different phases of worship.

The two most widely used approaches to worship within the contemporary movements are the "five-phase worship pattern" and the "four-phase worship pattern." The five-phase pattern of worship songs developed by the Vineyard Church leads the congregation through the following pattern:

Invitation Phase   Songs that serve as a call to worship. These songs are usually exuberant, are accompanied by hand clapping, spontaneous or choreographed dance, and a procession.

Engagement Phase   The people, having gathered, now sing songs to God, songs that express the purpose of coming before God such as "Come Let Us Worship, and Bow Down."

Exaltation Phase   Now the people are prepared to sing songs that extol and magnify the Lord. Usually these songs, such as "I Exalt Thee," are vigorous and directed to God.

Adoration Phase   Worship songs now become quieter and the pace is slower as the people sing songs like "Father, I Adore You."

Intimacy Phase   This phase of worship is the quietest, and the songs are more direct and relational, such as "I Love You Lord." In this phase most people will sing with uplifted hands. Some will kneel or lie prostrate on the floor.

Close Out   A traditional song that ends the intimate, quiet mood of worship, transitioning the congregation to the teaching time.[11]

The four-phase pattern of worship is not significantly different than the five-phase pattern. It is a model developed primarily from the pattern of the Old Testament tabernacle, a pattern that visualizes the worshiper moving from the courts into the Holy of Holies. Here is a chart picturing the flow of the four-phase pattern of worship:

Outside the Courtyard   The picture is of the worshipers outside the courtyard preparing to enter through the gates. Worship songs depict the preparation of the people, are usually joyful, and may be accompanied by dance. A favorite song is "I Will Enter His Courts with Thanksgiving in My Heart."

In the Outer Court   The content of the songs shifts to the experience of worship. These songs express how the congregation should respond: "Come, Let Us Worship and Bow Down."

In the Inner Court   Songs now emphasize worship *about* God. These songs declare God's worth and magnify the character and person of God: "I Exalt Thee."

In the Holy of Holies   Here the worship reaches an intense and intimate time of relationship. Songs directed *to* the Lord, such as "I Love You Lord," are sung quietly.

Congregations who wish to adopt either the five-phase pattern or the four-phase pattern of assembling the people for worship should recognize the difficulty of leading contemporary worship. One cannot simply pick up a guitar, assemble contemporary instruments, pick out the right songs, and expect it to go well. Worship leading requires certain skills, a good grasp of how to accomplish the transitions from one phase to another, an ability to make the right connecting comments between songs, a strong bond with the congregation, and a heart in tune with the Spirit.

THE CONVERGENCE OF TRADITIONAL AND CONTEMPORARY ASSEMBLING

For some, the liturgical assembling is too structured and formal; for others, the contemporary assembling is too dependent on music, particularly the contemporary choruses. Many congregations are developing acts of assembling the people that draw on both the traditional liturgical resources and the new contemporary choruses. While this new convergence of traditional and contemporary worshiping styles is still in its infancy, several configurations seem to be emerging.

First, there are those churches that sing gathering songs ten to twenty minutes before the announced beginning of the service. These songs follow the narrative of either the five-phase pattern or the four-phase pattern or some variation. Then, at the announced time, worship begins with an entrance hymn and procession followed by the elements of the more traditional approach to worship.

Next, some churches follow the traditional pattern of assembling, but in the place of the *Gloria,* they use acts of praise drawn from contemporary choruses and songs directed toward the character of God.

A third configuration draws together the acts of assembling and the service of the Word. The acts of assembling are shortened to an opening hymn and procession, a greeting, and an opening prayer, followed by the Scripture readings. Then, after the readings and before the sermon, the people engage in an extended time of singing, worshiping God through the words and music of contemporary song.

While these are simply three configurations that have gained some acceptance among the churches, each congregation should prayerfully and thoughtfully develop its own approach to the acts that assemble the people for worship.

While relevance is an important feature of worship, worship leaders should be very careful to maintain dignity and reverence as they come into the presence of the Holy One.

CONCLUSION

Because we are living in a time of transition in worship, it is important to pay careful attention to the acts of worship that assemble the people.

There was a time when the pattern of assembling was predictable, but that is no longer true. Consequently, as a congregation begins to develop new patterns, it should keep in mind that the essential nature of the assembling of the people is a divine call and a human response.

How, then, should the acts of assembling the people and preparing them to hear the Word of the Lord be ordered? Remembering that these acts are characterized by a narrative quality, a movement of the people toward the God who is present, each congregation should study the traditional, contemporary, and convergence models. After choosing one of these models, a congregation may experiment with it, teaching the people to make an intentional pilgrimage into the manifest presence of God, preparing their hearts to hear God speak.

1. *The Book of Common Prayer* (New York: Church Hymnal, 1979), 355–357.

2. Rudolf Otto, *The Idea of the Holy* (New York: Oxford Univ. Press, 1958), 211–12.

3. See "Procession," J. G. Davies, ed., *Westminster Dictionary of Worship* (Philadelphia: Westminster, 1972), 323ff.

4. Abraham Millgram, *Jewish Worship* (Philadelphia: The Jewish Publication Society, 1971), 98–99.

5. Bard Thompson, *Liturgies of the Western Church* (New York: New American Library, 1974), 197.

6. Thompson, *Liturgies of the Western Church*, 357.

7. Thompson, *Liturgies of the Western Church*, 417.

8. See "Gloria in Excelsis Deo," in *New Catholic Encyclopedia* (New York: McGraw, 1967), 7:510–11.

9. See Joseph Jungmann, *The Mass of the Roman Rite* (New York: Benzinger Brothers 1959), 222ff.

10. Brian Doerksen, "Vineyard," *The Renewing of Sunday Worship* (Nashville: Abbott Martyn, 1993).

11. For a more full explanation of the five-phase pattern of worship, see Barry Leisch, *People in the Presence of God* (Grand Rapids: Zondervan, 1988), 91–94.

Chapter 15

Listen and Respond to the Word

From the first instance of public worship described in Scripture and throughout the history of the church, the proclamation of the Word of God has been a central act of worship.

However, the nature of the service of the Word has always differed from that of the assembling. The act of assembling is, as we saw in the previous chapter, characterized by a narrative quality. The people travel toward the place where they are going to dwell for a while, listening to and responding to the Word of God.

Once the congregation has arrived at the place of the Word, the acts of worship shift into a new mood. The words that capture the mood of the service of the Word are "instruction," "teaching," "formation," and words such as "hearing," "listening," "responding." These words capture the nature of what God does in the service of the Word. God's action in the service of the Word differs strikingly from his action in the assembling. The assembling is full of joyful movement; the service of the Word demands quiet, meditative listening.

In this chapter we will look at the state of the service of the Word in traditional worship, then provide some suggestions for the incorporation of contemporary aspects of worship.

THE PROCLAMATION OF GOD'S WORD

The public reading of Scripture goes all the way back to Mount Sinai. It was the emphasis of Ezra the scribe that made the Scripture central to Jewish worship, especially in the synagogue. Ezra was a Babylonian Jew who led the second wave of immigrants to Palestine. Upon discovering the weak spiritual condition of the people of Jerusalem, he rent his garments, fasted, and prayed for renewal. Ezra instituted extensive reforms, including the renewal of worship.

> Ezra opened the book. All the people could see him because he was standing above them; and as he opened it, the people all stood up. Ezra praised the LORD, the great God; and all the people lifted their hands and responded, "Amen! Amen!" Then they bowed down and worshiped the LORD with their faces to the ground.
> The Levites . . . instructed the people in the Law while the people were standing there. They read from the Book of the Law of God, making it clear and giving the meaning so that the people could understand what was being read.
>
> Nehemiah 8:5–8

It is interesting to note all that is going on in this incident: the reader standing in a place where he can be seen; the people standing as the book was opened, lifting their hands, saying "Amen," and bowing to the ground; the Levites reading, making it clear, giving the meaning; the people understanding. This was no passive mumbling of Scripture, no mere preliminary to the sermon! This strong emphasis on Scripture was carried directly from the temple to the synagogue and on into Christian worship.

There is little direct evidence prior to Justin Martyr (A.D. 150) concerning the methods of reading Scripture in Christian worship. Nevertheless, the allusion to the reading and use of Scripture in the New Testament literature (see Acts 2:42; 13:5; Col. 4:16; 2 Tim. 3:16) and in early Fathers (1 Clement 13:1; 14:2; Epistle of Barnabas 21:1, 6) leaves little doubt that the description of Christian worship in Justin Martyr refers to a well-established tradition.

> And on the day called Sunday there is a meeting in one place of those who live in cities or the country, and the memoirs of the Apostles or the writings of the prophets are read, as long as time permits; then when the reader has finished, the president in a discourse urges and invites [us] to the imitation of these noble things.[1]

By the third century the liturgy of the Word included readings from the Law, Prophets, Epistles, Acts, and Gospels, with Psalms sung by cantors between the lections. Reading was characterized by an active involvement on the part of the people. Special attention was given to the reading of the Gospel as indicated by the canons of Addai: "At the conclusion of all the scriptures let the gospel be read, as the seal of all the scriptures; and *let the people listen standing up on their feet*, because it is the glad tidings of the salvation of all men[2] (emphasis added).

The people responded by singing psalms between Scripture readings. There is abundant evidence of the use of the psalms in the records of the third century.[3] Eusebius (260–340), bishop of Caesarea and author of the classic *Ecclesiastical History*, wrote, "The command to sing psalms in the name of the

Lord was obeyed by everyone in every place: for the command to sing is in force in all the churches which exist among the nations."[4] Athanasius referred to Psalms as "a book that includes the whole life of man, all conditions of the mind, and all movements of thought."[5] The Reformers, especially John Calvin, advocated the increased use of the psalms in worship.

The sermon is the final and climactic point in which God speaks to the people. The real meaning of preaching is set forth by the apostle Paul in the first chapter of 1 Corinthians. He came to preach the gospel (1:17), which he identifies as the message of the cross (1:18) or of Christ crucified (1:23). He assures his readers that this message was not his own (1:17). Instead, he came with a demonstration of the Spirit's power so that faith would rest on God's power (2:4–5). Paul's theology of preaching sees the kerygma as basic to preaching. In this sense preaching in the context of worship reenacts the event of Christ, the event that gives shape and meaning not only to worship but also to the lives of the worshipers.

But Paul also speaks about teaching in preaching, especially in the Pastoral Epistles. This teaching is referred to as "sound doctrine" (1 Tim. 1:10) and "good teaching" (1 Tim. 4:6). In this it may be seen that teaching belongs to the kerygma and ought not to be separated from it. The preaching of the Gospel always contains teaching, and teaching always contains the preaching of the Gospel. They both belong to the same Word of God. One is the initial preaching of the Gospel, while the other is a more advanced teaching that conforms to the proclamation of the Gospel.

Throughout history, preaching has frequently been accommodated to the prevailing patterns of cultural rhetoric. In some churches much of the simplicity of early preaching has been replaced by long, tedious, and sometimes complicated explanations of the text. Other congregations, particularly those strongly influenced by revivalism, have swung the other way toward the simple representation of the Gospel week after week. These two extremes illustrate the tension between kerygma and teaching. Having falsely separated the two, we fail to preach in such a way that both are present in every proclamation.[6]

A TRADITIONAL SERVICE OF THE WORD

Old Testament Reading
Responsorial Psalm (usually sung)
Epistle reading
Psalm, hymn, or anthem
Gospel reading
Sermon
Nicene Creed
Prayers of the people

Passing of the peace

The underlying structure of the service of the Word, like that of the assembling, is that God initiates and the people respond. While the assembling was God's calling the people to worship, and the people's obediently assembling in light of God's call, the service of the Word is God's proclaiming, and the people's responding in faith. For example, the reading and preaching of the Word is proclamation, while the psalms, hymns, reciting of the Nicene Creed, prayers of the people, and the passing of the peace are all responses.

THE RESPONSE OF THE PEOPLE TO THE WORD OF THE LORD

The people's response to God's Word is clearly seen in the responses to the Word, the creed, the prayers of the people, and the passing of the peace.

First, regarding the response to the Scriptural readings, the church has always shown respect to the Scripture through the use of a preface and a response to the reading of Scripture. This practice, attested to in the liturgies of the fourth century, intends to call attention to the importance of the reading and to engage the hearer in attentive listening. There is no absolute fixed formula for the preface and response. Here is an example:

Reader: A reading from the book of the prophet Isaiah. Following the readings:
Reader: The Word of the Lord.
People: Thanks be to God.

Because the Gospel carries the special privilege of communicating the legacy of Jesus, a different formula for introducing the Gospel reading developed. It became customary to kiss the Gospel and to have a procession accompany the reader to the place where the Gospel was to be read. This procession generally included lights (candles) held by acolytes and incense carried by a thurifer. In the introductory acclamation the reader expressed special honor to Christ himself.

Reader: The Gospel of our Lord Jesus Christ as recorded in . . .
People: Glory to Thee, O Lord.(reading)
Reader: (raising the gospel book over his head, he may say)The Gospel of our Lord.
People: Praise to Thee, O Christ.

It is not Roman or pagan to express love for the Scriptures and to give them a place of honor in worship through the use of physical signs. These signs are ways of expressing an inner conviction regarding the value and significance of God's Word.

Traditionally, the sermon has been followed by the Nicene Creed, the best known creed of the patristic era, in which the deity of Christ and the doctrine of the Trinity are affirmed and proclaimed. It was introduced into worship by Peter the Fuller at Antioch in 473 as a way of emphasizing the true faith. The Nicene Creed gained universal acceptance in the Western church as a credal recital of God's saving acts. As the people say the creed they are affirming their faith in the actions of God through which God, to use a phrase of the creed, acted "for us and for our salvation."

The prayers of the people come next. The true meaning of prayer is found in the relationship it expresses between human beings and God. In prayer the posture of dependence is assumed. Therefore, in the Scriptures and in the history of Christian thought, the church has recognized five kinds of prayer: adoration, confession, petition, praise, and thanksgiving. In *adoration* we worship God for who he is; in *confession* we recognize that forgiveness comes from God; in *petition* we supplicate or intercede on behalf of others; in *praise* we give outward expression of worship through words, music, and ceremony; and in *thanksgiving* we give an offering of thanks for the goodness of God.[7]

In worship all of these prayers are offered to God. Adoration is specifically offered when God is recognized for who he is (e.g., the *Gloria in excelsis Deo*). Confession is expressed when we recognize ourselves for who we are (e.g., the *Kyrie*). Praise is declared frequently throughout the service in the offering of music, the singing of the Psalms, the response of Alleluia, and the like. Thanksgiving is especially fulfilled in the Eucharist, which in the early church came to be known as the Great Thanksgiving. This leaves only one aspect of prayer yet to be treated—petition.

Petition should not be treated exclusively as the prayer of a pastor. It is also the prayer of the church. The early church was extremely conscious of the responsibility the whole church bore for prayers of petition.[8] In addition, the prayer of petition was regarded as the exclusive right of believers. Unbelievers or unbaptized persons were dismissed before the prayer of petition began.

The method of prayer in the early church should also be a matter of interest. The prayer of petition was designed to be a corporate act involving the whole church. All persons—the officiants, the deacons, and the laity—had their part. Furthermore, the prayers (as in the synagogue) were not haphazardly voiced. The leaders announced some matters of prayer, the people prayed, and then they went on to the additional matters of prayer.

Gregory Dix, one of the foremost liturgists of the twentieth century, sets forth an example of these prayers in his classic work, *The Shape of the Liturgy*.

First, a subject was announced, either by the officiant (in the West) or the chief deacon (in the East), and the congregation was bidden to pray. All prayed silently on their knees for a while; then on the signal being given, they rose from their knees, and the officiant summed up the petitions of all in a brief collect. They knelt to pray as individuals, but the corporate prayer of the church is a priestly act, to be done in the priestly posture for prayer, standing. Therefore all, not the celebrant only, rose for the concluding collect.

The following is the scheme of the old Roman intercessions still in use on Good Friday.

Officiant: Let us pray, my dearly beloved, for the holy church of God, that our Lord and God would be pleased to keep her in peace, unity and safety throughout the world, subjecting unto her principalities and powers, and grant us to live out the days of a peaceful and quiet life in glorifying God the Father Almighty.

Deacon: Let us bow the knee (*All kneel and pray in silence for a while*).

Subdeacon: Arise.

Officiant: Almighty everlasting God. Who hast revealed Thy glory unto all nations in Christ, preserve the work of Thy mercy; that Thy church which is spread abroad throughout all the world may continue with a firm faith in the confession of Thy holy Name: through. . . .

Prayers followed for the bishop, the clergy, and all the holy people of God; for the government and the state; for the catechumens; for the needs of the world and all in tribulation (a particularly fine collect, which has inspired one of the best of the official Anglican prayers for use in the present war [World War II]; for heretics and schismatics; for the Jews, and for the pagans. These prayers probably date from the fourth and fifth centuries in their present form, but may well be only revisions of earlier third century forms.

Or we may take an Eastern scheme from the Alexandrian liturgy, probably of much the same date as these Roman prayers.

The deacon proclaims first: Stand to pray. (All have been "standing at east" or sitting on the ground for the sermon.)

Then he begins: Pray for the living; pray for the sick; pray for all away from home.

Let us bow the knee. (*All pray in silence.*) Let us arise. Let us bow the knee. Let us arise again. Let us bow the knee.

The people: Lord have mercy.[9]

This "people's prayer" derives from the profound understanding that the early church had an organic sense of the body of Jesus Christ. Unfortunately, this approach to prayer began to fade away in the fifth century and became nonexistent by the medieval period. Prayer became increasingly clericalized, with the people having no more part than an "amen" here and there. Neither did the Reformers or Puritans recapture this sense of a "people's prayer." Rather, they kept the prayers of the church in the control of the minister by means of the pastoral prayer. This has begun to change as a result of liturgical scholarship and the renewed sense of worship as the work of the entire congregation.

Finally, the kiss of peace is a gesture that communicates peace with God and with each other.[10] In the New Testament there are a number of references to a kiss of greeting. Paul instructs the Roman Christians to "greet one another with a holy kiss" (Rom. 16:16). Peter appears to connect the kiss with the peace of God: "Greet one another with a kiss of love. Peace to all of you who are in Christ" (1 Peter 5:14).

How is this command carried out? The method depends somewhat on local custom. The officiant may say, "The peace of the Lord be with you," and to this everyone would respond, "And also with you," and then turn to those around them, grasping their hand or embracing them, saying, "The peace of the Lord be with you." If the church is small enough, everyone in the congregation may "pass the peace" to everyone else. In a large church the pastor may proceed down the center aisle, passing the peace to the person at the end of the row who in turn passes the peace to the next person.

The use of the kiss in worship appears in the writing of Justin Martyr and in other writers thereafter. However, it fell into disuse after the ancient period and was not revived until recently. Although the position of the kiss of peace appears in various places in the liturgy, the earlier accounts place it at the end of the liturgy of the Word, before the beginning of the Eucharist. So Justin wrote in his *First Apology*, "on finishing the prayers we greet each other with a kiss. Then bread and a cup of water and mixed wine are brought to the president of the brethren."[11] In the Eastern church the kiss was moved to the beginning of the eucharistic prayer. In either case it was seen as serving a transitional function between the Word and the Eucharist.

INCORPORATING CONTEMPORARY ASPECTS OF WORSHIP INTO THE SERVICE OF THE WORD

It is not possible to outline a contemporary order of the service of the Word. Most contemporary churches simply read a Scripture and preach, which constitutes the whole of the service of the Word. This truncated order reflects the current misunderstanding of the acts of worship that assemble the people. For example, in many contemporary churches the acts of assembly are regarded as the *worship* of the people, while the reading and preaching of the Word are regarded as *teaching*. In this way a division is made between worship and teaching so that the service of the Word is not seen as worship. From a biblical and historical perspective, the reading of Scripture and preaching have always been regarded as acts of worship. Consequently, there is a need to restore the service of the Word and to recognize that the service of the Word is also an act of worship, but one which is different than the acts that assemble the people. Once it is recognized that the service of the Word is worship, we must ask: What kind of worship acts should we do in the service of the Word?

The central feature of the service of the Word is the Scripture. Many churches that proclaim their allegiance to Scripture have no more than one Scripture reading, and some churches actually gather for worship on occasions when no Scripture is read. At least two Scriptures may be read and one of them should be a gospel lesson. Many churches are making the clear communication of Scripture a priority. For example, some churches have established a core of readers who offer their communication talents to God through clear Scripture reading and through the occasional use of drama presentation or storytelling. When the latter two are employed, care should be given so that storytelling and drama do not become overbearing or jarring to the flow of worship. Drama and storytelling should never be a performance to entertain, but an act of communication to express the message of God more effectively. More and more contemporary churches are using the Scripture reading guidelines offered by the *New Common Lectionary*, which organizes readings from the Old Testament, the Psalms, the Epistles, and the Gospels in a thematic form through the seasons of the Christian year.[12]

Next, the singing of psalms is most appropriate in the service of the Word, because the psalms relate to the mood of the more instructive atmosphere. Contemporary Christians may want to do what was done in the ancient church and sing the psalms between the readings of Scripture. Today there are numerous new settings of the psalms ranging in style from the more formal approach of Taizé music to the informal music of the heirs of the Jesus movement, who have turned many psalm verses and phrases into popular music.

Next, worshipers within the contemporary style may want to develop a response to the sermon such as a sung Nicene Creed or hymn that expresses the content of faith. Or, like the independents of the seventeenth and eighteenth centuries, contemporaries may want to occasionally follow the sermon with discussion and feedback. Even in formal settings of worship, people can turn to each other and briefly discuss the sermon or in smaller settings stand and speak a word of response or exhortation.

Also, the prayers of intercession do not have to be done through the pastoral prayer, which is an approach to prayer developed in modern times. Prayers may be offered in intimate circles, in litanies led by a layperson with written responses by the people, or in bidding prayers in which the prayer leader bids the people to pray for this or that concern and the people respond out loud in extemporaneous prayer.

Finally, the passing of the peace. Many churches have adopted what they call the ritual of friendship, a ritual of greeting and welcome to all. Churches should consider replacing the ritual of friendship or adding to it the ritual of the passing of the peace, which is rooted in biblical worship and has deeper spiritual meaning than the secular greeting introduced by many churches.

CONCLUSION

In this chapter the profound meaning of the service of the Word has been explored. Because worship cannot happen apart from the Word, and because some contemporary worshiping communities neglect the reading of the Word, worshiping communities must pay greater attention to the service of the Word.

1. See Cyril Richardson, *Early Christian Fathers* (Philadelphia: Westminster, 1953), 287; William Maxwell, *An Outline of Christian Worship* (London: Oxford Univ. Press, 1939), 14ff.

2. See Joseph Jungmann, *The Mass of the Roman Rite*, trans. Francis A. Brunner and Rev. Charles K. Riepe (New York: Benzinger Brothers, 1959), 260ff.

3. Quoted in "Psalmody," J. G. Davies, ed., *Westminster Dictionary of Worship* (Philadelphia: Westminster, 1977), 326.

4. Quoted in "Psalmody," Davies, *Westminster Dictionary of Worship*, 326.

5. See Jungmann, *The Mass of the Roman Rite*, 284ff.

6. For a hermeneutic of preaching see David Buttrick, *The Renewal of Sunday Worship* (Nashville: Abbott-Martyn, 1993) 326–29.

7. See Donald Coggen, *The Prayers of the New Testament* (New York: Harper, 1967).

8. See Jungmann, *The Mass of the Roman Rite*, 391ff., and Hughes Oliphant Old, *The Patristic Roots of Reformed Worship* (Zurich: Tehologischer Verlag Zurich, 1975), 240ff.

9. Gregory Dix, *The Shape of the Liturgy* (London: Dacre, 1945), 42–43.

10. See "Gestures," Davies, *Westminster Dictionary of Worship*, 185ff.

11. Richardson, *Early Christian Fathers*, 285–86.

12. *The New Common Lectionary* (Nashville: Abingdon, 1992).

Chapter 16

Remember and Give Thanks

In the previous two chapters we have discussed the underlying structure of both the service of assembling and the service of the Word as proclamation and response. God calls the people to assemble and they gather; God speaks to the people through the Word and they listen and respond.

This two-way action between God and the worshiper is the underlying structure of the service of the Eucharist. Coming to the table is a response of thanksgiving. The people, responding to the Word, "give thanks" or to use the Greek word "make Eucharist."

But how does the church make thanks? The purpose of this chapter is to look at the order of worship in the Eucharist in the early church. This order has shaped the renewal of the Eucharist in contemporary liturgical churches. And it has the power to inform and give meaning to the celebration of the Lord's table in the contemporary free church tradition.

THE ORDER OF THE EUCHARIST
IN THE ANCIENT CHURCH

The order of giving thanks at the Eucharist begins in the New Testament. The New Testament accounts suggest a "seven-action scheme." Jesus (1) took bread, (2) gave thanks (Eucharist) over it, (3) broke it, and (4) distributed it with certain words. Then he (5) took a cup, (6) gave thanks (Eucharist) over it, (7) and, saying certain words, handed it to his disciples.

173

In the extant early liturgies of the church, this sevenfold action has been compressed to a fourfold action. By bringing together the "taking," the "giving thanks," and the "handing it to his disciples," the result is a fourfold action of (1) taking, (2) blessing, (3) breaking, and (4) giving.[1] This is the order followed in the table experience of the early disciples with Jesus after the Resurrection. Here "he took bread, gave thanks, broke it and began to give it to them" (Luke 24:30). Because of this action "their eyes were opened and they recognized him" (Luke 24:31). They then hurried to Jerusalem to tell the other disciples that Jesus had risen from the dead and "how Jesus was recognized by them when he broke the bread" (Luke 24:35). This "Emmaus road" experience may have shaped the earliest eucharistic order of the Jerusalem church (Acts 2:46) and accounts for the association of the special presence of Christ in the worshiping community through the breaking of the bread.

This fourfold sequence provides the framework in which the essential prayers and actions of eucharistic worship took place in the early church. An examination of the eucharistic liturgies of the early church evidences a common basic structure of ten parts. They are (1) introductory dialogue and the prayer of thanksgiving that includes (2) the preface, (3) the *Sanctus*, and (4) the post-*Sanctus* prayers of thanksgiving. This is followed by (5) a preliminary invocation, (6) the narrative of institution, (7) the *anamnesis* (remembrance), (8) the *epiclesis* (an invocation of the Holy Spirit), (9) the intercessions, and (10) the concluding doxology. It should be noted that not all ten parts are found in all liturgies. The preliminary epiclesis and the intercessions are often omitted, except in the East. Also, there is some variety in the sequence of these ten parts.[2]

The common structure of all the eucharistic liturgies is found in *The Apostolic Tradition* of Hippolytus. In the forthcoming examination of the order of eucharistic worship, the text will be given in full because of the importance of the prayers, both in terms of their antiquity and with reference to the influence this text played in giving shape to the ancient structure of Christian worship.

We turn now to an examination of the order of the eucharistic liturgy. Although our major concern is with the primitive liturgy, it should be noted that the order of worship and the content of the prayers and actions in Reformation liturgies are not significantly different. Unfortunately, space does not permit an extensive inclusion of Reformation liturgies. However, similarities, differences, and issues will be sufficiently noted so that the interested reader may make comparisons.[3]

He Took

The first part of eucharistic worship is primarily a wordless action. Following the kiss of peace, the celebrant *takes* the bread and wine that are offered. This is an important action because it signifies the involvement of the whole worshiping community.

The earliest records indicate that each person or family brought bread and wine as well as other gifts (food to be distributed to the needy) and placed them on the table. Gradually, because of the increased size of the worshiping congregation, a representative brought the bread and wine for the entire congregation.

The significance of this symbol is that the people present themselves through the offering of bread and wine. Thus the entire worshiping community is involved in the action of "bringing," "presenting," and "offering." The canons of the synod of Ancyra in 314 recognized this symbolic action and prescribed that the communicant "brings," the deacon "presents," and the bishop "offers." The real significance of this action is caught by Gregory Dix in these words:

> Each communicant from the bishop to the newly confirmed gave *himself* under the forms of bread and wine to God, as God gives Himself to them under the same forms. In the united oblations of all her members the Body of Christ, the church, gave herself to *become* the Body of Christ, the sacrament, in order that receiving again the symbol of herself now transformed and hallowed, she might be truly that which by nature she is, the Body of Christ, and each of her members, members of Christ.[4]

Two other actions were adopted by the ancient church to communicate the meaning of the offering. First, the washing of the hands (in keeping with Psalm 26:6: "I wash my hands in innocence, and go about your altar, O LORD") signified the innocence of those who serve the altar. This action was first recorded by Cyril of Jerusalem in the fourth century and ought not be regarded as an early custom. Second, the imposition of hands on the elements may have been derived from the Old Testament practice of laying hands on the sacrificial animal (e.g., Lev. 4:14–15). It could have been used to signify the blessing conferred or to recognize that these elements represent the people who brought them and who, through the consuming of bread and wine, are blessed. The first occurrence of the act is recorded by Hippolytus in the third century.[5]

During the Reformation era there were traces of the offertory, but for the most part it appeared in the background and it was often dropped. In Calvin's *Strasbourg Liturgy*, reference is made to the minister's preparing the bread and wine.[6] Luther also makes a similar reference in his *Formula Missae* and *Deutsche Messe*.[7] In the *Westminster Directory* all hints of an offertory are dropped and ministers are instructed to have "the Table . . . decently covered before the service of communion begins."[8] There is no hint of either the washing of hands or the imposition of hands on the elements.

The Reformer's rejection of the offertory and the dropping of the symbolic action of "taking" probably stemmed from the late medieval notion of the Eucharist as a sacrifice. Unfortunately, the Reformer's strong reaction resulted in the continued loss of the original notion of offering.

He Blessed

The prayer of blessing over the bread and wine was the universally accepted practice of the ancient church. Justin informs us that "the president . . . offers prayers and thanksgivings."[9] The later liturgies of the church give us insight into the content of these prayers that were offered "according to his ability." The parts that belong to the "blessing" include the introductory dialogue, the preface, the *Sanctus,* and the main body of the prayer of thanksgiving, frequently referred to as the post-*Sanctus* prayer. Each of these aspects will be treated briefly.

First, the *introductory dialogue* contains both the *salutation* and the *Sursum corda.* The salutation has already been discussed in the previous chapter, so we will discuss only the *Sursum corda* here. This preface (in varying forms) is found in all the liturgies of both East and West.[10] Here is the *Sursum corda* from Hippolytus, with a few interpretive remarks:

SURSUM CORDA	COMMENTARY
Celebrant: Up with your Hearts. *People:* We have them with the Lord. *Celebrant:* Let us give thanks to the Lord.	The purpose of this response was to emphasize that true worship takes place in the heavenlies in Jesus Christ (Eph. 2:6–7). The bidding brought the congregations into the heavens (Rev. 4 and 5). Because thanksgiving (Eucharist) was made by the entire congregation, the response to "Let us give thanks" was the permission and command of the congregation to bring the offering of praise and thanksgiving.[11]

Second, after the worship had begun, the assembly moved into the *preface* and to the great prayer of thanksgiving. The Latin *prefatio* does not mean a preliminary but a proclamation. The purpose of the preface was to offer a brief explanation of why thanksgiving and praise were being offered. In Hippolytus, the preface was a very brief statement: "We render thanks to you, O God, through your beloved child Jesus Christ, whom in the last times you sent to us as savior and redeemer and angel of your will."[12] Although this statement was terse, it went right to the heart of the matter, indicating that worship was being offered because of the redemption.

Normally the preface was concluded with the *Sanctus* (from Isa. 6:3 and Rev. 4:8), the third part of the thanksgiving. This is certainly proper, considering the image of going up into the heavens to join the worship of eternity, which is characterized by the continual singing of "Holy, holy, holy is the Lord God Almighty, who was, and is, and is to come." The *Sanctus* is not found in Hippolytus, though it is found in all the later liturgies, and as early as 1 Clement. Here, for example, is the preface and *Sanctus* taken from the liturgy of John Chrysostom (380):

PREFACE AND SANCTUS

Celebrant: (Preface) It is fitting and right to hymn you (to bless you, to praise you), to give thanks to worship you in all places of your dominion. For you are God, ineffable, inconceivable, invisible, incomprehensible, existing always and in the same way, you and your only-begotten Son and your Holy Spirit. You brought us out of not being into being; and when we had fallen, you raised us up again; and did not cease to do everything until you had brought us up to heaven, and granted us the kingdom that is to come. For all these things we give thanks to you and to your only-begotten Son and to your Holy Spirit, for all that we know and do not know, your seen and unseen benefits that have come upon us. We give you thanks also for this ministry; vouchsafe to receive it from our hands, even though thousands of archangels and ten thousands of angels stand before you, cherubim and seraphim, with six wings and many eyes, flying on high (aloud) singing the triumphals hymn (proclaiming, crying and saying):
People: (Sanctus)
Holy, Holy, Holy, Lord of Saboath, heaven and earth are full of your glory. Hosanna in the highest. Blessed is he who comes in the name of the Lord. Hosanna in the highest.[13]

COMMENTARY

Eastern prayers were more poetic than Western ones, which were more precise and terse. This brief prayer contains the essence of the gospel message. It describes the major reason for giving thanks and praise. This praise joins in the great company of heavenly worship.

The *Sanctus* of the earthly church joins the heavenly in singing the eternal praise.

Immediately after the *Sanctus,* the congregation is led in the body of the prayer of thanksgiving. This prayer enacts the whole Gospel, because that is the content of the church's praise and thanksgiving. Here is that prayer from Hippolytus. Lengthier and more flowery ones are found in other extant canons.

PRAYER OF THANKSGIVING

Who is your inseparable Word, through whom you made all things, and in whom you were well pleased.

You sent him from heaven into the Virgin's womb; and, conceived in the womb, he was made flesh and made manifested as your Son, being born of the Holy Spirit and the Virgin.

Fulfilling your will and gaining you a holy people, he stretched out his hands when he should suffer, that he might release from suffering those who have believed in you.

And when he was betrayed to voluntary suffering that he might destroy death, and break the bonds of the devil, and tread down hell, and shine upon the righteous, and fix the limit, and manifest the resurrection. . . .[14]

COMMENTARY

It is particularly instructive to note how this prayer sweeps from creation to resurrection.

He begins by stating the position of the Son with the Father. He extols the Son for creation, moves on to the incarnation, and then emphasizes the destruction of the powers through Christ's death. Next, he makes reference to the resurrection.

Most liturgies make specific reference to the Fall. Here, he refers to the Fall by mentioning "death" and "the bonds of the devil."

Hippolytus does not have a preliminary epiclesis in his liturgy. Here is an example found in the fifth-century liturgy of Mark: "Fill, O God, this sacrifice also with a blessing from you through the descent of your (all-holy Spirit)."[15] This prayer recognizes the place of the Holy Spirit in empowering the worship of the church.

The Reformers retained parts of the ancient "blessing" or prayer of thanksgiving. Luther retained the salutation, the *Sursum corda,* and the preface but dropped the *Sanctus* and even the body of the prayer of thanksgiving, as well as the preliminary epiclesis in his *Formula Missae* of 1552. Calvin, in the *Form of Church Prayers* written for the church in Geneva in 1542, dropped the entire section in favor of an exhortation after the words of institution.[16]

Calvin rejected the element of thanksgiving in favor of a personal examination of faith. This marks a significant shift in the meaning of worship. In the ancient church, the emphasis at the table was on the objective work of Jesus Christ, who by his death was the sacrifice of God for humanity (the Eucharist being the offering of praise and thanksgiving for the work of Christ). Because this original notion had been corrupted by the medieval church and turned into a *re-sacrifice*, Calvin, Zwingli, and the majority of Protestants after them dropped the entire prayer of thanksgiving. They shifted the emphasis of the Eucharist from praise and thanksgiving for God's actin in Christ to man's faith, self-examination, and pursuit of good works.

In this new emphasis, Calvin lost and gained something. What he lost was the sense of praise and thanksgiving evoked by the ancient Eucharist. What he gained was the Pauline emphasis in 1 Corinthians 11:28–29: "A man ought to examine himself before he eats of the bread and drinks of the cup. For anyone who eats and drinks without recognizing the body of the Lord eats and drinks judgment on himself."

The *Westminster Directory* retained a prayer of thanksgiving and instructed the ministers "to give thanks to God for all his benefits, and especially for that great benefit of our redemption, the love of God the Father, the sufferings and merits of our Lord Jesus Christ the Son of God, by which we are delivered."[17] It is a normal practice in most evangelical churches to offer an extemporaneous prayer during the Eucharist that gives thanks for the broken body and shed blood and gift of salvation that comes through the death of Jesus. Renewal churches give more careful attention to the entire history of salvation in the prayer of thanksgiving by moving from the triune God through creation, to the Fall, and finally to incarnation, death, resurrection, and second coming of Christ.

There is no reason why the salutation, the *Sursum corda*, the preface, and the *Sanctus* should not be restored by the free church. These parts of the prayer of thanksgiving are deeply rooted in biblical truth and add a dignity to the offering of the great thanksgiving of the church. A slavish reproduction of the exact prayer of Hippolytus is not necessary. The pastor may use the extemporaneous approach to prayer to which free churches are committed while drawing from the ancient traditions.

In this way both the form and freedom that were the intent of Hippolytus would find a good balance. His prayer was not given to be memorized. Rather it was to serve as a model. It was expected that the extemporaneous approach to prayer as in Justin's report would be continued.

He Broke

The third action of the Eucharist is the breaking of the bread. The original breaking of the bread in the Jewish background probably had no meaning other than that of distribution. However, in the course of Christian history, the action of breaking the bread attained several meanings.

The earliest meaning concerned church unity. Paul interpreted it this way to the Corinthians, who were torn by strife. He wrote, "Because there is one loaf, we, who are many, are one body, for we all partake of the one loaf" (1 Cor. 10:17). This same notion is seen in Ignatius[18] and the *Didache*.[19] By the third century the emphasis on unity seems to have been replaced by the symbol of Christ's broken body and his death on the church's behalf. This latter notion seems to have been retained by most Protestant churches today.

The breaking of bread (fraction) is the climax of the prayer belonging to the "breaking." Other parts include the narrative, the anamnesis, the prayer of intercessions, and the epiclesis.

The narrative of institution is simply the repetition of the words of Jesus. Hippolytus put this quite simply, as do the other liturgies of the ancient church:

> He took bread and gave thanks to you, saying, "Take eat; this is my body, which shall be broken for you." Likewise also the cup, saying, "This is my blood, which is shed for you; when you do this, you make my remembrance."[20]

The concept of remembrance generally contains statements of *memorial* and *offering*. Here is an example from *The Apostolic Constitutions* (375):

THE APOSTOLIC CONSTITUTIONS

Remembering therefore what he endured for us, we give you thanks, almighty God, not as we ought but as we are able, and we fulfill his commands.

For in the night he was betrayed, he took bread in his holy and blameless hands and, looking up to you, his Father, he broke it and gave it to his disciples, saying, "This is the mystery of the new covenant; take of it, eat; this is my body which is broken for many for forgiveness of sins."

Likewise also he mixed the cup of wine and water and sanctified it and gave it to them, saying, "Drink from this, all of you; this is my blood which is shed for many

COMMENTARY

In the early church the anamnesis was regarded as more than a memorial. It was an objective act in which the event commemorated was actually made present.

The memorial always mentioned the passion, the resurrection, and the Ascension, and frequently included the Incarnation, the burial, the mediation of the ascended Christ, and the Second Coming.

The offering explicitly offered the bread and wine in identification with the offering of Jesus and as being representative of the whole created order that he redeemed.

for forgiveness of sins. Do this for my remembrance; for as often as you eat this bread and drink this cup, you proclaim my death, until I come."

Remembering then his passion and death and resurrection from the dead, his return to heaven, and his future second coming, in which he comes to judge the living and the dead, and to reward each according to his works, we offer to you, King and God. . . [21]

This portion of the prayer completes the drama of the work of Jesus. The focus is on the eschatological aspects of the Christian faith—the Ascension, the Second Coming, and the Judgment.

A word needs to be said about the anamnesis. We tend to translate this word as "memory," a mental action that brings to mind something from the past. This is questionable. The word may also mean "re-calling" or "re-presenting" before God an event, so that its effects become operative here and now.[22] In this sense the remembrance places before God the once-for-all sacrifice of Christ and makes it operative in the present to the believer who by faith receives Christ under the signs of bread and wine. In this way the remembrance is no empty act but a powerful proclamation of the sacrifice of Christ.

Next comes the epiclesis (invocation of the Holy Spirit), a prayer for the coming of the Holy Spirit on both the elements of bread and wine and on the people who worship. This prayer recognizes the Holy Spirit as the agent who confirms and makes worship real, a fact evident in the following prayer of Hippolytus:

> And we ask that you would send your Holy Spirit upon the offering of your holy Church; that, gathering them into one, you would grant to all who partake of the holy things for the fullness of the Holy Spirit for the confirmation of faith in truth.[23]

Then comes the prayer of intercession. There is a strong divergence of opinion here between the East and the West. The Eastern liturgy places the prayer of intercession at this point because the worshiping community is at the very throne of God. Alexander Schmemann, an Orthodox theologican, writes:

> It is the very joy of the Kingdom that makes us *remember* the world and pray for it. It is the very communion with the Holy Spirit that enables us to love the world with the love of Christ. . . Intercession begins here, in the glory of the messianic banquet, and this is the only true beginning for the church's mission.[24]

The typical place for the intercession in the Western church is in the liturgy of the Word, after the sermon. While the West recognizes the theological validity of the Eastern viewpoint, a major concern has been for the rhythm of worship. The Western church regards the intercession at this point as a major distraction from the emphasis on praise and thanksgiving.

Nevertheless, the West has placed the Lord's Prayer in the prayer of thanksgiving as a recognition of the value of intercession when the people of God are before the throne. By limiting prayer to the Lord's Prayer, the West retains the focus of the Eucharist as an act of praise and thanksgiving.[25]

Finally, the fraction occurs.[26] Here, the bread may be lifted up for all to see so that worship occurs through the senses of sight and sound. The Reformers kept most of the parts of the "breaking," though their service was organized quite differently.[27]

He Gave

The final "movement" of worship in the Eucharist is the giving of bread and wine. Careful attention has been paid to the giving and the receiving of the elements in worship renewal. In the original drama Jesus handed over the bread and the cup saying: "Take and eat; this is my body" and "Drink from it [the cup], all of you. This is my blood of the covenant, which is poured out for many for the forgiveness of sins" (Matt. 26:26–28). The earliest liturgies record this tradition of Jesus. The officiant hands the bread and the cup to each person and says either the exact words of Jesus or a paraphrase of them. Here is an example from *The Apostolic Constitutions*:

Officiant: The body of Christ.
Person: Amen.
Officiant: The blood of Christ, the cup of life.
Person: Amen.[28]

The reason for such careful attention to detail is that this is the point of *communion*. It is a sacred moment. Paul reminded the Corinthians of the meaning of communion: "Is not the cup of thanksgiving for which we give thanks a participation in the blood of Christ? And is not the bread that we break a participation in the body of Christ?" (1 Cor. 10:16). At this point in the worship, the offering and remembrance become a communion, a mystical communication between Christ and the believer. This is not an ordinary act to be defiled by a haughty or irreverent attitude. It is the moment when the transcendent God, who sent his Son into the world so that human beings may be saved, meets with his people.

For this reason the ancient church treated this moment with the utmost dignity and reverence. Cyril of Jerusalem in his *Catecheses* instructed candidates for baptism to take the following care as they came to receive the elements:

After this, you hear the cantor inviting you with a divine melody to the communion of the holy mysteries, and saying, "Taste and see that the Lord is good."

Do not entrust your judgment to your bodily palate, but to undoubting faith; for what you taste is not bread and wine, but the likeness of the body and blood of Christ.

When you approach, do not come with your hands stretched or your fingers separated; but make your left hand a throne for the right, since it is to receive a king. Then hallow your palm and receive the body of Christ, saying after it, "Amen." Carefully sanctify your eyes by the touch of the holy body, then partake, taking care not to lose any of it. . . .

Then, after having partaken of the body of Christ, approach also the cup of his blood. Do not stretch out your hands, but bowing, and saying "Amen" in the gesture of adoration and reverence, sanctify yourself by partaking of the blood of Christ also. While the moisture is still on your lips, touch it with your hands and sanctify your eyes and forehead and the other senses. Then wait for the prayer, and give thanks to God who has deemed you worthy of such great mysteries.[29]

APPLICATION TO CONTEMPORARY WORSHIP

The study of the eucharistic prayer in the early church has shaped the approach to communion in the contemporary church. This impact is most clearly seen among those churches that use written texts. One of the best examples of a contemporary approach to the Eucharist is the liturgical setting from the *Book of Common Prayer*.

A LITURGICAL EUCHARISTIC PRAYER

The people remain standing. The Celebrant, whether bishop or priest, faces them and sings or says:
> The Lord be with you.

People: And also with you.
Celebrant: Lift up your hearts.
People: We lift them up to the Lord.
Celebrant: Let us give thanks to the Lord our God.
People: It is right to give him thanks and praise.

Then, facing the Holy Table, the Celebrant proceeds:
> It is right, and a good and joyful thing, always and everywhere to give thanks to you, Father Almighty, Creator of heaven and earth.

Here a Proper Preface is sung or said on all Sundays, and on other occasions as appointed.

Therefore we praise you, joining our voices with Angels and Archangels and with all the company of heaven, who for ever sing this hymn to proclaim the glory of your Name:

Celebrant and People:

Holy, holy, holy Lord, God of power and might,
heaven and earth are full of your glory.
    Hosanna in the highest.
Blessed is he who comes in the name of the Lord.
    Hosanna in the highest.

The people stand or kneel.

Then the Celebrant continues:

Holy and gracious Father: In your infinite love you made us for yourself; and, when we had fallen into sin and become subject to evil and death, you, in your mercy, sent Jesus Christ, your only and eternal Son, to share our human nature, to live and die as one of us, to reconcile us to you, the God and Father of all.

He stretched out his arms upon the cross, and offered himself, in obedience to your will, a perfect sacrifice for the whole world.

At the following words concerning the bread, the Celebrant is to hold it, or lay a hand upon it; and at the word concerning the cup to hold or place a hand upon the cup and any other vessel containing wine to be consecrated.

On the night he was handed over to suffering and death, our Lord Jesus Christ took bread; and when he had given thanks to you, he broke it, and gave it to his disciples and said, "Take, eat: This is my Body, which is given for you. Do this for the remembrance of me."

After supper he took the cup of wine; and when he had given thanks, he gave it to them, and said, "Drink this, all of you: This is my blood of the new Covenant, which is shed for you and for many for the forgiveness of sins. Whenever you drink it, do this for the remembrance of me."

Therefore we proclaim the mystery of faith:

Celebrant and People:

Christ has died.
Christ is risen.
Christ will come again.

The Celebrant continues:

We celebrate the memorial of our redemption, O Father, in this sacrifice of praise and thanksgiving. Recalling his death, resurrection, and ascension, we offer you these gifts.

Sanctify them by your Holy Spirit to be for your people the Body and
Blood of your Son, the holy food and drink of new and un-
ending life in him. Sanctify us also that we may faithfully receive this holy Sacrament, and serve you in unity, constancy,
and peace; and at the last day bring us with all your saints
into the joy of your eternal kingdom.
All this we ask through your Son Jesus Christ. By him, and with him,
and in him, in the unity of the Holy Spirit all honor and
glory is yours, Almighty Father, now and forever. Amen.
And now, as our Savior Christ has taught us, we are bold to say,
People and Celebrant:

Our Father, who art in heaven,
hallowed be thy Name,
thy kingdom come,
thy will be done,
on earth as it is in heaven.
Give us this day our daily bread.
And forgive us our trespasses,
as we forgive those who trespass against us.
And lead us not into temptation,
but deliver us from evil.
For thine is the kingdom,
and the power, and the glory,
for ever and ever. Amen.

The Breaking of the Bread

The Celebrant breaks the consecrated bread.
A period of silence is kept.
Then this may be sung or said.
[Alleluia.] Christ our Passover is sacrificed for us;
Therefore let us keep the feast [Alleluia.]
In Lent, Alleluia is omitted, and may be omitted at other times except during
Easter Season.
In place of, or in addition to, the preceding, some other suitable anthem may
be used.
Facing the people, the Celebrant says the following invitation:
The Gifts of God for the People of God.
He may add: Take them in remembrance that Christ died for you, and
feed on him in your hearts by faith, with thanksgiving.
The ministers receive the Sacrament in both kinds, and then immediately de-
liver it to the people.

The Bread and the Cup are given to the communicants with these words:
The Body (Blood) of our Lord Jesus Christ keep you in everlasting life.
>   [*Amen*]

or with these words:
The Body of Christ, the bread of heaven. [*Amen*]
The Blood of Christ, the cup of salvation. [*Amen*]
*During the ministration of Communion, hymns, psalms, or anthems may be
>   sung.*

After Communion, the Celebrant says:
Let us pray.
Celebrant and People:
Eternal God, heavenly Father,
you have graciously accepted us as living members
of your Son our Savior Jesus Christ,
and you have fed us with spiritual food
in the Sacrament of His Body and Blood.
Send us now into the world in peace,
and grant us strength and courage
to love and serve you
with gladness and singleness of heart;
through Christ our Lord. Amen.[30]

ADAPTATION OF THE LITURGICAL EUCHARISTIC PRAYER FOR CONTEMPORARY FREE CHURCH WORSHIP

Some free churches are using liturgical resources for eucharistic worship and creating communion services that draw on liturgical resources. There is growing interest among many free churches to create an extemporaneous eucharistic liturgy that follows the pattern of the ancient church. In these churches an outline of worship similar to the following outline has been adopted. Music and responses are frequently displayed on a screen.

1)   The service begins with a communion hymn. If the bread and wine have not been prepared before the service, the bread and wine are now brought to the table. The deacons or elders may gather around the table with the minister, who stands at the center. The people stand.

2)   The minister and the people say the *Sursum corda* (Lift up your hearts).

3)   The minister prays a brief preface prayer that states why the church has gathered (to give thanks) and with whom the church has gathered (angels, archangels, cherubim, seraphim, the company of the saints, etc.).

4)   The minister and people join together in the heavenly song, singing one of the many variations of the *Sanctus* (Holy, holy, holy). Here a contemporary *holy* is appropriate.

5)   The minister now prays the prayer of thanksgiving over the bread and wine. This prayer is a commemoration of salvation history and recounts God's saving activity through Abraham, the patriarchs, the Exodus, the prophets, the coming of Christ, his death and resurrection (one prayer may be prayed over both bread and wine).

6)   The minister says the words of Institution followed by the people's proclamation of the mystery of faith said or sung:

> Christ has died
> Christ has risen
> Christ will come again.

7)   The minister continues to pray, *recalling* the death and resurrection of Christ, *offering* the gifts of bread and wine as the congregational act of praise and thanksgiving, and *invoking* the presence of the Holy Spirit.

8)   The minister and congregation may now pray the Lord's prayer.

9)   The minister now breaks the bread. "Christ our Passover is sacrificed for us" (or a contemporary song) may be said during this action. The bread and wine will be lifted for all to see.

10)   The people come forward to receive the bread and wine. As the reception is taking place, the people may sing contemporary songs that describe the death, resurrection, and exaltation of Jesus. At the same time leaders of the church may anoint with oil those who seek healing.

11)   After all have received, a concluding prayer may be said that gives God thanks for the spiritual food and asks for the blessing of God's Spirit.

CONCLUSION

The celebration of communion has always been a vital part of Sunday worship. Today, many churches have lost both the meaning of the Eucharist and the art of its celebration. However, worship renewal has succeeded in helping congregations rediscover both the theology and practice of communion. A deep and lasting worship renewal will restore communion to its rightful place in the life of worship and will find that the Eucharist, properly celebrated, will shape the peoples' spirituality and make them a people of thanksgiving.

1. See Gregory Dix, *The Shape of the Liturgy* (London: Dacre, 1945), 48ff.

2. See "Anaphora," J. G. Davies, ed., *Westminster Dictionary of Worship* (Philadelphia: Westminster, 1972), 10ff.

3. The basic sources for comparison are found in Cheslyn Jones, Geoffrey Wainwright, and Edward Yarnold, eds., *The Study of Liturgy* (New York: Oxford Univ. Press, 1978); Bard Thompson, *Liturgies of the Western Church* (New York: New American Library, 1974); Hughes Oliphant Old, *The Patristic Roots of Reformed Worship* (Zurich: Theologische verlag Zurich, 1975); and R. C. D. Jasper and G. C. Cumings, *Prayers of the Eucharist: Early and Reformed*, 2d. ed., (New York: Oxford Univ. Press, 1980).

4. Dix, *The Shape of the Liturgy*, 117.

5. Dix, *The Shape of the Liturgy*, 124–25.

6. Thompson, *Liturgies of the Western Church*, 204.

7. Thompson, *Liturgies of the Western Church*, 111.

8. Thompson, *Liturgies of the Western Church*, 369.

9. Justin Martyr, *First Apology*, 67.

10. Dix, *The Shape of the Liturgy*, 126ff.

11. Hippolytus, *Apostolic Tradition*, 1, 4, 3.

12. Hippolytus, *Apostolic Tradition*, 1, 4, 3.

13. See Jasper and Cumings, *Prayers of the Eucharist*, 89.

14. Hippolytus, *Apostolic Tradition*, 1, 4, 4–8. To compare with the eucharistic prayer of the Reformers see Old, *Patristic Roots*, 283ff; Jasper and Cumings, *Prayers of the Eucharist*, 130–92; Thompson, *Liturgies of the Western Church*, 95–374.

15. See Jasper and Cumings, *Prayers of the Eucharist*, 130ff.

16. Jasper and Cumings, *Prayers of the Eucharist*, 153ff.

17. Thompson, *Liturgies of the Western Church*, 369.

18. Ignatius, *Letter to the Ephesians*, 20:1.

19. *Didache*, 9:4.

20. Hippolytus, *Apostolic Tradition*, 1, 4:9–10.

21. *The Apostolic Constitutions*, Book 8, see Jasper and Cumings, *Prayers of the Eucharist*, 76.

22. See Dix, *The Shape of the Liturgy*, 161.

23. Hippolytus, *Apostolic Tradition*, 1, 4:12.

24. Alexander Schmemann, *For the Life of the World* (Crestwood, N.Y.: St. Vladimir's Press, 1973), 44.

25. Dix, *The Shape of the Liturgy*, 161.

26. *The Shape of the Liturgy*, 131.

27. See Thompson, *Liturgies of the Western Church*, 95–104.

28. *The Apostolic Constitution*, Book 8, 78–79.

29. See Henry Bettenson, *Later Church Fathers* (New York: Oxford Univ. Press, 1970), 46–47.

30. *The Book of Common Prayer* (New York: Seabury Press, 1979), 361–65.

Chapter 17

Go Forth to Love and Serve the Lord

The final action of public worship is to send the community of worshipers forth. While this aspect of worship differs in content from the assembling, the hearing of the Word, and the celebration of the Eucharist, the structure of divine action and human response does not change.

As God called the people to worship, so God sends them forth. Like the assembling, which expressed movement, the dismissal also expresses movement—the vision of the church is directed outward toward the world, rather than inward toward a special meeting with God.

In this chapter we will look at the traditional structure of the dismissal and compare it with the dismissal in the contemporary church.

THE TRADITIONAL STRUCTURE OF THE DISMISSAL

The early church ended worship with a benediction. In the course of time, the dismissal of worship developed to include additional features, but it has always been the shortest of the acts of worship. Traditional forms of the dismissal include benedictions, recessional hymns, and words of dismissal.

The benediction is a pronouncement of blessing. It originated with the benediction given to Aaron and his sons. In this act they were to communicate God's name and, therefore, the blessing of his presence on the people (see Num. 6:22–27).

In the New Testament a parallel to the Aaronic blessing is found in the apostolic blessing (2 Cor. 13:14, note also the holy kiss in v. 12). The main difference between the Old and New Testament blessings is that it is now in the name of the Father, Son, and Holy Spirit.

In both of these benedictions the blessing comes from God and is communicated through his servants. Thus the benediction has always been a part of Christian worship. It recognizes that the one who has met with God has indeed been blessed!

The recessional hymn signifies "going out from." Because the worshipers have been with God, the recessional ought to be marked by great joy, a freeing exuberant note of praise. The final hymn is important, therefore, because it is a means of expressing this irrepressible urge to shout. In fact, it ought to be a kind of shout—a final "amen" and "alleluia" to the Lord!

The words of dismissal are usually as follows:

Minister: Go forth to love and serve the Lord.
People: Thanks be to God.

With these words the gathering of the people has ended and their service in the world (the continuation of worship) has begun. For in this work the members of the church act as salt and light to transform the world.

APPLICATION TO THE CONTEMPORARY WORLD

Worship leaders have come to recognize that worship is a vision of what the world will be like without evil. As an application of Christ's work to the entire creation, it summons up images of the world to come.

Worship is a vision of the new creation. This dimension of worship has been described in Revelation 4 and 5. Here, the imagery presents eternity, the ongoing worship of God's creation. This eternal vision is emphasized on earth through the setting apart of nature. The use of space, stained glass windows, materials of the building (wood, brick, stone, mortar, et al.) involve elements of the creation in worship, transforming the present into an image of the future. Here nature is doing what it was created to do—give glory to God. People too are employed in service, doing what they have been created to do. This image of man and nature expressing the transformation of the world in worship is expressed in the words of Norman Pittenger in his work *Life as Eucharist.*

> In worship the right relationship between God and his creation is manifested. The Eucharist shows us the utter dependence of all things on God, the adoration of God through the created order (as in the *Sanctus*), where through men's lips and by their lives they are ready to kneel in his presence, to sing his praise, and to offer to him their oblation of love and service. The created order is here doing what it is meant to do; for

heaven and earth are united, living and departed are at one, and the creation is ordered for its own great good and for God's great glory. Man is in his place, nourished by the life that comes from God; he is man as God means him to be, the crown of the creation and the image and likeness of God himself. All that he does is related to God as he meets men in Christ and unites them with himself. Sin and failure are forgiven, strength is imparted, a redeemed and transfigured cosmos is both signified and present. Whenever the Body of Christ gathers its members for eucharistic worship, all this is seen, as men worship God the Father through Christ the Son in the power of the Holy Spirit.[1]

Worship also reveals the action that the body of Christ must take to participate in the transformation of the world. This action is hinted at in the Lord's Prayer: "Your will be done *on earth* as it is in heaven." The Lord's prayer shows that there is a place where God's will is fully carried out—heaven. The hope of worship is clearly indicated as the worshiper prays that the earth may become a place where the will of God is also fulfilled.

In this sense the Eucharist contains a radical side. The Old Testament roots of the Eucharist lie in the liberation of the people of Israel from Egypt. This sense of liberation is also carried through in the Eucharist. For the Eucharist is the symbol of the potential liberation of the whole creation in Christ.[2]

Paul tells us that the entire creation (humans also) "was subjected to frustration, not by its own choice, but by the will of the one who subjected it, in hope that the creation itself will be liberated from its bondage to decay and brought into the glorious freedom of the children of God" (Rom. 8:20–21). The Eucharist is the sign of this liberation. The elements have a twofold reference. Both bread and wine represent redemption in Christ. When these two images are brought together, the relationship between redemption and creation is clearly seen in worship. The redemption accomplished by Christ transforms the entire creation.

This transformation first takes effect within the worshiping community, which may be called the eucharistic community. The vision of the earliest Christian community is one of a people who take the social implication of the Eucharist seriously. Theologian Tissa Balasuriya comments on the early Christian community in these words:

> The early Christians thus understood the deep meaning of the symbol instituted by Jesus. Its social impact was the main criterion of its value and credibility. That is why the early Christians were so acceptable to many, especially the poor, and so detested by some of the powerful, particularly the exploiters. Christianity was then a dynamic movement of human liberation from selfishness and exploitation. All were to be equal in the believing community and this was symbolized by the eucharistic meal.[3]

The question for us, then, is to recover the social implication of the Eucharist. It was lost in the medieval period when the Eucharist was turned into an action to be observed. The reformers tended to interpret the Eucharist in terms of personal devotion, a tradition still found among many Protestants (and also Catholics) today. In the modern era the social and eschatological dimensions of the Eucharist have been lost in the notion of the Eucharist as a memorial. Contemporary liturgical scholarship, however, is helping today's church return to the full implications of the Eucharist through the study of ancient practices.

CONCLUSION

We must always remember that worship has a horizontal as well as a vertical dimension. It is important for us to enact the work of Christ as an offering of praise and thanksgiving to the Father. But it is equally important that we *act on* what we have enacted. If we really praise God for the redemption of the world through Jesus Christ, then we must do as Paul instructs: "Offer your bodies as living sacrifices, holy and pleasing to God—this is your spiritual act of worship. Do not conform any longer to the pattern of the world, but be transformed by the renewing of your mind" (Rom. 12:1–2). The pattern of this world is one of injustice, inequality, discrimination, war, hate, immorality, and all those human abuses that the New Testament and the early church fathers described as the way of death (see Rom. 1:21–32; Gal. 5:19–21; Col. 3:5–9; *Didache* 5–6). The true worship of God inevitably leads the people of God into positive social action. Our calling is to worship God not only with our lips but with our lives.

---

1. Norman Pittenger, *Life as Eucharist* (Grand Rapids: Eerdmans, 1973), 80–81.

2. Tissa Balasuriya, *The Eucharist and Human Literature* (Maryknoll, N.Y.: Orbis, 1979).

3. Balasuriya, *The Eucharist and Human Literature,* 25.

Chapter 18

The Role of Music in Worship

We have already seen that the two central foci of Christian worship are Word and Eucharist. In preaching and in the celebration of bread and wine, God's work of salvation in Jesus Christ is remembered, proclaimed, enacted, and celebrated.

A third component of biblical and historical worship is music. Music is the wheel upon which the Word and the Eucharist ride. Music proclaims the Scriptures in a heavenly language and provides a means through which the mystery of God in Christ is approachable.

THE PURPOSE OF MUSIC IN WORSHIP

Music witnesses to the transcendence of God and to his work of salvation. God's heavenly court uses music to praise him. Music in worship draws the earthly worshiper into the heavens to stand with the heavenly throng as they offer praise to God. This posture of worship was recognized by the early church especially in the singing of the *Sanctus*.

Music also induces an attitude of worship. It elicits from deep within a person the sense of awe and mystery that accompanies a meeting with God. In this way music releases an inner, nonrational part of our being that mere words cannot set free to utter praise.[1]

Music also affirms the corporate unity of the body of Christ because it is something that the entire congregation does together. Ignatius, in one of his many musical metaphors, offered the following image of the church unified in song:

The psalm which occurred just now in the office blended all voices to-

195

gether, and caused one single fully harmonious chant to arise; young and old, rich and poor, women and men, slaves and free, all sang one single melody. . . All the inequalities of social life are here banished. Together we make up a single choir in perfect equality of rights and of expression whereby earth imitates heaven. Such is the noble character of the Church.[2]

PURPOSES THAT VARIOUS KINDS OF SOUND FULFILL

A service of worship witnesses a variety of sounds. These sounds support the words and actions of worship. Because worship is an action, it takes on the dimension of a congregational performance. Consequently, the moods and meaning of each part of worship are conveyed in the sound made as well as in the words spoken or the actions carried out by the congregation.

One type of sound is called "proclamation." By this means a message is conveyed to God by the congregation or from God through the designated member of the congregation. These tones occur in prayer, in the reading of Scripture, in prefaces, blessings, benedictions, and sermons. Although everyday speech is used, elements of rhythm and melody are present as a way of proclaiming the meaning and urgency of the words.[3] Tones that betray listlessness and apathy convey such. But a tone of enthusiasm and clarity creates excitement and anticipation.

Rhythmic cadences with a formalized tone pattern express the spirit of meditation. The sound itself allows the worshiper to savor the meaning of the text. This is the sound used in singing the Lord's Prayer, singing responses to the intercessions, and especially in singing the psalms. Here the sound fits the words in such a way that one worships in the unity of word and sound. For example, in the early church, psalms were sung in a responsorial manner so that the congregation repeated the refrain (and sound) of the cantor, allowing a psalm in an antiphonal manner to be sung twice.[4]

A third sound is known as "chant." In this musical expression the shape of the sound evolves from the words and refrains. Chant is a natural way to pronounce the words musically. In this way the full meaning of the text is always the focal point of interest, not the sound itself. This musical expression is highly conducive to Christian worship.[5] It was derived from the Old Testament and was used in the early Christian congregations in the reading of Scripture and the singing of responses.

Acclamation is a fourth kind of sound. In this action the vocal activity itself is of final importance. For this reason acclamations are generally retained in their original language (Hebrew, Greek, or Latin). The acclamation is like the cry of help (e.g., Maranatha, Hosanna), the prayer recognizing one's sinfulness (*Kyrie eleison*), the heartfelt response affirming the Word of God or the action of prayer (Amen), or the joyous response of a people to salvation (Alleluia).[6]

In the hymn, the musical elements become extremely important. Here the melody, because of its rhythm and cadences, leads the worshiper. In the hymn, the worshiper is drawn into a unified act of offering vocal praise to God.

Finally, there is sound without words, what was known as *jubilus* in the early church.[7] Initially this was developed from the last vowel of the alleluia that was continued spontaneously by the worshiping community. In our time, the *jubilus* is fulfilled by charismatic singing in the Spirit, by the more formal sound of organ music or that of instruments played by musicians and offered to God as an act of worship.

A HISTORY OF MUSIC IN WORSHIP

A brief survey of music in the church will demonstrate how sound has been offered to God as an act of worship and serves as an aid in the application of sound to the contemporary church.

The New Testament Church

The roots of sound in the early church are found in the Old Testament heritage. Among these are (1) the monodic system of chanting with cadences, (2) congregational song with repetition as in the antiphon and responsory, and (3) elaborate melodies on a single vowel (as in the Alleluia). In the Jewish synagogue these styles of sound were used in the scripture reading, the prayers, and the psalms.[8]

The New Testament provides ample evidence of sound in worship. Paul admonished the Ephesians to: "Speak to one another with psalms, hymns and spiritual songs. Sing and make music to the Lord" (5:19; see also Acts 16:25; 1 Cor. 14:15; Col. 3:16; James 5:13). In the New Testament itself there are a number of identifiable lyrics such as the *Amen*, *Alleluia* and *Holy, holy, holy*. Revelation contains hymns to the Lamb. There are also a number of canticles in Luke that have become major musical statements in Christian worship: *Ave Maria* (1:28–29), *Magnificat* (1:46–55), *Benedictus* (1:68–79), *Gloria in excelsis deo* (2:14), and *Nunc Dimittis* (2:29–32). Besides these, other passages such as John 1:14 and Philippians 2:6–11 have been identified as hymns of the early church.[9]

The Ancient Church

During this period there were frequent references to music in the church as well as a number of hymn texts. The most interesting feature of this period is the rise of syllabic tendencies of hymnody. This gave music a more popular character and emphasized the text rather than the sound itself. As a result, many hymns were written to spread teaching, both heretical and orthodox. This was particularly true of Arianism (the denial of the deity of Christ), which spread its heresy by marching through the streets singing its viewpoint in a popularized form of music.

During the fourth and fifth centuries, when the liturgy was developing along a more elaborate Roman and Byzantine style, music in the church became more highly developed. The most important development during this period was the spread of the responsorial psalm. A soloist sang the psalm and the congregation responded at the end of each verse with a refrain chosen from the psalm. The psalms, and this way of singing them, became exceedingly popular throughout the Christian world. They were sung not only between Scripture readings but also at the Eucharist, during vigils, and in morning and evening prayer. They were also sung in the home and fields. These psalms became a vital spiritual force in the lives of many Christians.

Another important development was the rise of hymnody. Ambrose, the bishop of Milan, is known as the "father of hymnody in the Western church" because he developed a large body of church music based on four scales that became known as the Ambrosian chant. Two centuries later, Gregory the Great added four more scales to the Ambrosian system, creating what came to be known as the Gregorian chant.[10]

In the meantime the responsorial psalm underwent significant changes: The assembly was divided into two choirs or choruses that repeated the refrains. Eventually the refrain was no longer repeated after each verse. Rather, the verses were recited alternatively by two choirs so that singing eventually became the privilege of the monks and clerics, and the congregation was relegated to the position of watching and listening.

The Medieval Church

The musical developments of the ancient church were expanded and became more sophisticated in the medieval church. This was particularly true of the chant and overall hymnody.[11]

The medieval church produced a number of hymns that are still used today: Gregory the Great (540–604), "Father We Praise Thee"; Theodulph of Orleans (ca. 750–821), "All Glory, Laud, and Honor"; Bernard of Clairvaux (1090–1153), "Jesus, the Very Thought of Thee"; and "O Sacred Head, Now Wounded"; and an anonymous twelfth-century writer, "O Come, O Come, Emmanuel." The blot on the medieval record is that the singing of hymns in the church by the lay person was banned. The Council of Constance in 1415, which ordered the burning of the Bohemian reformer John Hus at the stake, also decreed: "If laymen are forbidden to preach and interpret the scripture, much more are they forbidden to sing publicly in the church."[12]

The most important contribution to church music in the medieval period was the development of the Gregorian chant. Formed by the chanters of the eighth century, Gregorian chant has been called "the greatest revolution in the history of Christian singing."[13] It spread rapidly throughout the entire West and gave a beauty, dignity, and solemnity to the liturgy of the church.

The value of medieval music is, of course, in its professionalism. The music is indeed beautiful and inspiring, but the fact that it was taken away from the people and put into the category of performance was undesirable for worship. Worship was no longer the action of the congregation; it was now the work of a privileged few.

The Reformation

One of the most important contributions made by the Reformers to worship was the restoration of congregational music. The earliest Protestant hymnbooks were published by the Bohemian Brethren (later known as the Moravians), one in 1501 (containing eighty hymns) and the other in 1505 (containing four hundred hymns). In 1522 these Brethren contacted Luther, who received them warmly and later used some of their hymns in his own hymnbook.[14]

Luther's influence on music in worship was revolutionary. He himself was a music lover and well trained in music. He also had the gift of writing and created music close to the hearts of the common people. His work was so effective that one of his enemies wrote, "Luther's songs have damned more souls than all his books and speeches."[15]

Luther's contribution was in the area of chorale music. His hymns were characterized by "a plain melody, a strong harmony and a stately rhythm."[16] This type of music continued to develop in the church and was perfected by Johann Sebastian Bach (1685–1750).[17]

Calvin's contribution to music in the church was in the restoration of psalm singing. He viewed hymns as manmade, whereas the psalms were the inspired Word of God. At first Calvin permitted only unison singing (as opposed to Luther's advocacy of singing in parts) and rejected the use of accompanying instruments as worldly (he later changed his mind). Calvinists produced a number of psalm books. The best known work is *The Genevan Psalter* (1562). It was the major psalm book of the Reformation and regarded by many as the most famous book of praise produced by the church. There were at least 1,000 editions and it was translated into many languages. Other well-known books include the *Bay Psalm Book* (Boston, 1640) in America and the *Scottish Psalter* (1650) used by the Scottish Presbyterian churches.[18]

The Modern Period

The birth of modern hymnody is associated with the genius and influence of Isaac Watts (1674–1748). He reacted against the limited use of psalm singing, which he believed had grown cold and lifeless. Furthermore, he was convinced that the slavish reproduction of the psalms was frequently not in the spirit of the gospel. So he set out to write hymns that reflected the devotion and encouragement of the Psalms combined with the New Testament fulfillment and joy of the resurrection.[19] He wrote:

> It is necessary to divest *David* and *Asaph* etc. of every other character but that of a *psalmist* and a *saint*, and to make them *Always speak the common sense of a Christian*. When the Psalmist describes Religion by the *Fear* of God, I have often joined *Faith* and *Love* to it. Where he talks of sacrificing *Goats* and *Bullocks*, I rather choose to mention the sacrifice of *Christ, the Lamb of God*. When he *attends the Ark with shouting in Zion*, I sing the *Ascension of my Savior into heaven*, or *His presence in His Church on earth*.[20] (emphasis original)

An example of this method is found in his use of Psalm 72:

Jesus shall reign where'er the sun
Doth his successive journeys run.

Through the influence of Isaac Watts, who wrote more than six hundred hymns, the eighteenth century became the first age of hymn singing in England. Watts was followed by John and Charles Wesley, two of the most prolific hymn writers of all times. With the Wesleys, however, there came a noticeable shift toward the subjective. For the most part, singing in the church had been God-centered. The emphasis was on the perfection of God, the glory of his works, and the graciousness of his acts in Jesus Christ. Now, however, with the whole tenor of Christianity in revivalism shifting toward subjective experience, the use of sound was put to the service of personal experience and evangelism. This shift is clearly discernable in the second preface to the *Collection of Hymns for the Use of the People Called Methodists* (1780). Here Wesley wrote:

> The hymns are not carelessly jumbled together, but carefully ranged under proper heads, according to the experience of real Christians. So that the book is, in effect, a little body of experimental and practical divinity.[21]

Although the revival songs of the eighteenth century were concerned with personal experience, they still retained a healthy objective emphasis on God. Many hymns such as "Love Divine All Loves Excelling" (Charles Wesley), "The God of Abraham Praise" (Thomas Olivers), "All Hail the Power of Jesus' Name" (Edward Perronet), and "Glorious Things of Thee Are Spoken" (John Newton) exhibited a good balance between the subjective and the objective.[22]

The trend toward a preoccupation with subjective experience is exhibited in many (not all) of the gospel songs that came into use in the late nineteenth century. These songs have a great popular appeal and have been widely used in revival meetings. They frequently contain references to "I" and "me" and dwell on the state of personal feeling. Fanny Crosby is probably the best known of the gospel song writers (e.g., "Rescue the Perishing"). Other well-known gospel songs included "Just As I Am Without One Plea" (Charlotte Elliott), "Take My Life and Let It Be" (Frances Ridley Havergal), and "Jesus Loves Me, This I Know" (Anna B. Warner).[23]

Contemporary Music

Music in worship, as we have seen in the above survey, is closely connected with culture.[24] In the twentieth century the world has experienced a major cultural shift toward what has become known as mass culture. Mass culture has influenced the shape of a new musical form known as pop music. Pop music is characterized by novelty and entertainment and is, therefore, a kind of throwaway music, having little enduring or lasting value.

Pop music has influenced the church and Christian music through the rise of chorus music. This music generated through the Pentecostal, Charismatic, and Jesus movements has become widespread and is now sung in nearly every denomination. It has created a virtual revolution in worship that is hailed by some as return to biblical worship and by others as a sellout to commercialism and entertainment.

A negative view of the steady diet of choruses is expressed by Calvin Johansson, a music specialist from the Pentecostal tradition. He writes:

> Exclusive use of choruses tends to produce a people who have the same depth of spirituality as the music they sing. The result is a faith which lacks depth, is simplistic, pleasure-oriented, emotionalistic, intellectually weak, undisciplined, and prone to the changeability of feelings. The end result of nothing else but chorus singing is immaturity.[25]

Johannson has a good point. An *exclusive* use of Christian pop choruses cuts the church off from the treasuries of Christian music given to the church throughout the centuries. However, choruses, like gospel music or other forms of music given to the church, should not be excluded from worship but incorporated at the appropriate places in worship and added to the use of hymns, psalms, and other musical forms. For example, below is an order of worship that brings together both the old and the new and specifies where choruses as well as other kinds of music could be appropriately integrated into worship.

ACTS OF ENTRANCE

Gathering Song (choruses)
Entrance Song (hymn)
Greeting
Call to Worship

Invocation
Act of Praise (*Gloria in excelsis Deo*; canticle; hymn; or appropriate
        choruses)
Confession
Opening Prayer

SERVICE OF THE WORD

Old Testament Lesson
Responsorial Psalm (Many psalms have been put to contemporary
        sound; Gregorian chants fit well here.)
Epistle Reading
Musical Response (hymn, ancient or contemporary alleluia)
Gospel Reading
Sermon
Creed (The creed has been put to contemporary musical sound. There
        are also hymns and songs that are expressions of faith that can
        be used in place of the creed.)
Prayers of the People (In some churches prayers are sung.)

SERVICE OF THE EUCHARIST

Offering (As bread and wine are brought to the table and as money is re-
        ceived, a choir anthem or congregational hymn is appropri-
        ate.)
Prayers of thanksgiving
Reception of bread and wine (As communion is being received hymns
        and choruses about the death, resurrection, and exaltation of
        Jesus may be sung.)
Closing Prayer

ACTS OF DISMISSAL

Benediction
Closing Song (Hymns or gospel song expressing the work of the church
        in the world may be sung.)

CONCLUSION

This brief survey of the role of music in worship may be summarized in the
following principles:

1)   Music is the means through which the church in worship joins the
       heavenly song, offers otherwise unutterable praises, and experiences
       the unity of the body of Christ.

2)   Music expresses the worship of proclamation, meditation, and praise and thus affects the attitude of the worshiper.

3)   The use of music has undergone a number of significant changes throughout history. Consequently, there are a variety of musical sounds in the church, many of which are reflective of particular historical periods or ethnic groups. Thus, the church has a rich depository of music from which to draw for worship renewal.

The challenge of future worship is to identify those choruses and spiritual songs that have lasting value, to retain the music from the past that is characterized by depth and a power, and to combine these many forms of music into an order of worship that remembers, proclaims, enacts, and celebrates the story of salvation. While some churches will continue to remain hymn-singing churches only, and other churches will insist on being chorus-singing churches only, the majority of churches are likely to find ways to incorporate both the richness and dignity of the hymns of the church with the inspiration and relevance of gospel songs and contemporary choruses.

---

1. See "The Numinous in Poetry, Hymn, and Liturgy," Rudolf Otto, *The Idea of the Holy* (New York: Oxford 1977), 186ff.

2. Ignatius, *Letter to the Ephesians*, 4.

3. Jones, Wainwright, and Yarnold, *The Study of Liturgy* (New York: Oxford Univ. Press, 1978), 451.

4. Jones, Wainwright, and Yarnold, *The Study of Liturgy*, 451–52.

5. Jones, Wainwright, and Yarnold, *The Study of Liturgy*, 452.

6. Jones, Wainwright, and Yarnold, *The Study of Liturgy*, 452–53.

7. Jones, Wainwright, and Yarnold, *The Study of Liturgy*, 453–54.

8. For a discussion of the relationship between music in the Old Testament and the New see especially Eric Werner, *The Sacred Bridge: Liturgical Parallels in Synagogue and Early Church* (New York: Schocken, 1970).

9. See "Hymns and Spiritual Songs," Ralph P. Martin, *Worship in the Early Church* (Grand Rapids: Eerdmans, 1976), 39–52.

10. See "Gregorian Chant," in Hugh Leichtentnitt, *Music History and Ideas* (Cambridge Mass.: Harvard Univ. Press, 1961), 22ff.

11. See Ellsworth, *Christian Music in Contemporary Witness,* 35–44.

12. Quoted in Lester Hostetler, *Handbook to the Mennonite Hymnary* (Newton, Kans.: General Conference of the Mennonite Church of North America, 1949), xv.

13. Jones, Wainwright, and Yarnold, *The Study of Liturgy,* 444.

14. Hostetler, *Handbook,* xv.

15. Hostetler, *Handbook,* xvi.

16. Hostetler, *Handbook,* xvii.

17. See Erik Routley, *Church Music and the Christian Faith* (Carol Stream, Ill.: Agape, 1978), 50ff.

18. See "Psalmody and Hymnody" in Hughes Oliphant Old, *The Patristic Roots of Reformed Worship* (Zurich: Theologischer Verlag Zurich, 1975), 251ff.

19. For a brief but helpful survey of this period see Robert G. Rayburn, *O Come Let Us Worship* (Grand Rapids: Baker, 1980), 223ff.

20. Quoted in Alan Dunstan, "Hymnody in Christian Worship," in Jones, Wainwright, and Yarnold, *The Study of Liturgy,* 458.

21. See "Eighteenth Century Music," Ellsworth, *Christian Music in Contemporary Witness,* 65ff.

22. See "Eighteenth Century Music," Ellsworth, *Christian Music in Contemporary Witness,* 65ff.

23. Ellsworth, *Christian Music in Contemporary Witness,* 103ff.

24. For an excellent survey of music and its relation to cultures see Andrew Wilson-Dickerson, *The Story of Christian Music* (Oxford: Lion, 1992).

25. Calvin M. Johansson, *Disciplining Music Ministry* (Peabody, Mass.: Hendrickson, 1992), 136.

Chapter 19

The Role of the Arts in Worship

During the latter part of the twentieth century, there has been a virtual explosion of the arts in worship initiated by the Roman Catholics with the publication of *The Constitution on the Sacred Liturgy* published in 1963. In a section titled "Sacred Art and Sacred Furnishings" the *Constitution* states:

> The fine arts are deservedly ranked among the noblest activities of human genius and this applies especially to religious art and to its highest achievement, sacred art. These arts, by their very nature, are oriented toward the infinite beauty of God, which they attempt in some way to portray by the work of human hands. They are dedicated to advancing God's praise and glory to the degree that they center on the single aim of turning the human spirit devoutly toward God.[1]

Since 1963 the revolution in the arts has touched every major mainline denomination and has resulted in significant changes in the use of the arts in worship. In addition to the Catholic and subsequent Protestant renewal of the arts, new art forms have been introduced into worship through the Charismatic renewal and through the emergence of the praise and worship tradition. While the Catholic Church has given primary attention to environmental art, the charismatic and praise and worship traditions of worship have recovered dance and drama.

THE BIBLICAL BACKGROUND

A Biblical Theology of the Arts

The biblical approach to the arts is grounded in the basic story line of Scripture: creation, fall, incarnation, redemption, and consummation.

In the act of creation God demonstrated his own creativity by bringing into being everything from nothing. God originated all forms, patterns, colors, and configurations. God's creativity extends from the blade of grass and the form of an insect to the shapes of the clouds, stars, and human persons. In these and all other forms and shapes of the created order we see God's creative power.

Persons made in the image of God are gifted by him with creativity. Human creativity produces new forms from the existing forms to communicate truth. Because of the Fall, the human mind and hands may also create forms that misuse God's good creation. These forms of creativity, instead of inciting the praise of God, may result in the elevation of self or may degenerate into such things as pornography.

While the arts are rooted in a theology of creation, the theology of the fall, which affects human creativity in a negative way, is reversed in the theology of the incarnation. Christians confess that God became enfleshed in the Incarnation and became one of us, a full participant in the created order. By virtue of Christ's death and resurrection, the powers of evil that distort the human creative impulse have been dethroned. Consequently, the Resurrection constitutes a second act of creation, a new beginning that points toward the consummation of all things in the new heavens and the new earth. This means that the creative activity of the Christian is not only based in creation but in the *re-creation* of the world accomplished by God in Christ. Thus, the artist in the service of God (the creator) displays redemption through artistic creativity and sets creation free to worship God. Therefore, environmental art, the visual arts, and the movement arts are not primarily presentational or witness arts in worship, but acts of worship that serve the goal of pointing all of creation toward the praise of God.

The Arts in Scripture

The greatest concentration on the arts in Scripture is found in the Old Testament. This has led some theologians to conclude that the arts were primarily for use in Old Testament worship but abolished in the New Testament, where worship becomes spiritual and independent of physical symbols and artistic renderings.

To reject the physical side of spirituality is to deny the unity of the Scriptures. This falls into the Gnostic denial of the goodness of the created order. It is not consistent with the biblical theology of creation and does not deal with the fact that there is no explicit teaching in the New Testament against the use of physical artistry in worship. While this chapter draws its examples of the arts from the Old Testament, the appropriate use of the arts in Christian worship will be assumed.

The Scripture affirms the visual arts, particularly through the use of the arts in the temple (2 Kings 6–7). The temple artists, under the direction of God, brought theological themes into the temple so that God's people could actually see God's truth.

> The Temple was really an architectural microcosm of the whole of creation, of "Heaven and earth." In it the worshiper encountered God enthroned in the heavens (Ps. 123:1), establishing the earth (Ps. 96:10) and preserving its creatures (Ps. 36:6–7), defeating the enemies of his people (Ps. 76:2–3), and blessing the land as the source of the river of life (Ps. 46:4; Ezek. 47:9).[2]

While the visual arts play an important part in biblical worship, they assume a position of lesser importance than the other arts. This may be because the visual arts have a static character and are prone to be made into objects of veneration and worship rather than signs that inspire the worship of God.

Other arts, such as the movement and literary arts, require the participation of the community in a way that the visual arts do not. These arts represent the dynamic character of God, a God who acts to deliver the people from their bondage.

Movement art, whether in dance; the gestures of bowing, kneeling, and lifting the hands; or in a procession, is a choreographed expression of the dynamic God whose saving actions are being enacted in worship.

For example, in the Old Testament pattern of bringing a sacrifice before the Lord, the people and priest went through a series of choreographed movements of presenting the sacrifice, laying hands on the sacrifice, offering the sacrifice to God, burning it, and eating it. All these movements and gestures were laden with meaning and were means through which the people communicated with God.

The literary arts were also used in biblical worship. The solemn recitation of covenant laws and the reading of the Psalms, the decalogue, and other parts of Scripture (Ex. 22:18–22; 23:1–9; 34:11–26; Lev. 18:7–18; Deut. 27:15–26) were often arranged for metrical group readings.

THE HISTORICAL DEVELOPMENT

The Ancient Church

In the early church the Gnostics rejected the physical side of spirituality, insisting on a nontangible faith. Among orthodox believers the visual arts flourished. For example, scenes from the Bible were painted on the walls of the Roman catacombs and Christian burial chambers. Christian symbolism was also used generously. Favorite themes were the Resurrection, depicted by Jonah and the great fish, and the Eucharist, illustrated by the loaves and fish. In the catacombs one could find pictures depicting the early church at worship, particularly scenes of men and women with their arms and heads lifted heavenward. The introduction of large basilicas for worship allowed for the flourishing of artistic activity. Mosaics began to appear on the walls and ceilings of the churches, the most famous of which pictures Jesus as the ruler of all and is centered in the apse of the building.

Drama in early Christian worship was expressed primarily in worship itself, which was a kind of drama—for example, the dramatic retelling of the Gospel story in readings and sermons and in the great drama of the Eucharist. The Eucharist was always celebrated with a sense of drama and mystery. From the fourth century onward, as worship became public and was celebrated in large basilicas and later churches and cathedrals, the dramatic nature of the entire service was stressed through an increase of processions and ceremonial actions that centered around primary aspects of the liturgy, such as the reading of the Gospel and the celebration of the Eucharist. However, the actual dramatic arts were not acceptable within worship in the early church. During the Roman era theater was crude and contained considerable amount of immorality. Christians, therefore, rejected all theater and would not allow it in the context of worship.

Dance in worship, which is rooted in the Old Testament festivals, continued into the New Testament era and on into the early church. Later, Christian dance came into conflict with pagan dance. In the second century, dance was connected with the dance of heaven; dance in the present symbolized a future dance with the angels of heaven. Although there is no description of the actual dance in worship, there are references to dance in worship by various Fathers of the church. However, after the conversion of Constantine and the influx of many former pagans into the church, the attitude of the Fathers shifted toward a negative view of dance. Unlike Old Testament and early Christian dance, pagan dance was lewd and sexually suggestive. Because pagan dance crept into the Christian festivals, the leaders of the church exorcised the dance from worship.

The Medieval Era

After the fall of Rome in A.D. 410, Christianity became divided between the Eastern church in Byzantium and the churches in Western Europe. By 1054 the divisions became formalized, with mutual anathemas separating the churches.

The Eastern church perfected icons, frescos, and mosaics, creating an interior that joined earth with the heavens and the great company of God's people who lived in eternal praise. The religious art of the Orthodox Church is two dimensional, so that it functions as a window to God. The Orthodox reject all three dimensional art as the breaking of the second commandment, "You shall not make for yourself an idol in the form of anything in heaven above or on the earth beneath or in the waters below" (Ex. 20:4). Timothy Ware, an Orthodox historian, defends the use of icons in worship.

> The icons which fill the church serve as a point of meeting between heaven and earth. As each local congregation prays Sunday by Sunday, surrounded by the figures of Christ, the angels, and the saints, these visible images remind the faithful unceasingly of the invisible presence of the whole company of heaven at the Liturgy. The faithful can feel that the walls of the church open out upon eternity, and they are helped to realize that their liturgy on earth is one and the same with the great Liturgy of heaven. The multitudinous icons express visibly the sense of "heaven on earth."[3]

The Western church perfected the basic cathedral, which expressed the systemized view of the universe held in the medieval world. The view of a divinely ordered world was expressed in the well-ordered church building. In the medieval universe every person had a specific place and function that had been ordained by God. Closest to God was the priest, who moved about the holy places of the sanctuary; furthest from God was the laity, who stood and watched worship from a distance. The arts flourished not only in the architectural setting of the building, with its exquisite stained glass and ornate holy places, but also in the liturgical furniture such as pulpits, altars, baptismal fonts, highly decorative liturgical books, artistically designed chalices, ciboriums, remonstrances, and beautiful vestments.

During the medieval era the Catholic church restored drama as a way of communicating the stories of faith and educating the people. The earliest forms of drama were developed around the events of Holy Week. On Palm Sunday the church would hold a procession with a person riding on a donkey. On Good Friday a cross would be wrapped in cloth and laid inside an empty tomb in the chancel and then dramatically displayed as an expression of the Resurrection on Easter Sunday. Another early form of drama known as the *trophe* (phrase or clause) developed as a dramatic insertion in the liturgy. For example, the following trophe, known as the *Quen Queritas* (whom seek ye), is found in the introductory portion of the mass as early as 925.

Angel: Whom seek ye in the tomb, O Christian?
The Three Marys: Jesus of Nazareth, the crucified, O Heavenly Beings.
Angel: He is not here, he is risen as he foretold. Go and announce
           that He is risen from the tomb.

Soon plays like the *Quen Queritas* were expanded into fully developed dramatic events and eventually spread all over Europe, expanding beyond their liturgical starting points into the medieval marketplace. Eventually, three kinds of plays were developed. *Mystery* plays dramatized Bible events such as creation and the lives of Bible characters. *Miracle* plays featured Christian saints such as St. Nicholas and Joan of Arc. *Morality* plays probed human conduct and dealt with the clash between vices and virtues, the most famous of which was *Everyman*. While drama had its start in the church and flourished in the liturgy and the courtyards of churches, it eventually became increasingly bawdy and secular. In 1250 Pope Innocent III expelled drama from the church, though players continued to perform outdoors.

Dance during the medieval era shifted from the festivals to the sacred Mass itself. In 633 the Council of Toledo forbade the Festival of Fools in the churches because its singing, dancing, and feasting had incorporated pagan elements. The church's self-understanding also underwent a significant change. It shifted from the concept of community to a more hierarchical concept that elevated the priesthood and relegated the people to a passive role in worship. Soon the people's celebration of God's saving events yielded to the mysterious sacred drama of the Mass.

The Modern Era

The most significant shift in the church's attitude toward the arts resulted from the Renaissance and the Reformation of the sixteenth century. Both of these movements sought to shape the direction of society.

The Renaissance affirmed the arts while the Reformation frowned on them. The Reformers, particularly Calvin and Zwingli, viewed the arts as worldly and as having no place in the church and in its worship. This attitude was carried forth by the Puritans, the Pietists, and the Evangelicals and through them into the twentieth century.

Meanwhile the arts were encouraged by Renaissance humanism. The visual arts, drama, and dance developed largely under the influence of a humanistic and secular outlook. While the church retained its love for music, the secular world developed its own style of music. The twentieth-century Protestant church woke up to the unfortunate realization that by its neglect of the visual arts, drama, and dance the world now owned what rightfully belonged to the church.

The Protestant church had not exercised its calling in the arts and now had to recover from four hundred years of neglect. Meanwhile both the Orthodox church and the Roman Catholic Church had remained fixed in the visual art forms of the medieval era.

ARTS IN THE TWENTIETH CENTURY

The Visual Arts

The restoration of the visual arts to worship found a new impetus in the publication of the document *Environment and Art in Catholic Worship*, a statement issued by the Bishops' Committee on the Liturgy in 1977. In the Introduction to the document, the Committee challenges the church with these words:

> Like the covenant itself, the liturgical celebrations of the faith community (church) involves the whole person. They are not purely religious or merely rational and intellectual exercises, but also human experiences calling on all human faculties: body, mind, senses, imaginations, motions, memory. Attention to these is one of the urgent needs of contemporary liturgical renewal.[4]

This Catholic document does not endorse particular visual arts. Rather, it sets down principles for the use of visual arts in worship. It advocates that "the art of our own days, coming from every race and region, shall also be given free scope in the Church, provided that it adorns the sacred buildings and holy rites with due reverence and honor; thereby it is enabled to contribute its own voice to that wonderful chorus of praise."[5] The document grounds liturgy in the action of the assembly, the gathered people who worship. It then discusses the house for the liturgy; personal gestures; posture; processions; ease of movement; furnishings for the liturgical celebration such as chairs, benches, the altar, the pulpit, and the baptismal pool; and objects used in liturgical celebrations such as the cross, candles, books, vestments, vessels, images, decorations, and audio visuals.

This complete examination of the visual environment of worship has prompted mainline churches and free churches to look more seriously at their own environment of worship. The free church interest in the visual arts is represented by LeRoy Kennel's *Visual Arts and Worship*. Kennel reminds us that the "Bible speaks of the employment of visual arts both in informal and in formal worship: stars lead; rainbows announce; clouds guide; stone tablets declare; ark of covenant reminds; and temples and synagogues symbolize."[6]

Free church people who have rejected the visual arts in worship are increasingly recognizing that the visual arts help the worshiper see what is otherwise hidden; that the visual arts therefore assist us in praising God; and that the visual arts provide a form of witness.[7] Assuming that free church people will accept the basic premise that God is known and worshiped through the visual arts, we may ask: What should the free church do about the visual arts? The scope of this book does not allow an extensive discussion of this matter. The following paragraphs point to the areas of renewed interest in the visual arts among members of the free church community.

New attention is being paid to church architecture. New or refurbished church buildings need to facilitate the relationships of people to one another, renew the holy, and allow for appropriate use of artistic symbols, sights, and sounds. Above all, the church building must express hospitality and acceptance.

The place of worship furniture is important. The primary liturgical furnishings are the pulpit, the communion table, and the baptismal font or pool. Concern for the rightful place of worship furniture among the assembled people is becoming a high priority for those concerned with the visual. In addition to the assembly of the people, these furnishings are the primary visuals of the worshiping church.

Secondary visuals that assist the function of worship such as stained glass windows, sculptures, crosses, paintings, banners, bulletin graphics, and audio visuals have become a priority to many. Each of these is a matter of local style. Therefore, they are less likely to become standardized.

The seekers' service introduced by the Willow Creek Community Church in the suburbs of Chicago presents a curious philosophy regarding the visual arts. Willow Creek believes that the place where unchurched people gather should be completely free from all Christian symbolism that may make the unchurched feel uncomfortable. Consequently, it advocates corporate looking buildings with an interior auditorium that resembles a theater.

In order to evaluate this movement appropriately, it should be remembered that the seekers' service is not worship but evangelism, and a bare auditorium is appropriate for evangelistic services. What the church does when it gathers for worship is completely different than what it does when it gathers for evangelism. Therefore, the question of the place of the visual arts remains valid, even for the seeker-centered churches that use their main gathering for evangelism and move their worship to a mid-week service. As long as worship remembers, proclaims, and enacts God's saving deeds, it is appropriate for churches to consider what kind of visuals assist the worshiping people.

Drama

In the twentieth century drama within worship has gone full circle. Currently, drama is making a comeback. In current worship renewal the dramatic nature of every service of worship, as well as the dramatic character of the great festivals of the church year, and the use of mini-dramatic presentations within worship are all matters of high interest.

Worship is a drama played out before God by all the people. The worship leaders are the prompters, the people are the players, and God is the audience. In this sense, worship is not a drama done for the people as in the Middle Ages, but a return to the drama of the early church in which the biblical story of the drama of redemption is the true content of worship.

The tension that is basic to any drama needs to be present in contemporary worship. The Scripture story is the subject of worship. In it we find the dramatic conflict between good and evil. The readings of Scripture and the celebration of the Eucharist address the tension that is the subject of worship. The object of worship is the triune God, who resolves the conflict between good and evil through the work of Christ.

The contemporary church is also rediscovering the dramatic nature of the services of the Christian year. While the church dramatizes the Gospel story every Sunday, the reestablishment of the Christian year allows for the festive drama of particular saving events. The entire Christian year flows out of the dying and rising of Christ. This is the chief saving act of God's salvation, which defines and gives meaning to all other events of the Christian year. Advent dramatizes the coming of the Messiah. Christmas heralds the birth of Jesus. Epiphany declares Christ as Savior of the whole world. Lent prepares the people for the death of the redeemer. Holy Week brings the people into the passion of our Lord. Easter celebrates Christ's resurrection and victory over the powers of evil. Pentecost announces the coming of the Holy Spirit. In these special saving events the drama of the entire work of God's salvation is played out by all the people.

The church is also recovering the mini-drama within worship. Because the great drama of the Christian faith is expressed through Word and Eucharist, the use of mini-drama must always highlight these two focal points and never overshadow them. The kind of drama recommended among contemporary renewalists is choral reading, storytelling, and chancel drama. These forms of drama are especially useful in the service of the Word.

Choral reading is a written dialogue of Scripture that involves the entire congregation. Sometimes the reading may be done in an antiphonal manner; other times a reading may involve several individual parts and a part for the congregation as a whole. These readings can be easily prepared by anyone in the congregation with a sense of the dramatic. A good example is the use of the passion narrative on Palm Sunday. This drama includes the narrator, Jesus, Pilate, Peter, and the crowd, which is played by the congregation.

Storytelling is most appropriate for the Gospel lesson. The storyteller may read and reread a passage until it forms as a story in his or her mind. Instead of reading the Gospel, it is told through story. Storytelling may be used frequently, as long as it is carefully prepared and done with dignity.

Chancel drama is a mini-drama performed during worship, usually during the service of the Word and often before the sermon to illustrate the point the sermon will make. Chancel drama is appropriate when it has been carefully chosen, well rehearsed, and is suitable to the atmosphere of the service. Short dramas of three to five minutes in length are more appropriate than longer more complicated dramas.

There are certain forms of drama that are inappropriate within worship, yet appropriate in educational (Sunday school) or recreational settings (church parties, family worship). For example, youth plays, drama games, skits, puppets, clowns, and parades are all forms of drama that ably communicate truth but are not generally acceptable within a morning worship of Word and Eucharist.

Presentational drama is used particularly in seeker-centered services. Presentational drama differs from the drama of worship itself, from telling the Gospel in story, and from chancel drama in that it does not address inherent tension within the text of the story that the worshiping community enacts each week. Presentational or witness drama used in seeker-centered service is designed particularly to gain the hearing of the unchurched. It raises questions, poses problems, and stimulates interest rather than proclaim the Gospel.

All these forms of drama have their place in the church and in its worship and are gaining in popularity as the church is gradually reclaiming the dramatic nature of worship and of the Gospel it enacts.

Dance

Dance, which has long been repudiated in worship, is now in the process of being redeemed in worship. Although liturgical churches have reclaimed dance, charismatic churches have championed its renewal.

Thomas Kane has identified five kinds of dance.[8] Processional dance is the movement from one place to another. It includes movements such as entrance processionals, processionals related to the Gospel readings, the procession of bringing the bread and wine to the table (in those churches where the elements are not prepared before the service), and the closing procession.

A second form of dance is proclamation movement. This dance accompanies the reading or the storytelling of the Scriptures. As the Scripture is read or told, a dance may express the core of the story, so that the message is not only expressed in words but embodied in action.

Prayer dance expresses the prayer of the assembled community. Kinds of prayer dance include acclamation and invocation. Acclamation dance expresses the assent of the community to God's Word. In liturgical worship an acclamation dance may accompany the *Kyrie, Sanctus,* the *Memorial Acclamation,* the *Amen,* or the *Doxology* to the Lord's Prayer. Invocation dances express prayers of praise or thanksgiving and may occur during the *Gloria* and the Lord's Prayer.

A fourth kind of dance, meditation dance, is more reflective by nature. It may occur after a Scripture reading or as an expression of thanksgiving for God's saving deed, as in a dance in response to communion.

Celebrative dance usually occurs at the beginning or at the close of worship. It works with the celebrative portions of worship to lift the text from an enslavement to words to find expression and meaning in movement.[9]

Charismatic worship may include any one of these five types but often dancing is more spontaneous and frequently includes the entire congregation. People will often "dance in the Spirit" in response to songs that are being sung, a message that has been proclaimed, or the communion that has been received.

For most free church people dance is still taboo. Prohibitions against social dancing, which reach all the way back to the negative attitude toward the "dancing, drinking, and gambling" days of the frontier, are etched deeply in the spiritual history of most free church people.

Nevertheless, dance in worship is gradually being understood as a movement of praise, a means of setting the body free to worship God. As this biblical understanding of movement in worship takes root, various communities of worship are becoming more comfortable with dance and movement within worship.

CONCLUSION

The church is in the process of rediscovering that the arts are a gift from God and meant for worship. The future of the arts in worship is uncertain. The church must recognize that the arts in worship are not performances as such, but vehicles that serve the text of worship. The text of worship is expressed in the place where the church assembles and in what the church does in its entrance, service of the Word, Eucharist, and dismissal every Sunday and in the great festivals of the Christian year. Because God created all things and became incarnate in Jesus Christ, all created realities are set free to worship. Thus the visual arts, dramatic reenactment, and dance all have their appropriate places in worship.

---

1. *The Constitution on the Sacred Liturgy*, Chap. 7, 122. See Mary Ann Simcoe, ed., *The Liturgy Documents* (Chicago: Liturgy Training, 1985), 32.

2. Richard Leonard, "Biblical Philosophy of the Worship Arts," *The Biblical Foundations of Christian Worship* (Nashville: Abbott Martyn, 1993), 219.

3. See Ronald Gagne, Thomas Kane, Robert Ver Eecke, *Introducing Dance in Christian Worship* (Washington, D.C.: Pastoral, 1984), 38–43; 45–51.

4. Timothy Ware, *The Orthodox Church* (New York: Penguin Books, 1994), 277–78.

5. *Environment and Art in Catholic Worship* (Washington, D.C.: United States Catholic Conference, 1978), 2.

6. Ibid., 3.

7. LeRoy Kennel, *Visual Arts and Worship* (Newton, KS: Faith & Life Press, 1983), 9.

8. For the development of these ideas, see Kennel, *Visual Arts and Worship*, 9–17.

9. For a discussion of these five types of dance, see Ronald Gagne, Thomas Kane, Robert Ver Eecke, *Introducing Dance in Christian Worship* (Washington, D.C.: The Pastoral Press, 1984), 99–115.

Chapter 20

The Services of the Christian Year

In Christian worship we not only remember, proclaim, enact, and celebrate the Christian story through Word and Eucharist, assisted by music and the arts, we also remember the story through commemorative time.

Commemorative time is not only the remembrance of Christ's death and resurrection, but a special time that brings the power and significance of the event into contemporary time and makes the saving and healing reality of the Christ event available to the worshiping community.

THE GREEK VIEW OF TIME

The Greek language had two words to describe time: *kairos* and *chronos*. *Kairos* designates a moment of time and may refer to special occasions rather than an extended period of time. *Chronos* refers to the time between special events and may be appropriately designated as the time of sequence or chronology. For this reason *kairos* is always looked upon as event time, the time of a special or significant moment.[1]

From a more philosophical point of view, there were two distinguishing characteristics of time among the Greeks. Greek philosophers separated time (as bound to creation) from timelessness (as above creation). Because of this separation, that which is eternal or above time cannot enter into time. Thus, time has no eternal or ontological meaning; it is a prison in which people are held.

The second emphasis among the Greeks was the notion that time is cyclical. It has no goal. It is not proceeding toward a final moment (*kairos*) that will give meaning and purpose to the chronology of time. Thus, history and people are doomed to an eternal recurrence of time. This pessimistic view sees time without meaning outside of those existential events in which people may find meaning for their existence.

THE HEBRAIC CONCEPT OF TIME

The ancient Israelites also made distinctions between different types of time. However, their view differed significantly from that of the Greeks because the Israelites held a theological worldview. They believed in the existence of a transcendent God who made himself present in time through various actions.

Therefore, Hebraic time was defined by historical events. These events were a series of special moments that represented the saving acts of God. For example, great attention was given to the time of Moses and the Exodus out of Egypt. Other significant events include the reign of David and the building of Solomon's temple. For the Israelites time was not empty of meaning, for it was in the time-oriented events of history that God was at work accomplishing his will and purposes through the people of Israel. Time for Israel was linear, moving in a particular direction.

A second aspect of Hebraic time emphasized prophecy. Time was marked not only by past events, such as the Exodus, but also by future events. Past events contained elements of expectation, of hope, of fulfillment, and even judgment. The prophets foretold the impending eschatological judgment of God against the nations and against Israel for its unfaithfulness (Jer. 4:11–12; Dan. 12:1; Joel 3:1–2). Nevertheless, beyond judgment lay the hope of a new age. Those who remained faithful would achieve everlasting salvation (Ps. 81:13–16; Isa. 60:20–22; Dan. 12:1–3; Zeph. 3:16–20).

A number of significant features of the Hebraic view of time resulted from the emphasis on historical events and prophecy. In the first place, unlike the Greek concept of time, the Hebraic approach recognized the presence of the eternal in time. Time and eternity were not antithetical concepts. Rather, God, who created time, was active in time, moving it toward the fulfillment that he intended. Time was an integral structure of God's reality. It was not the result of chance but an evidence of God's benevolent care and purpose for his creation.

One implication of the Hebraic concept of time is seen in the Old Testament view of worship. Because worship enacted past events, the marking of time in worship was an indispensable feature of Old Testament faith. The yearly cycle of the festivals of Passover, the Feast of Weeks, the Feast of Tabernacles, and the lesser feasts, the weekly cycle of the Sabbath, and the daily cycle of prayers all celebrated the action of God in history. The reenactment of these historic events sanctified the present moment, gathering it up in the eternal meaning of the event that represented the presence of the transcendent and eternal

God in time. Furthermore, Israel anticipated the fulfillment of worship in the dawning of the new age.[2]

THE CHRISTIAN SYNTHESIS

The Christian understanding of time incorporated the concepts of *chronos* and *kairos,* maintaining the distinctions given to them by the Greeks but viewing them in a manner similar to the Israelites.

The Christian conception was governed by a major event through which all other times and events found their meaning. This unique moment was the incarnation, death, and resurrection of Christ. Thus, in Christianity, all time has a *center.* Paul developed this notion in his epistle to the Colossians by declaring that Christ is the creator of all things (1:16), the one who holds all things together (1:17), and the one who reconciles all things (1:20). Christ is the cosmic center of all history. Everything before Christ finds its fulfillment in him. Everything after Christ finds its meaning by pointing back to him.

From Christ, the center of time, three kinds of time are discerned. First, there is fulfilled time. The incarnation of God in Christ represented the fulfillment of the Old Testament messianic longings. Here, in this event, all the hopes rooted in the sequence of significant historical moments of the Old Testament were completed. For in Christ the new time (*kairos*) had arrived, as Jesus himself announced: "The time has come.... The kingdom of God is near. Repent and believe the good news!" (Mark 1:15).

Second, the coming of Christ was the time of salvation. The death of Christ came at the appointed time, as Paul wrote to the Romans: "You see, at just the right time, when we were still powerless, Christ died for the ungodly" (Rom. 5:6; see also Matt. 26:18; John 7:6). Jesus' death was the moment of victory over sin: "Having disarmed the powers and authorities, he made a public spectacle of them, triumphing over them by the cross" (Col. 2:15). Consequently, the death of Christ introduced the time of salvation: "I tell you, now is the time of God's favor, now is the day of salvation" (2 Cor. 6:2).

Third, the Christ event introduces Christian anticipatory time. This aspect of time is based on the Resurrection, the Ascension, and the promise of Christ's return. The church, like the Old Testament people of God, lives in anticipation of the future. Now, the church awaits the final judgment (John 5:28–30; 1 Cor. 4:5; Rev. 11:18).

The Christian concept of time plays a significant role in the worship of the church. The Christ event gives meaning to all of time.[3] Therefore, in worship we sanctify the present by enacting the past, which gives shape to the future.[4] The church celebrates the Christ event in a daily, weekly, and yearly manner.

THE DAILY CYCLE OF TIME

The daily cycle of prayer is rooted in the worship practices of the Old Testament, where prayers were said at various times throughout the day.[5] Prayer occurred at certain times in the temple (1 Chron. 23:30), and Daniel prayed three times a day (Dan. 6:10). The sense of marking the day with times of prayer was carried over into the early Christian community. Luke, in the book of Acts, informs us that "Peter and John were going up to the temple at the time of prayer—at three in the afternoon" (Acts 3:1). Peter, Luke tells us later, "about noon ... went up on the roof to pray" (Acts. 10:9). Luke noted the coming of the Holy Spirit at the third hour (9 a.m.): "These men are not drunk, as you suppose. It's only nine in the morning!" (Acts 2:15). The time of these important events was significant and shows that the early church marked time by religious events.

There is, however, no direct evidence in the New Testament of a community-wide, daily worship. Nevertheless, it seems that the early Christians continued the practice of prayer at particular times of the day.

The most significant evidence of times for prayer in the ante-Nicene church comes from *The Apostolic Tradition* of Hippolytus. Because of allusions to times of prayer in the early Fathers, we may assume the practice detailed by Hippolytus precedes his description and dates perhaps to the middle of the second century.

> If at the *third hour* thou art at home, pray then and give thanks to God; but if thou chance to be abroad at that hour, make thy prayer to God in thy heart. For *at that hour Christ was nailed to the tree*, therefore in the old (covenant) the law commanded the shewbread to be offered continually for a type of the body and blood of Christ, and commanded the sacrifice of the dumb lamb, which was a type of the perfect Lamb; for Christ is the Shepherd, and he is also the Bread that came down from heaven.
>
> At the *sixth hour* likewise pray also, for, after Christ was nailed to the wood of the cross, *the day was divided* and there was a great darkness; wherefore let (the faithful) pray at that hour with an effectual prayer, likening themselves to the voice of him who prayed (and) caused all creation to become dark for the unbelieving Jews.
>
> And at the *ninth hour* let a great prayer and a great thanksgiving be made, such as made the souls of the righteous ones, blessing the Lord, the God who does not lie, who was mindful of his saints and sent forth his Word to enlighten them. *At that hour, therefore, Christ poured forth from his pierced side water and blood,* and brought the rest of the time of that day with light to evening; so, when he fell asleep, by making the beginning of another day he completed the pattern of his resurrection.
>
> *Pray again before thy body rests on thy bed.*[6] [emphasis added]

The unique feature of the prescription for prayer set forth by Hippolytus is the interpretation of time through the events of Jesus' death. He gives insight into the concept of time held by the ancient Christians. Time, this approach suggests, finds meaning through Jesus Christ, the center of all time.

This concept of time was the basis of the daily devotional life of the church. This is especially seen in the development of matins and vespers and the more complicated series of daily prayers that characterized the monastic movement. This approach to prayer was used by the Christian community (with some modifications) for centuries.[7] After the Reformation, particularly through the influence of the Pietists, the concept of hours of prayer (especially morning and evening prayer) shifted into the home. More recently, the same notion is stressed in the idea of morning and evening devotions.

THE WEEKLY CYCLE OF TIME

The weekly cycle of time, based on the church's observance of Sunday, is a highly complicated and somewhat controversial subject. Little more than an outline of the role of Sunday in the Christian understanding of time can be given here. We will note the relationship between the Sabbath and Sunday and summarize the various views of Sunday by early Christians.

To begin, we must ask how Sunday relates to the Sabbath. The Sabbath was an Old Testament institution that, like the temple, pointed to Jesus Christ. This was the conviction of the early church. Therefore, Paul included the Sabbath day as "a shadow of the things that were to come; the reality, however, is found in Christ" (Col. 2:7).

In the Old Testament, the Sabbath called for a day of rest on the seventh day (Ex. 16:26). In this sense the Sabbath was related to time. It was the symbol of sacred time as it looked to a future fulfillment.

Christ, of course, was the fulfillment of the Sabbath (Matt. 12:8). He brought the rest that the Sabbath anticipated: "Come to me, all you who are weary and burdened, and I will give you rest" (Matt. 11:28). This was the theme of the seventh day that the author to Hebrews so eloquently developed (Heb. 4:1–11). He saw three "rests" in the economy of God: the rest after the Creation, the rest that Israel sought in the Promised Land, and the rest that comes through Jesus Christ. The Sabbath, therefore, had an eschatological character. It pointed to the future, to Jesus Christ as its fulfillment. The Christian now lives in the Sabbath rest found in Christ.

Consequently, the Sabbath, like the temple, was abolished. But the principle of rest, like the principle of God's presence with his people, remains. The Christian lives in the age of rest. Nevertheless, the Christian has an external expression of inner rest, and this is manifested by Sunday observance.

The primary reason for Sunday worship is that Sunday was the day of the Resurrection. The early church gathered on this day, the Lord's day, as they called it, in remembrance of Christ's resurrection. Every Sunday was a celebration of the Resurrection. The significance of Sunday was subject to various interpretations for at least three reasons: It was the first day of the Jewish week, it fell on the day of the sun, and it was the eighth day. An examination of these three less obvious meanings shows how Sunday was related to the concept of time by the early Christians.[8]

Sunday was the first day of the Jewish week. Consequently, the early Christians regarded it as the anniversary of the creation of the world.[9] But Sunday was more than an anniversary; it represented the day that God began to create again—the beginning of the new creation. For that reason Sunday was also seen as a figure for the end of the first creation. As liturgical historian Jean Daniélou puts it: "On the sixth day creation was finished; on the seventh, God rested from all his works. But in the Gospel, the Word says: I have come to finish the work."[10] Sunday also symbolized the generation of the Word. All these concepts cluster around the notion of Sunday, the beginning and the end of the first creation. All these notions have to do with time and the meaning time has because of these events.

Sunday was the day of the sun in the astrological calendar. The ancient Christians made no attempt to synthesize Sunday with the day of the sun. However, they did seize it as an opportunity to Christianize the pagans through a reinterpretation of the day of the sun in keeping with the motif of a new creation. Regarding this, Jerome wrote,

> The day of the Lord, the day of the Resurrection, the day of the Christians is our day. And if it is called the day of the sun by the pagans, we willingly accept this name. For on this day arose the light, on this day shone forth the sun of justice.[11]

Some also considered Sunday to be the eighth day.[12] Although the origins of this notion are somewhat obscure, it appears to be of Christian origin, being found among the early church Fathers. The meaning of the term appears to have an eschatological flavor. While the seventh day signified rest, and the first day symbolized re-creation, the eighth day represented the future world. It preserved the eschatological expectation of the early church, which looked to the end of the present age and the beginning of the eternal age.

Even if one does not accept all the interpretations given to Sunday by the early church, the implication is obvious. It is a day that *marks time*. It is the end of one age and the beginning of another. Worship on Sunday therefore is not a mere coincidence; on this day the church enacts the Resurrection and thus reaffirms the meaning of the history of the world.

THE YEARLY CYCLE OF TIME

The most common term for the early celebration of time is the Christian year. The Christian year, developed in antiquity, was a vital part of worship until the Reformation.[13] The Reformers dropped it because of the abuses attached to it in the late medieval period (e.g., every day of the year had been named after a saint). The emphasis on these saints and the feasts connected with their lives overshadowed the celebration of the Christ event and the sanctification of time because of Jesus' death and resurrection. The Reformers abolished most of the Christian year, thereby losing the bad and the good. A return to the Christian year among evangelicals ought to advocate a very simple and unadorned year, similar to that of the early church, which accents the major events of Christ. The source of the Christian year is not paganism as some have supposed, but the life, death, resurrection, ascension, and second coming of the Lord Jesus Christ. The understanding of time was a part of Christian consciousness in the recognition that the death and resurrection of Jesus began the "new time." The fact that two major events of the church took place during Jewish celebrations—Passover and Pentecost—led early Christians to recognize that a new time had begun. Thus, like the Jews, the early Christians marked time, but, unlike the Jews, they marked their time by the events of the new age.[14]

The oldest evidence of a primitive church year is found in Paul's first letter to the Corinthians. Here Paul refers to "Christ, our Passover lamb" and urges the people to "keep the Festival" (1 Cor. 5:7–8). These references seem to suggest that the early Christians celebrated the death and resurrection of Christ during the Jewish Passover.

There is considerable information from the second and third centuries to describe the significance of what came to be called Easter. It became the major day of the year for baptism, which was preceded by a time of prayer and fasting. However, we do not have evidence of a fully developed Christian year until the fourth century.[15] Because space does not permit a full treatment of the origins and development of the Christian year, the following summary will outline the Christian year and touch on the origins and significance of each part.[16]

Advent. The word *advent* means "coming."[17] It signifies the period preceding the birth of Christ when the people anticipated the coming of the Messiah. Although it signals the beginning of the Christian year, it appears that Advent was established after other parts of the year as a means of completing the cycle. Its purpose was to prepare for the birth of our Lord. The Roman church adopted a four-week season before Christmas, a practice that became universally accepted.

Epiphany means "manifestation."[18] It was first used to refer to the manifestations of God's glory in Jesus Christ (see John 2:11) through his birth, baptism, and first miracle. Although the origins of the Epiphany are obscure, it is generally thought to have originated among Egyptian Christians as a way of counteracting a pagan winter festival held on January 6. Originally it probably included:

Christmas (celebrated on December 25 to replace the pagan festival of the

Sun). In the fourth century, Christmas became part of Advent, and the beginning of Epiphany on January 6 became associated with the manifestation of Jesus to the wise men (i.e., the Gentile world). The celebration of Epiphany is older than that of Christmas and testifies to the whole purpose of the Incarnation. Therefore, the emphasis in worship during Epiphany is on the various ways Jesus was manifested to the world as the incarnate Son of God.

Lent signifies a period of preparation before Easter.[19] The origins of Lent lie in the preparation of the catechumen before baptism. The setting aside of a time of preparation for baptism goes back as early as the *Didache* and is attested to in Justin Martyr and detailed in *The Apostolic Tradition* of Hippolytus. Gradually, the time of preparation was associated with the number forty: Moses spent forty years preparing for his mission, the Israelites wandered in the wilderness for forty years, and Jesus spent forty days in the wilderness. In addition, the congregation joined the catechumen in preparation, making it a special time for the whole church. Scriptural readings and sermons during this period highlight the ministry of Jesus, especially his teaching in parables and his miracles. Special emphasis is given to growing opposition toward Christ and the preparation he made for his death. The church joins Jesus in the recalling of this significant period of his life through the devotional disciplines of Lent.

The period of Lent was gradually marked by *Ash Wednesday*[20] at its beginning and Holy Week [21] at its ending. The beginnings of Ash Wednesday are obscure. It was in use by the fifth century, and the meaning of it was derived from the use of ashes as a penitential symbol, which originated in the Old Testament and was used in the church as early as the second century to symbolize repentance. The formula used for the imposition of ashes is based on Genesis 3:19: "Remember man, that you are dust and into dust you shall return." These words signal the beginning of a time dedicated to prayer, repentance, self-examination, and renewal. It ends in the celebration of the Resurrection when the minister cries, "Christ is risen!"

Before Easter, however, the church enacts the final week of Jesus. Although traces of a special emphasis during this week can be found in the third century, *Holy Week* was developed in the fourth century by the Christians of Jerusalem. Holy Week linked the final events of Jesus' life with the days and the places where they occurred. Jerusalem, of course, was the one place in the world where this could actually happen. For here were the very sites of his last days. As pilgrims poured into Jerusalem, the church of Jerusalem evolved this structure to provide them with a meaningful cycle of worship. The worship services that were developed during this time are still used today in some churches. The use of the ancient Maundy Thursday service, the Good Friday veneration of the cross, and the Saturday night vigil make Holy Week the most special time of worship in the entire Christian calendar.

The aim of Holy Week was to make the life of Christ real for the worshiper. Enacting his last days and entering into his experience was a way of offering worship to him. This liturgical realism made a significant impact on the Christian world. It served as a primary impetus toward the development of the church year as a way of manifesting the entire life of Christ in the life of the worshiper.

The *Easter* season stands out as a time of joy and celebration.[22] Unlike Lent, which is sober in tone, Easter is the time to focus on resurrection joy. Augustine said:

> These days after the Lord's Resurrection form a period, not of labor, but of peace and joy. That is why there is no fasting and we pray standing, which is a sign of resurrection. This practice is observed at the altar on all Sundays, and the Alleluia is sung, to indicate that our future occupation is to be no other than the praise of God.[23]

The preaching of this period calls attention to the postresurrection appearances of Jesus and the preparation of his disciples to witness to the kingdom. It is fifty days in length and ends with Pentecost.

The term *Pentecost* means fifty, referring to the fifty days after Passover when the Jews celebrated the Feast of Weeks, the agricultural festival that commemorated the end of the barley harvest and the beginning of the wheat harvest.[24] In the Christian calendar the term is associated with the coming of the Holy Spirit and the beginnings of the early church. Possible evidence for the celebration of Pentecost in the early church goes back to Tertullian and Eusebius. More reliable are the references made by Etheria to the celebration of Pentecost in Jerusalem during the latter part of the fourth century. Liturgical scholar A. A. McArthur describes the event in these words.

> Just after midday the people gathered at the sanctuary on the traditional site of the ascension, and the passages about the ascension from the gospel and Acts were read. A great candlelight procession came to the city in the darkness, and it was eventually about midnight when the people returned to their homes.[25]

The time after Pentecost is the longest season in the church, having twenty-seven or twenty-eight Sundays, lasting until Advent. Preaching during this time concentrates on the development of the early church and emphasizes the power of the Holy Spirit in the ministry of the apostles and the writing of the New Testament literature.

CONCLUSION

We must now ask whether there is a place for commemorative time in the contemporary church. While liturgical churches continue to observe the Christian calendar, and while the renewal leaders in mainline Protestant churches are calling for observance of the Christian calendar, those in the free church movement, including Protestant, evangelical, charismatic, and praise and worship churches, must consider adopting the Christian calendar.

There are good reasons to restore the Christian year. First, the Christian year is rooted in the biblical and historical tradition of worship. Practicing the Christian year is an act of remaining faithful to the Christian tradition. But second, and more important, the biblical concept of time arises out of the conviction that commemorative time brings the power of the event commemorated to the worshiping community. This "evangelical nature" of the Christian year is alone a compelling reason to recover the church year. Finally, Christian churches will find that the practice of the Christian year contrasts the community of worship with the secular community and its practice of time. Time in the Christian church is governed by the life, death, and resurrection of Jesus Christ, not civil or national holidays.

The recovery of the Christian year by many churches that had been indifferent or hostile to it shows spiritual courage and makes time a means by which the Christian story is remembered, proclaimed, enacted, and celebrated.

---

[1]See "καιρός," Colin Brown, ed., *Dictionary of New Testament Theology* (Grand Rapids: Zondervan, 1971), 3:833ff.

[2]See Abraham Millgram, *Jewish Worship* (Philadelphia: Jewish Publication Society, 1971).

[3]Oscar Cullman, *Christ and Time: The Primitive Conception of Time and History* (Philadelphia: Westminster, 1964).

[4]Marion J. Hatchett, *Sanctifying Life, Time, and Space* (New York: Seabury, 1976), 9ff.

[5]See Millgram, *Jewish Worship*, 143ff.

[6]Hippolytus, *The Apostolic Tradition*, 4, 36.

[7]Chesly Jones, Geoffrey Wainwright, and Edward Yarnold, *The Study of Liturgy* (New York: Oxford Univ. Press, 1978), 350–402.

[8]See "The Lord's Day," Jean Daniélou, *The Bible and the Liturgy* (Notre Dame: Univ. of Notre Dame Press, 1956), 242ff.

[9]Daniélou, *Bible and Liturgy*, 249.

[10]Daniélou, *Bible and Liturgy*, 251.

[11]Quoted by Daniélou, *Bible and Liturgy*, 255.

[12]See "The eighth day," in Daniélou, *Bible and Liturgy*, 262ff.

[13]See Peter G. Cobb, "The History of the Christian Year," Jones, Wainwright, and

Yarnold, *The Study of Liturgy*, 403–19.

[14]See the perceptive comments on this subject by Alexander Schmemann, *Introduction to Liturgical Theology* (Bangor, Maine: American Orthodox, 1970), 34ff.

[15]See "The Liturgical Year," Jean-Jacques von Allmen, *Worship: Its Theology and Practice* (New York: Oxford Univ. Press, 1965), 227–36.

[16]Helpful works on the origins of the Christian year include Adolf Adam, *The Liturgical Year* (New York: Pueblo, 1981), A. G. Martinmort, *The Liturgy and Time* (Collegeville, Minn.: Liturgical, 1986).

[17]See "Advent," J. G. Davies, ed., *Westminster Dictionary of Worship* (Philadelphia: Westminster, 1972), 1ff.

[18]See "Epiphany," Davies, *Westminster Dictionary of Worship*, 170ff.

[19]See "Lent," Davies, *Westminster Dictionary of Worship*, 212ff.

[20]See "Ash Wednesday," Davies, *Westminster Dictionary of Worship*, 41.

[21]See "Holy Week," Davies, *Westminster Dictionary of Worship*, 193ff.

[22]See "Easter," Davies, *Westminster Dictionary of Worship*, 166ff.

[23]Quoted in James F. White, *Introduction to Christian Worship* (Nashville: Abingdon, 1980), 53.

[24]See "Pentecost," Davies, *Westminster Dictionary of Worship*, 310ff.

[25]Quoted in "Pentecost," Davies, *Westminster Dictionary of Worship*, 310–11.

Chapter 21

The Sacred Actions of Worship

We have already seen that worship proclaims, enacts, remembers, and celebrates the biblical story of salvation. While this story of God's saving deeds is told in words and explained in concepts, it is also communicated through another kind of language called ritual or symbolic language.

A symbol is the language of the unconscious. These symbols, which are linked with the right side of the brain, deal with intuition, imagination, and emotion. They differ from words in that they have to be cultivated through meditation and concentration. While they speak a language that differs from words, they speak as powerfully as words.

Worship is rich with symbolic language, a language that has the Gospel as its point of reference and communicates a relationship with the Father, the Son, and the Holy Spirit. These symbols are called sacraments because they act in a commemorative way. They bring the reality that they represent to the worshiping community and express a relationship between God and the believing worshiper through sign-acts.

Although the term *sacrament* is greatly misunderstood by many Protestants, it is an appropriate word for these sign-acts. It is the Latin word that Jerome used in the fourth century to translate the Greek word for mystery found in the Scripture. *Sacrament,* therefore, refers to a mystery, the mystery of proclaiming salvation through sign-acts.

The mysterious nature of the sacraments is further enhanced by an understanding of the Latin meaning of *sacramentum,* a word derived from *sacra* meaning sacred or holy and the suffix *mentum* meaning to make. Thus sacrament means to "make holy." In this sense there is only one sacrament, Jesus Christ. Jesus Christ is *the* sacrament of the church because only Jesus Christ can make one holy. The power of Jesus Christ to make holy is communicated through the sign-acts of baptism, Eucharist, and other sacramental action. But water, bread, and wine do not save us; they are the signs of the salvation that comes from Jesus Christ, the one sacrament, the only means by which we are brought to God.

In this chapter we will look at the commemorative nature of baptism, the Eucharist, and other sacramental actions and search for ways these actions may empower contemporary worship.

BAPTISM

The Biblical Roots

Baptism is *the* initiation rite of the early church. When the Jews at Pentecost asked, "'Brothers, what shall we do?' Peter replied, 'Repent and be baptized, everyone one of you, in the name of Jesus Christ for the forgiveness of your sins. And you will receive the gift of the Holy Spirit'" (Acts 2:37–38).

As an initiation rite, baptism stands in connection with the Old Testament rite of circumcision (Gen. 17:11). Like circumcision, which was the sign of entrance into the covenant community, baptism is the sign of entrance into the church. While baptism also carries the sense of washing for cleansing, as in the ceremonial washings of the Old Testament, the most powerful biblical image associated with baptism is that of being transferred from one condition to another as in the case of Noah. Peter wrote of Noah and the ark:

> In it only a few people, eight in all, were saved through water, and this
> water symbolizes baptism that now saves you also—not the removal of
> dirt from the body but the pledge of a good conscience toward God. It
> saves you by the resurrection of Jesus Christ, who has gone into
> heaven and is at God's right hand—with angels, authorities and pow-
> ers in submission to him.
>
> 1 Peter 3:20–22

This transfer from one state to another lies at the heart of the Pauline teaching on baptism. Throughout his writings Paul teaches an identification with the death and resurrection of Jesus as the pattern of a life transferred from the domain of darkness to the kingdom of God. To be in Christ is to put to death the earthly nature (Col. 3:5–14), to live by the Spirit and not gratify the desires of the sinful flesh (Gal. 5:16–26), and to be a slave of righteousness (Rom. 6:15–23). Thus, Paul can say, "We were therefore buried with him through baptism into death in order that, just as Christ was raised from the dead through the glory of the Father, we too may live new life" (Rom. 6:4). Baptism is not only the sign-act of entrance into Christ, but also into the church.

The Historical Development

The full historical development of baptism is beyond the scope of this chapter. A brief excursion into the second century shows us that what emerges in the early church is consistent with the biblical understanding of water baptism as an initiation rite into the church. Baptism symbolizes the new convert's transfer of allegiance from the powers of evil to Christ and the new life of the Spirit.

These themes are expressed by Tertullian, a late second-century theologian, in his work entitled *On Baptism*. The focus of his treatise is on the theology of water, a sign of God's creative work. He argues that the age of water—it was there before the formation of the world—and the dignity of water—it was the seat of God's creative activity, for he called upon the waters "to bring forth living creatures"[1]—are a worthy vehicle through which the grace of God operates. The "material substance [water]," he says, "which governs terrestrial life acts as agent likewise in the celestial."[2]

Tertullian, like others in the early church, did not teach a doctrine of baptismal regeneration (salvation through baptism). Rather, he roots the necessity of baptism in the death of Christ—in the water and blood that flowed from his side. "He sent out these two baptisms from the wound in His pierced side that we might in like manner be called by a water and chosen by blood, and so that they who believed in His blood might be washed in the water."[3] Tertullian did teach the necessity of baptism. For him baptism does not save a person; it is the rite through which one is brought into the church, the community through which God's salvation in the world is being expressed.

The emphasis on baptism as a rite of initiation is best seen in the third-century writings of Hippolytus, who wrote *The Apostolic Tradition*.[4] By the third century the rite of initiation had developed into a two or three year process that culminated in baptism and an official reception into the full life of the church. The process entailed seven steps.

The inquiry. The first step in conversion was a formal inquiry. It was conducted for the specific purpose of weeding out those persons who were not willing to commit themselves to radical discipleship. As a result, persons who became Christians were required to give up vocations not compatible with the Christian faith. For example, Hippolytus tells us that "an enchanter, an astrologer, a diviner, a soothsayer, a user of magic verses, a juggler, a mountebank, an amulet-maker must desist or be rejected."[5]

The rite of entrance. After the converting person passed the inquiry by sufficiently persuading the local church leaders of his or her commitment to Christ and the Christian faith, he or she gained entrance into the church as a catechumen. The passage rite that signified the movement from inquiry into the catechumenate was known as the rite of entrance. Very little is known about the content of the rite of entrance. We do know of several symbolic acts that occurred during this service, one of the most important being the rite of signation (the sign of the cross made on the forehead of each candidate) which signified that the candidate now belonged to Christ, whose sign (the cross) he or she bore.

The catechumenate. The next stage, the catechumenate, was a period of personal testing and teaching, a time for the formation of Christian character. Hippolytus reports, "Let Catechumens spend three years as hearers of the Word. But if a man is zealous and perseveres well in the work, it is not the time but his character that is decisive."[6]

The rite of election. Having passed through the three-year period of instruction, the catechumen was ready to progress through the final stage toward baptism. A rite of election, which signified that God had chosen you, occurred on the first Sunday of Lent as a passage rite into the period of purification and enlightenment. The focus of this rite was the enrollment of names—each candidate stepped forward during the service and wrote his or her name in the Book of Life.

The period of purification and enlightenment. This period of time, which extended through Lent, was a period of intense spiritual preparation for baptism. The candidate underwent a series of exorcisms and rituals that signified the meaning and importance of baptism.

The rite of baptism. The rite of baptism occurred on Easter Sunday morning. It included prayers said over the water; removal of clothing as a sign of putting off the old nature; renunciation of the devil and all his works together with a final prayer of exorcism; creedal affirmations expressing faith in the Father, Son, and Holy Spirit; anointing with the oil of thanksgiving; the laying on of hands with a prayer for the gift of the Holy Spirit; entrance into the community of the faithful; and, for the first time, joining the congregation in the Eucharist.

Mystagogue. This final period of instruction, which occurred during the fifty days of the Easter season, explained the meaning of the Eucharist and integrated the convert into the full life of the church.

The preceding explanation of baptism in the third century shows how important baptism was in the early church. It was primarily for adults and signified their conversion and entrance into the church. Popular images of baptism among the early Fathers included the salvation of Noah in the ark and the passage of Israel from its bondage in Egypt across the Red Sea to the Promised Land. Baptism, more than anything else, meant release from the clutches of Satan into the domain where Christ rules.

During the middle ages the character and meaning of baptism underwent a significant shift. The process of initiation was lost, as baptism was administered primarily to infants. In addition, Thomas Aquinas interpreted baptism in terms of baptismal regeneration. Aquinas understood baptism and all the sacraments to be "remedies through which the benefit of Christ's death could somehow be conjoined to them." For him, the human condition is of such a nature that "spiritual remedies had to be given to men under sensible sign."

Consequently, baptism, as Aquinas claimed, has "the power to take away both original sin and all the actual committed sins."[7] This doctrine of *Ex opere operato* (it works the work), which argued that baptism even apart from faith brings salvation, was affirmed as Catholic teaching at the Council of Trent in 1545.

Both Luther and Calvin, who retained infant baptism, rejected the notion of *Ex opere operato* and insisted that baptism must be joined by faith.

For Luther, baptism was connected with the promise of God in the Word. For example, in *The Babylonian Captivity of the Church* he wrote, *"The first thing in baptism to be considered is the divine promise which says, 'He that believeth and is baptized shall be saved.'"*[8] Baptism is a sign of the promise derived from the Word. Therefore, it is the Word of God that is believed, and baptism is the sign of that Word.

While Luther connected the doctrine of baptism with justification by faith, Calvin understood baptism in relation to the biblical interpretation of predestination. His argument was that God always takes the initiative to come to us. We do not initiate grace. Rather, it starts in God's choosing that finds further expression in baptism. God's grace precedes the sign. Therefore, he defined a sacrament as "an outward sign by which the Lord seals on our consciences the promises of His good-will toward us, in order to sustain the weaknesses of our faith; and we in turn attest our piety toward Him in the presence of the Lord and of His angels and before men."[9] Therefore, baptism may be defined as "the sign of initiation by which we are received into the society of the church in order that, ingrafted in Christ, we may be reckoned among God's children."[10] Calvin, like Luther, argued for infant baptism, rooting it in the nature of grace as related to God's covenant and in the example of circumcision in the old covenant through which infants were included in the saving context of Israel.

The Anabaptists of the sixteenth century offered a radical alternative to both Luther and Calvin. They insisted that infant baptism was an invention of the church and that the only scriptural form of baptism was adult baptism by immersion.

The central verse on which the Anabaptist doctrine of baptism was based is 1 Peter 3:21: "This water symbolizes baptism that now saves you also—not the removal of dirt from the body but the pledge of a good conscience toward God." They emphasized the word *pledge*. According to Robert Friedmann, Anabaptist thinking about *pledge* had three connotations: (1) a covenant between God and man, (2) one between man and God, and (3) one between man and man in which the church is established.[11] Leonhard Schlemer, a sixteenth-century Anabaptist leader, had this to say about the covenant established in baptism.

Baptism with water is a confirmation of the inner covenant with God. This might be compared to a man who writes a letter and then asks that it be sealed. But nobody gives his seal or testimonial unless he knows the contents of the letter. Whoever baptizes a child seals an empty letter.[12]

In short, Anabaptist theology viewed baptism as a personal act of faith rather than God's sign of grace. In the sixteenth century, immersion of an adult signified renunciation of the false doctrine of the Catholic Church. It was also an entrance into and an embracing of the life of the new community of God.

The view of the Anabaptists gave rise to questions about the issue of infant versus adult baptism. The Anabaptists argued that because no record of infant baptism could be found in the New Testament, the baptism of infants was always wrong (this view is shared by many Protestants, particularly of the separatist tradition). It must be conceded that no actual description of the baptism of an infant can be found in the pages of the New Testament and that the earliest actual description of the baptism of an infant did not appear until the writing of Hippolytus in 215. While the absence of infant baptisms constitutes a strong argument against the baptism of infants, those who would baptize infants based their practice on a covenant theology—God includes children in the covenant—and the Israelite precedent of circumcising a male child at the age of eight days. Even as children were not excluded from Israel, so children of believers are not to be excluded from the church and the kingdom.

While we cannot solve this battle, we can clearly state one thing upon which most Christians agree: The New Testament calls for the baptism of both the heart and the body—an internal and an external baptism. The question is, which comes first? Those who baptize children (paedobaptists) believe that external baptism may precede the baptism of the heart (signified by confirmation), whereas those who do not support infant baptism argue for a heartfelt conversion first, followed by baptism as an act of obedience. The paedobaptists see baptism primarily as God's act, to which the child is called to respond (a sacramental view). While these two views have never been compromised into a third alternative, Christians have simply agreed to disagree on the issue, agreeing upon the need for conversion and baptism, the internal and external acts of salvation.[13]

BAPTISMAL RENEWAL IN THE TWENTIETH CENTURY

Because studies in the early church have brought about the rediscovery of baptism as a rite of initiation and a pattern of spirituality, the twentieth-century church has witnessed a renewed understanding and practice of baptism.

First, baptism as a rite of initiation has received considerable attention by the Catholic Church in what is known as the Rites of Christian Initiation

(RCIA). The work of the Roman Catholics in this area has influenced the Episcopal Church and other mainline denominations to study both the early church and the current initiation practices of the Roman Church. The seven steps of initiation practiced in the early church have been adapted to modern culture. Renewal churches in particular have found this approach to evangelistic outreach and spiritual nurture to be particularly effective in helping the unchurched encounter Jesus in a saving way. It has also been used successfully as a way to bring the lapsed back into the fellowship of Christ and his church.[14]

Recent studies in baptism have resulted in the recovery of the theological nature of baptism. Identifying baptism with the death and resurrection of Christ has resulted in significant insights into spirituality. Baptism is seen as bringing death to the powers and principalities and of evil and giving birth to the desire to following after the Spirit. The evangelical and charismatic substance of this theology is deeply rooted in the biblical and early church traditions and holds enormous appeal to renewalists who wish to emphasize the centrality of Christ to Christian faith and spirituality.

Finally, this renewed interest in baptism has resulted in new forms of baptismal worship.[15] In the early church baptism was highlighted by the renunciation of evil and by the threefold acceptance of the Father, Son, and Spirit, as expressed in the interrogatory creed (later developed into the Apostles' Creed). Today the new baptismal liturgies of the Roman Catholic Church and of the Protestant mainline churches reflect this ancient structure.

These new insights have much to offer the free church. In most free churches baptism is seen as the person's expression of faith. While the subjective side of baptism should not be denied, it is important to recover the biblical and historical emphasis on baptism. The ancient understanding of baptism recognizes it as a rite of initiation characterized by a divine action through which God initiates a relationship with the new believer. This relationship empowers the believer to live a life that renounces evil and embraces truth.

THE EUCHARIST

The Biblical Roots

What Christians do at the table of the Lord is described in the New Testament as the "breaking of bread" (Acts 2:42), the "Lord's Supper" (1 Cor. 11:20), and "the cup of thanksgiving" (1 Cor. 10:16).

The word *Eucharist*, which means to give thanks, became the prominent designation used by Christians in the beginning of the second century. This word became the norm because what Christians do at the table of the Lord is rooted in the Jewish thanksgiving prayers. Blessings were offered over food, particularly bread and wine, in Jewish homes. The *prayers of blessing* that Christians pray at the table of the Lord grew out of these *blessing prayers,* particularly those of the

Sabbath and the Passover. For Jews, these meals remembered, proclaimed, and enacted God's saving deeds. As Christians developed prayers over the bread and wine, which commemorated God's saving work in Jesus Christ, it was natural for them to follow the pattern already established in the Jewish tradition.

Theological Reflection

Since the Eucharist has become a matter of division within the church, a brief reflection on the theological issues surrounding the Eucharist seems in order. First, the Eucharist is understood as a thanksgiving for the victory of Christ over the power of evil. Paul teaches that "having disarmed the powers and authorities, [Christ] made a public spectacle of them, triumphing over them by the cross" (Col. 2:15). Worship enacts and celebrates this victory. All the liturgical prayers of the early church are careful to include a prayer of thanksgiving that mentions Christ's victory over evil. This motif is clearly set forth in the eucharistic prayer of Hippolytus.

> And when he was betrayed to voluntary suffering that he might destroy death, and break the bonds of the devil, and tread down hell, and shine upon the righteous, and fix the limit, and manifest the resurrection. . . "[16]

The Eucharist anticipates the judgment of evil. Jesus implied this when he said, "I will not drink of this fruit of the vine from now on until that day when I drink it anew with you in my Father's kingdom" (Matt. 26:29). The future judgment against sin was already present in every celebration of the Eucharist. Paul was clear about this in his letter to the Corinthians. Their sins of division and gluttony had already been judged in the Eucharist. For by eating unworthingly they were eating and drinking judgment upon themselves (see 1 Cor. 11:27–34). But each Eucharist anticipates the future and points to the end of the world as well. In this way the Eucharist foreshadows the complete destruction of evil (Rev. 20) and the creation of the new heavens and the new earth (Rev. 21–22). This is also seen in the liturgical prayer of the early church, "maranatha" (Our Lord, come).

The Eucharist may be regarded as an offering of Jesus Christ to the Father. This notion was developed by the writer of Hebrews in 10:11–14.

> Day after day every priest stands and performs his religious duties; again and again he offers the same sacrifices, which can never take away sins. But when this priest had offered for all time one sacrifice for sins, he sat down at the right hand of God. Since that time he waits for his enemies to be made his footstool, because by *one sacrifice* he has made perfect forever those who are being made holy. (emphasis added)

It is clear from this passage that there is only one offering or sacrifice for sin—the offering Jesus Christ made of himself.

Several questions concerning the relationship between this offering and what is done in the Eucharist may arise: (1) Do the elements of bread and wine symbolize the offering of Jesus Christ? (2) How may the presentation of bread and wine by the congregation through the minister be regarded as an offering? (3) What effect does this offering have on the elements of bread and wine? And (4) what effect does the notion of an offering have on the worshipers?[17]

First, does the offering of bread and wine symbolize the offering of Jesus Christ? There is no direct answer to this question in the New Testament.[18] However, the early church Fathers universally and unequivocally regarded the offering of bread and wine as symbolic of the sacrifice of Jesus Christ. Clement, the bishop of Rome in the last decade of the first century, referred to Christ as "the high priest of our oblations,"[19] and described the bishop as one whose office is to "offer the gifts."[20] Sixty years later Justin informed the emperor that after the intercessions and the kiss, bread was "offered."[21] Another sixty years later, in the beginning of the third century, Hippolytus instructed the church to "let the deacons bring up the oblation offering, and he with all the presbyters laying his hand on the oblation shall say. . . ."[22]

Secondly, the idea of sacrifice is clearly connected with the elements of bread and wine. The *Didache* states:

> On every Lord's Day—his special day—come together and break bread and give thanks, first confessing your sins so that your *sacrifice* may be pure. Anyone at variance with his neighbor must not join you, until they are reconciled, lest your *sacrifice* be defiled. For it was of this *sacrifice* that the Lord said, "always and everywhere offer me a *pure sacrifice* for I am a great King," says the Lord, "and my name is marveled at by the nations."[23] [emphasis added]

Ignatius, the bishop of Antioch, in 110 referred to the eucharistic assembly of the church as *thusiasterion,* "the place of sacrifice."[24]

The terms *sacrifice* and *offering* used in connection with the Eucharist are especially repugnant to some Protestants. This is so because of the late medieval association of these terms with a continuing sacrifice of Christ, or because of the notion that Jesus is sacrificed in an unbloody manner again and again for salvation. This medieval notion is clearly unbiblical and was rightfully rejected by the Reformers. However, it needs to be made clear that this was not the theology of the early church Fathers. For them the notion of offering and sacrifice, while associated with the offering and sacrifice of Christ, contained no notion of *re*sacrifice.

This is the case in an early eucharistic prayer found in the writings of Hippolytus: "We *offer* to you the bread and cup . . . and we ask that you would send your Holy Spirit upon the *offering* of your holy church . . . *that we may praise and glorify you* through your child Jesus Christ" (emphasis added).[25] In this prayer, bread and wine are the temporal symbols that transcend time and find their true meaning in the atonement of Jesus Christ. This answers the second question, namely, that the presentation of bread and wine is an offering, not in the sense of a sacrifice, but in the sense of an offering of praise and thanksgiving for the sacrifice of Christ.

The third question considers what effect the offering of bread and wine has on the elements. Do they *change* into the body and blood of our Lord when they are offered to the Father?[26] This question has been a divisive issue in the church. Space does not permit a detailed examination of it here. Let it be sufficient to say that the early church knew no notion of transubstantiation as developed in the medieval church and rejected by the Reformers. On the other hand, the early church had a stronger view than the memorialism adhered to by some Protestant groups.[27]

The position of the early church may be described this way: Because the elements of bread and wine have been offered to the Father, they are no longer common bread or common drink. Instead they represent to us the death and resurrection of Christ for our salvation. Thus, they proclaim to us the saving power of Jesus Christ. When we receive them by faith, we receive not only bread and wine, but mysteriously receive the saving grace that comes from the once-for-all sacrifice of Jesus Christ.[28]

This observation raises the fourth and final question: What effect does this offering have on the worshiper? The answer to this question is based on the recognition that the offering of bread and wine is also an offering of self. Bread and wine are the first fruits of creation and as such represent the fruits of human labor. Thus, the offering of bread and wine represents the offering of one's whole being. This is an offering made by the whole congregation, one body of Christ. But it is made in and through Christ and his offering to the Father. Consequently, the Eucharist, or the church's thanksgiving, includes the offering of oneself as an act of thanksgiving. This personal giving of self ought to result in the confession of Christ's lordship and the living of a life of personal sacrifice. For this reason the following words from Hebrews are to be interpreted in the context of worship: "Through Jesus, therefore, let us continually offer to God a sacrifice of praise—the fruit of lips that confess his name. And do not forget to do good and to share with others, for with such sacrifices God is pleased" (13:15–16).[29]

This early conviction of the Eucharist as an "offering of praise and thanksgiving," rediscovered as a result of modern liturgical scholarship, enriches the church's understanding of worship. Nothing in this view is incompatible with the Scriptures nor with an evangelical commitment to the Gospel. The restoration of this teaching will prove to be a means of recovering the joy and triumph of celebrating Christ's victory over evil.

The Historical Development

The Ancient Church

One of the earliest interpretations of what happens at the table of the Lord was provided by Justin Martyr (150). In a letter written to the Emperor Titus in defense of the Christian faith, he explained the meaning of Eucharist in the following words:

> This food we call Eucharist, of which no one is allowed to partake except one who believes that the things we teach are true, and has received the washing for forgiveness of sins and for rebirth, and who lives as Christ handed down to us. For we do not receive these things a common bread or common drink; but as Jesus Christ our Savior being incarnate by God's word took flesh and blood for our salvation, so also we have been taught that the food consecrated by the word of prayer which comes from him, from which our flesh and blood are nourished by transformation, is the flesh and blood of that incarnate Jesus.[30]

Several observations about this quote will clarify the early Christian view of the Eucharist. First, Justin was describing something that happened weekly and not monthly or quarterly as in some churches today. Next, note that Justin's description of the bread and wine as the body and blood of the Lord was neither the later Catholic doctrine of transubstantiation nor the Protestant concept of memorialism. The bread and drink, Justin writes, is more than common food or drink. The key to understanding what Justin means by this statement is found in the comparison between the Incarnation and the consecration. As Christ by God's Word became incarnate, so by the power of prayer, bread and wine are more than mere food. The general consensus among liturgical scholars is that Justin's understanding may be described as "real presence." That is, there is a mystery at work here, whereby Jesus becomes savingly present to us through the action represented by the rite of bread and wine. It is not a mere human memory that is invoked at the table, but a real action on the part of God whereby the elements represent an actual and saving communication of Christ's work on the cross.

Hippolytus

Seventy years after Justin's description of the Eucharist, Hippolytus provided a detailed account of an actual eucharistic prayer used in Rome. This prayer, one of the oldest extant eucharistic prayers of the church, not only gave evidence of the structure, content, and spirit of early Christian worship at the table, but it is also the model for liturgical reform in the twentieth century. Its value for liturgical scholarship and worship renewal cannot be overestimated. We have included the entire prayer because of its unparalleled significance.

We render thanks to you, O God, through your beloved Child Jesus Christ, whom in the last times you sent to us a savior and redeemer and angel of your will; who is your inseparable Word, through whom you made all things, and in whom you were well pleased. You sent him from heaven into the Virgin's womb; and, conceived in the womb, he was made flesh and was manifested as your Son, being born of the Holy Spirit and the Virgin: Fulfilling your will and gaining for you a holy people, he stretched out his hands when he should suffer, that he might release from suffering those who have believed in you. And when he was betrayed to voluntary suffering that he might destroy death, and break the bonds of the devil, and tread down hell, and shine upon the righteous and fix the limit, and manifest the resurrection, he took bread and gave thanks to you, saying, "Take, eat; this is my body, which shall be broken for you." Likewise also the cup, saying, "This is my blood, which is shed for you; when you do this, you make my remembrance." Remembering therefore this death and resurrection, we offer to you the bread and the cup, giving you thanks because you have held us worthy to stand before you and minister to you, and we ask that you would send your Holy Spirit upon the offering of your holy Church; that, gathering them into one, you would grant to all who partake of the holy things (to partake) for the fullness of the Holy Spirit for the confirmation of faith in truth; that we may praise and glory you through your Child Jesus Christ, through whom be glory and honor to you, to the Father and the Son with the Holy Spirit, in your holy Church, both now and to the ages of ages. (Amen).[31]

This eucharistic prayer follows the pattern and structure of the Jewish Berakhah—praise, historical recitation, and petition. It begins with praise, continues with a historical recitation of God's saving deeds in Jesus Christ, and ends with a petition for the coming of the Holy Spirit.

Furthermore, the prayer of blessing contains the entire confession of the Christian church. Note that it begins with the essence of the Christian message and then emphasizes the unity of the Son with the Father, creation, incarnation, obedience, suffering (for the church), victory over evil through the Resurrection, recitation of the institution of the Supper as a remembrance (the word *anamnesis* means recalling, not mere memory), the power of the Holy Spirit to sanctify the elements and the congregation, and finally a recognition that the offering is one of praise to the Father *through* the Son.

The Fourth and Fifth Centuries

It is generally recognized that the early church did not seek to explain the mystery of "real presence" through the bread and wine. However, this changed somewhat in the late fourth and early fifth centuries when leading churchmen sought to be more specific about what actually happened to the bread and wine after the prayer of consecration. Two primary differences of opinion were set in motion by the writings of Ambrose and Augustine. Ambrose's view is known as *realism*, whereas the description of Augustine has been called *symbolic realism*.

The realism of Ambrose suggests that the bread and wine become the actual body and blood of our Lord. Commenting on the relationship between the nature miracles of the Bible and the power of the prayer of consecration he writes:

> But if a human blessing had the power to effect a change in nature, what are we to say of the divine consecration where the very words of the Lord and Savior are in operation? For the sacrament that you receive is effected by the words of Christ. Now if the words of Elijah had the power to call down fire from heaven, will not the words of Christ have power to change the character [species] of the elements?[32]

Augustine shuns such strong realism and describes the presence of Christ in the elements in a more symbolic way. In one of his sermons Augustine says, "The reason why these [the bread and wine], are called sacraments is that one thing is seen in them, but something else is understood. That which is seen has bodily appearance; that which is understood has spiritual fruit."[33] Elsewhere he states, "Christ was once sacrificed in his own person; and yet he is mystically [*in sacramento*] sacrificed for the peoples, not only throughout the Easter festival, but every day."[34] While Augustine's symbolic realism is closer to the less defined early church's "real presence" than is the realism of Ambrose, the debates of the next centuries resulted in the medieval Catholic view of transubstantiation, the seeds of which are found in Ambrose.

The Medieval Church

Paschasius Radbertus, the abbot of the monastery of Corbie (844–53), began a controversy regarding the presence of Christ in the elements of bread and wine that continued for four centuries and culminated in the medieval view of transubstantiation affirmed at the Fourth Latern Council in 1215.

Radbertus, in a work entitled *The Lord's Body and Blood*, argued that the bread and wine truly turn into the body and blood of the Lord. Interpreting the words "This is my body" (Matt. 26:26) in a literal way, he wrote:

> If you truly believe that the flesh was without seed created from the Virgin Mary in her womb by the power of the Holy Spirit so that the Word might be made flesh, truly believe also that what is constructed in Christ's Word through the Holy Spirit is his body from the virgin. If you ask the method, who can explain or express it in words? . . . The power of divinity over nature effectively works beyond the capacity of our reason.[35]

One can see here that Radbertus was following the train of thought begun by Ambrose.

But the view of Radbertus was not the only conviction in the ninth century. Ratramnus, a rival monk from Corbie, in his work *Christ's Body and Blood*, argued in the tradition of Augustine for a more symbolic view. He wrote, "That bread which through the ministry of the priest comes to be Christ's body exhibits one thing outwardly to human sense, and it proclaims another thing inwardly to the minds of the faithful."[36]

In 1215 the debate between Ambrosian and Augustinian tradition about the presence of Christ in bread and wine came to an end through the pronouncement of the church. The Fourth Latern Council declared:

> There is one universal church of believers outside which there is no salvation at all for any. In this church the priest and sacrifice is the same Jesus Christ Himself, whose body and blood are truly contained in the sacrament of the altar under the figures of bread and wine, the bread having been transubstantiated into His body and the wine into His blood by divine power, so that, to accomplish the mystery of our union, we may receive of Him what He has received of us. And none can effect this sacrament except the priest who has been rightly ordained in accordance with the keys of the church which Jesus Christ Himself granted to the Apostles and their successors.[37]

Aquinas interpreted transubstantiation to mean that the external characteristics of the bread and wine remained the same while the substance became the body and blood of the Lord.

> The complete substance of the bread is converted into the complete substance of Christ's body, and the complete substance of the wine into the complete substance of Christ's blood. Hence this change is not a formal change, but a substantial one. It does not belong to the natural kinds of change, and it can be called by a name proper to itself —"transubstantiation" . . . It is obvious to our senses that, after the consecration, all the accidents of the bread and wine remain.[38]

This doctrine of transubstantiation was intricately tied into the broader medieval developments within the Catholic Church. It fit the institutional concept of the church, which had the power to turn the elements into the body and blood through the prayer of consecration; it fit the liturgical shift into the notion that Christ was sacrificed anew at every mass, and it served the sacramental notion of salvation; that is, that the body of the divine Christ conjoined with the human body through the Eucharist secured the salvation of the sinner.

Consequently, when the pre-Reformers of the late medieval period began to attack the doctrine of transubstantiation, they were inadvertently attacking the whole system of which it was a part—the church, its concept of sacrificial worship, and salvation through the sacrament. An example of this multifaceted attack is found in the writings of John Wycliff, who issued the *de Eucharistia* in 1381 with a scathing attack on the doctrine of transubstantiation.

First it is contrary to Scripture. Second, it is unsupported by early church tradition. "Since the year of our Lord one thousand, all the doctors have been in error about the sacrament on the altar, except perhaps Berengar of Tours." Third, it is plainly opposed to the testimony of the senses. Finally, it is based upon false reasoning. "How canst thou, O priest, who art but a man, make the Maker? What! The thing that growth in the fields—that ear which thou pluckest today, shall be God tomorrow! As thou canst not make the works which he made, how shall ye make him who made the works?"[39]

The debate over transubstantiation reached its climax in the sixteenth century when Luther, Calvin, and the Anabaptists defined the Lord's Supper in ways that differed radically from the medieval Catholic view. Roman Catholicism kept its ground, and in the decree of Trent reaffirmed once again the doctrine of transubstantiation.

The Reformation Era

Luther and the Lutheran Tradition

We have already seen how Luther's battle with Roman Catholicism centered on works-righteousness. Luther was convinced that a doctrine of salvation by works extended into every aspect of Roman Catholic thought and practice, including worship and the sacraments.

Luther rejected the Catholic concept of a sacrificial mass and the doctrine of transubstantiation. For Luther, the idea of a priest's sacrificing Christ at the altar emphasized human achievement and works, and he did not find the doctrine of transubstantiation to be scriptural.

Luther argued that it is the Word, not the sacrament, that is the source of new life. Therefore the salvation that Christ brings through his Word is proclaimed in the Lord's Supper. When we take the bread and the wine, we are receiving his Word of promise that is "given and shed for you for the remission of sins." Luther's view is succinctly stated in the *Small Catechism*:

What is the sacrament of the Altar? It is the true body and blood of our Lord Jesus Christ, under the bread and wine, instituted by Christ himself for us Christians to eat and drink. Where is this written? The holy Evangelists, Matthew, Mark and Luke, together with St. Paul, write thus: "Our Lord Jesus Christ, in the night in which he was betrayed, took bread; and when he had given thanks, he brake it, and gave it to his disciples, saying, Take, eat; this is my body, which is given for you; this do in remembrance of me. After the same manner, when he had supped, he took also the cup, and when he had given thanks, he gave it to them, saying, Drink ye all of it; this cup is the New Testament in my blood, which is shed for you, for the remission of sins; this do, as oft as ye drink it, in remembrance of me." What benefit is such eating and drinking? It is shown us by these words: "Given and shed for you, for the remission of sins"; namely, that in the Sacrament, forgiveness of sins, life and salvation are given us through these words. For where there is forgiveness of sins, there is also life and salvation. How can bodily eating and drinking do such great things? It is not the eating and drinking indeed that does it, but the words which stand here: "Given and shed for you, for the remission of sins." These words, together with the bodily eating and drinking, are the chief thing in the Sacrament; and he that believes these words has what they say and mean, namely the forgiveness of sins. Who then receives this Sacrament worthily? Fasting and bodily preparation are indeed a good outward discipline; but he is truly worthy and well prepared for who has faith in these words: "Given and shed for you, for the remission of sins." But he who believes not these words, or doubts, is unworthy and unprepared; for the words, "For you," require only believing hearts.[40]

Although Luther rejected transubstantiation and placed the saving action of Christ in the Word, he did not reject the real presence of Christ in the bread and wine. He argued that the word *is* in the words of institution. "This is my body" can be interpreted with integrity only when it is understood literally. He thus argued against the figurative interpretation of the word, espoused by Andreas Carlstadt and Zwingli, and maintained the unity of the spiritual and the physical, a unity that is best exemplified in the Incarnation.

Calvin and the Reformed Tradition

Like Luther, Calvin also rejected the Catholic notions of the mass as a sacrifice and the transubstantiation of the bread and wine into the body of Christ. Nevertheless, Calvin was a full step away from Luther regarding the presence of Christ in the bread and wine. Calvin's position is closer to a figurative and symbolic interpretation of Christ's presence in the bread and wine.

There are two fundamental differences between Luther and Calvin that help us understand how they differ on the question of "real presence." First, Luther believed in the ubiquity of the body of Christ; that is, he was convinced that Christ is everywhere. Calvin, on the contrary, believed that Christ is in heaven and therefore in a particular localized place. For Calvin, Christ could not be present both in heaven and in the bread. Second, Calvin tended to maintain a distinction between the spiritual and the material. This view is expressed in a Calvinistic formula: "The finite cannot contain the infinite." Therefore Calvin and his followers tended toward the more figurative interpretation of the words "This is my body."

Zwingli, who generally stands in the Calvinist tradition, has been called the father of the memorialist view. This view regards the Lord's Supper as a commemoration done by the church so as to trigger in the mind of the individual a recollection of God's act of salvation in the death of Christ. Its emphasis is not so much on what God does, as in Calvin (God's sign, pledge, testimony), but rather on what the worshiper does. The worshiper remembers, meditates, thinks upon, and recalls God's great act of salvation. Zwingli's memorialist view sees the Eucharist as a devotional act on the part of the worshiper. Bread and wine are not God-given vehicles of grace, as in the understandings of Luther and Calvin. The Lord's Supper is not a sacrament—God's action—but an act of piety on the part of the believer.

Calvin's emphasis in the Lord's Supper is on what it is and what it effects. What it is may be best expressed in words such as *sign, witness, testimony*. In these ways the bread and wine signify what Christ has done. What the bread and wine effect is best expressed in the terms *participation* or *communion* (1 Cor. 10:16). Calvin put these ideas this way in his *Institutes of the Christian Religion*:

> Since, however, this mystery of Christ's secret union with the devout is by nature incomprehensible, he shows its figure and image in visible signs best adapted to our small capacity. Indeed, by giving guarantees and tokens he makes it as certain for us as if we had seen it with our own eyes. For this very familiar comparison penetrates into even the dullest minds: Just as bread and wine sustain physical life, so are souls fed by Christ. We now understand the purpose of this mystical blessing; namely, to confirm for us the fact that the Lord's body was once for all so sacrificed for us that we may now feed upon it and by feeding feel in ourselves the working of that unique sacrifice; and that his blood was once so shed for us in order to be our perpetual drink. And so speak the words of the promise added there: "Take, this is my body which is given for you" (1 Cor. 11:24; cf. Matt. 26:26; Mark 14:22; Luke 22:19). We are therefore bidden to take and eat the body that was once for all offered for our salvation, in order that when we see ourselves made partakers in it, we may assuredly conclude that the power of his life-giving death will be efficacious in us.[41]

Menno Simons and the Anabaptist Tradition

We have already seen that the Anabaptist wing of the Reformation differed quite significantly from that of the Lutheran and Reformed. Menno Simons and the Anabaptists were not reformers, but restitutionists. They wanted to restore what they believed to be the biblical and ancient practice of the church.

For them the Lord's Supper was a memorial. They rejected and even ridiculed such ideas as transubstantiation or consubstantiation. However, it would be a mistake to think that their memorialism resulted in a low view of the Lord's Supper. One could hardly assume such a thing when the Anabaptists risked life and limb to gather in secret to worship and partake of the bread and the cup.

Anabaptist theology saw the overriding theme of the Lord's Supper as eschatological. It was a fraternal meal that represented a foretaste of the kingdom to come. In the new heavens and the new earth, God's people will gather at the table of the Lord to celebrate Christ's victory over evil and enjoy the community of love that Christ has established. For the Anabaptist, that experience was available in the here and now in the worship of the church, especially in the meal of bread and wine.

However, in this world the experience of the kingdom to come is bittersweet. The church is under persecution, and God's people may be put to death. The Anabaptist's images of the bread and the wine were that of wheat being ground into the loaf or of the grapes crushed into wine. These images spoke of Christ's suffering, of the suffering of his disciples, and of the unity of God's people. Here is what Hans Nadler, an Anabaptist martyr, had to say at his trial in 1529:

> We celebrated the Lord's Supper at Augsburg in 1527, the Lord's wine and bread. With the bread the unity among the brethren is symbolized. Where there are many small kernels of grain to be combined into one loaf there is need first to grind them and to make them into one flour . . . which can be achieved only through suffering. Just as Christ, our dear Lord, went before us, so too we want to follow him in like manner. And the bread symbolizes the unity of the brotherhood.

> Likewise with the wine: many small groups came together to make the one wine. That happens by means of the press, understood here as suffering. And thus also the wine indicates suffering. Hence, whoever wants to be in brotherly union, has to drink from the cup of the Lord, for this cup symbolizes suffering.[42]

The Armenian Tradition and John Wesley

James Arminius stood in the Reformed tradition and defined the Lord's Supper in terms similar to those of Calvin. He rejected the transubstantiation of the Catholics, the consubstantiation of the Lutherans, and the figurative understanding of the Anabaptists. Instead, he emphasized that in the sacrament "the death of Christ is announced and the inward receiving and enjoyment of the body and blood of Christ are signified."[43]

On the other hand, John Wesley's view of the Lord's Supper differed somewhat significantly from the Reformed tradition. He believed that grace was received *through* the sacrament, not *from* it. That is to say, he saw the sacrament as an occasion for an encounter with the saving reality of Christ. He argued that the Lord's table could be seen as a "converting ordinance." Because he viewed faith in stages of development, he felt "the purpose of the Lord's Supper conveyed to persons according to their need, whether preventing, justifying, or sanctifying grace."[44] Furthermore, he stated, "No fitness is required at the time of communicating, but a sense of our state, of our utter sinfulness and helplessness; everyone who knows he is fit for hell, being just fit to come to Christ, in this as well as all other ways of his appointment."[45]

EUCHARISTIC RENEWAL IN THE CONTEMPORARY CHURCH

Until recently, the various denominations remained fixed in their theological understandings of the Eucharist, and in the structural forms in which the Eucharist was practiced. However, a renewed interest in worship has reopened old questions about the understanding, the structure, and the practice of the Eucharist in nearly every denomination. A considerable amount of agreement now exists among the churches.

Regarding the understanding of the Eucharist, current studies have emphasized a number of common themes. (1) The Eucharist is a celebration offered to God by the whole church. (2) It is a remembrance of the saving event which is mysteriously made present in all its saving power to the community gathered in worship. (3) The presence of Christ rather than being localized in bread and wine is a presence in the assembled people, in the presiding ministers, in the Word proclaimed, and in the songs sung. (4) The sacrificial nature of the Eucharist is understood in terms of Christ's action, which is not repeated but *remembered* through words, symbols, and actions of thanksgiving. (5) The eschatological aspect of the Eucharist has been recovered as the Eucharist is seen as a foretaste of the future kingdom, a momentary earthly experience of the future glory in heaven.[46]

These ideas, which first emerged in the Catholic Church through the *Constitution on the Sacred Liturgy*, are now fairly common in the renewal worship of mainline churches and are increasingly discussed within the free church traditions.

Another shift taking place has to do with the structure of the eucharistic prayer. Studies in the early church tradition, particularly in the prayer of Hippolytus, and in the Jewish roots of the prayer of thanksgiving in the *berakhah* prayers have revolutionized the structure of the modern prayer.

Berakhah prayers were ordered around (1) praise, (2) commemoration, and (3) petition. Contemporary worship has recovered this basic structure and has restored the *Sursum Corda* (Lift up your hearts), the prayer of thanksgiving (a commemoration of the history of salvation), and the *epiclesis* (an invocation calling upon the Holy Spirit to be present). This common form of giving thanks at the table of the Lord is now advocated in the prayer books of all mainline denominations and is now increasingly used among renewal churches in the free tradition.

The contemporary church is also rethinking the way in which the Eucharist is practiced. In many renewal churches the people now walk forward to receive the bread and wine, sing during the communion, and are anointed for healing and empowerment.

SUGGESTIONS FOR THE PRACTICE OF THE EUCHARIST IN THE FREE CHURCH TRADITION

Free church worship may benefit significantly from recent scholarship pertaining to the understanding and practice of the Eucharist. There is no reason not to join in the consensus that has grown out of liturgical scholarship, especially when this scholarship has reached back into the biblical and historical traditions of worship. The following suggestions for free church worship are based on this scholarship.

Free church worshipers should seek to improve the prayer of thanksgiving over the bread and wine. Every worship leader utters some kind of prayer over the bread and wine. In most cases, it is a prayer thanking God for the death of his Son and for the salvation that comes from the broken body and shed blood. The content of this prayer can be expanded and enhanced by following an order of the prayer of thanksgiving that was used in the ancient church and is still used in many churches today. This ancient order derives from the Jewish berakhah prayers and includes a prayer of praise, a prayer of commemoration, and a prayer of petition.

For example, if a Jew prayed, "Blessed be God who brought us up out of Egypt, bring us to the Promised Land," all three elements of praise, commemoration, and petition are there.

When a free church minister stands before the people and prays a prayer of thanksgiving over the bread and wine, the ancient order may be followed in an extemporaneous prayer. First, praise God for the work of the Son and express the desire to join with the angels, archangels, cherubim, and seraphim who stand around the throne of God singing, "Holy, holy, holy" (the congregation may join in singing one of the many versions of this song).

Next, give thanks to God for his mighty deeds of salvation by briefly reciting the history of God's acts of salvation expressed throughout the Old Testament and in the death and resurrection of Jesus. Conclude this prayer with the words of Jesus in Matthew 26:26–28, the breaking of the bread, and the pouring or lifting of the cup.

Finally, ask God to bless the congregation with the fullness of the Holy Spirit and for the confirmation of faith. These words may be followed by the invitation to receive the bread and the wine.

Invite the people to come forward to receive the bread and wine. Worship renewal emphasizes participation and involvement. By asking the people to stand, walk down the aisle, and receive the bread and then the wine, you are inviting them to reaffirm their identification with the death and resurrection of Christ.

While the people are coming to receive the bread and wine—sing! Singing breaks through the passive character of the Eucharist as it is observed in many churches. Singing allows the whole community of faith to express the mystery of faith and the joy of Christ's saving and healing presence at the table. Sing songs of the death, then songs of the resurrection, and finally songs of the exaltation of the Lord. This progression of song orders the experience of the worshiping church past the death of the Lord (where too many churches remain) and into the joy of the Resurrection and exaltation.

Provide a time of ministry with the anointing of oil and the laying on of hands for healing and empowerment. This act of ministry extends the meaning of Christ's death and resurrection—God's acts of salvation and healing—and allows the congregation to experience the power of Christ's death and resurrection.

In conclusion, let me say once again that worship needs to strive toward biblical fullness, and this means more frequent celebrations of the Eucharist. What worship renewal is experiencing is not the old funeral approach to the Eucharist but a powerful, joyful experience of the resurrected Christ, who is present at bread and wine to touch, to heal, and to make whole. This is celebration worship.[47]

CONCLUSION

In this chapter we have looked at those two central commemorative actions that bring us to the saving action of Jesus Christ. Baptism is the rite of initiation into the church. The Eucharist is the church's celebration of Christ's death and resurrection and anticipation of the new heaven and the new earth.

While these are the two major commemorative actions of worship, there are others that the church in its history and tradition have recognized as special, sacred actions in which the presence of Christ is active. These include confirmation, or the sealing of the Spirit; confession, or what is now known as the rite of reconciliation; marriage; ordination; and the anointing of oil. While these acts have been singled out by the church to express a vital connection with the life, death, and resurrection of Jesus, the church also recognizes the sacred character of all life. God is present with us in prayer, Scripture study, relationships, and in all that we do. The sacredness of life is a vital theme of worship to be kept in our minds and hearts. For God meets us not only in the special rituals of worship but in all of life.

1. Tertullian, "On Baptism," *The Ante-Nicene Fathers*, Vol. 3, Tertullian, trans. S. Thelwall (Grand Rapids: Eerdmans, 1978), 670.

2. Tertullian, *On Baptism*, 670.

3. Tertullian, *On Baptism*, 677

4. *The Apostolic Tradition of St. Hippolytus*, ed. Gregory Dix and Henry Chadwick (2d ed., Harrisburg, Penn.: Morehouse Publishers, 1991).

5. Hippolytus, *Apostolic Tradition*, for full text see 23–28.

6. Hippolytus, *Apostolic Tradition*, for full text see 28–30.

7. Cited from Robert Ferm, *Readings in the History of Christian Thought* (New York: Holt, Rinehart and Winston, 1964), 446–69.

8. Hugh T. Kerr, ed., *A Compend of Luther's Theology* (Philadelphia: Westminster, 1966), 166.

9. John Calvin, *Institutes of the Christian Religion*, ed., John T. McNeil (Philadelphia: Westminster, 1960), 4.1.1277.

10. Calvin, *Institutes*, 4.1.1303.

11. Robert Friedman, *The Theology of Anabaptism* (Scottdale, Penn.: Herald, 1973), 135.

12. Friedman, *The Theology of Anabaptism*, 137.

13. Much of the material on baptism has been adapted from Alan Johnson and Robert Webber, *What Christians Believe* (Grand Rapids: Zondervan, 1989), 389–397.

14. For an explanation of an adaptation of the RCIA for Protestants, see Robert Webber, *Liturgical Evangelism* (Harrisburg, Penn.: Morehouse, 1993).

15. See, for example, *The Book of Common Prayer*.

16. Hippolytus, *The Apostolic Tradition*, 4, 2.

17. See the discussion on this question in Gregory Dix, *The Shape of the Liturgy* (London: Dacre, 1945), 48–102; see also "Was the Last Supper a Passover Meal?" in Joachim Jeremias, *The Eucharistic Words of Jesus* (Philadelphia: Fortress, 1977).

18. See Dix, *The Shape of the Liturgy*, 110–23.

19. Clement, *First Letter*, chap. 36.

20. Ibid., chap. 44.

21. Justin, *First Apology*, 2, 65.

22. Hippolytus, *Apostolic Tradition*, 4, 2.

23. *Didache*, 14.

24. Ignatius, *Letter to the Ephesians*, 5, 2.

25. Hippolytus, *Apostolic Tradition*, 4, 12–13.

26. For a history of eucharistic theology see Joseph M. Powers, *Eucharistic Theology* (New York: Seabury, 1967); see also Cheslyn Jones, Geoffrey Wainright, and Edward Yarnold, eds., *The Study of Liturgy* (New York: Oxford Univ. Press, 1978), 147–288.

27. See Hughes Oliphant Old, *The Patristic Roots of Reformed Worship* (Zurich: Theologischer Verlag Zurich, 1975), 101ff.

28. See the eucharistic prayers and teaching of the early Church Fathers in R. C. D. Jasper and G. C. Cumings, *Prayers of the Eucharist: Early and Reformed*, 2d ed. (New York: Oxford Univ. Press, 1980), esp. Justin Martyr, 17–20.

29. See the comments on this by Dix, *The Shape of the Liturgy*, 114ff.

30. Cyril C. Richardson, ed., *Early Christian Fathers* (Philadelphia: Westminster, 1953), 286.

31. Jasper and Cumings, *Prayers of the Eucharist*, 22–25.

32. See Henry Bettenson, *The Later Christian Fathers* (London: Oxford Univ. Press, 1970), 185.

33. Bettenson, *The Later Christian Fathers*, 244.

34. Bettenson, *The Later Christian Fathers*, 245.

35. Quoted from Robert Ferm, *Readings in the History of Christian Thought* (New York: Holt, Rinehart and Winston, 1964), 459.

36. Ferm, *Readings*, 461.

37. See John H. Leith, *Creeds of the Churches* (New York: Doubleday, 1963), 58.

38. Thomas Aquinas, *Summa Theologiae*, 58:73, 75.

39. Quoted by Donald Bridge and David Phypers, *Communion: The Meal that Unites?* (Wheaton, Ill.: Shaw, 1981), 80.

40. Kerr, *A Compend of Luther's Theology* (Philadelphia: Westminster, 1966), 170–71.

41. Calvin, *Institutes*, 4.17.3, 1363.

42. Quoted from Friedmann, *The Theology of Anabaptism*, 140–41

43. James Arminius, *The Works of James Arminius*, 3 vols. (Grand Rapids: Baker, reprint of 1875), 1.161.

44. Arminius, *Works*, 1.280.

45. The material on the historical development of the Eucharist was adapted from Johnson and Webber, *What Christians Believe*, 399–408.

46. See Peter E. Fink, "Eucharist, Theology of" *The New Dictionary of Sacramental Worship* (Collegeville, Minn.: Liturgical, 1990), 431–47.

47. These suggestions were published previously in Robert Webber, "The Table of the Lord Is a Time for Celebration," *Worship Leader* (August-September, 1993): 9.

Chapter 22

Worship and Related Ministries

In recent years, scholars and practioners of worship have recognized that worship is not an activity of the church that stands alone or even alongside the other ministries of the church. Recognizing that worship is central to the entire life of the church, liturgical scholars have begun to explore how worship relates to all the ministries of worship. Since these new fields of worship inquiry are vast and complicated, this chapter will only introduce those fields of study and provide direction for further reading and study.[1]

LANGUAGE

In recent years the women's movement has forced the church to face its use of language in worship. This matter has become highly divisive in some denominations and local churches, and no easy solution seems to be at hand. On the one hand, radical feminist theologians are calling for a language that not only excludes the use of male pronouns, but eliminates all male language and images of God such as Father, Lord, and King. On the other hand, some conservatives are advocating the continued use of male pronouns for God. They argue that words such as *man* and the consistent use of the pronoun *he* are generic forms that include both men and women.

Some churches have reached a compromise by continuing to use male language for the Godhead but adopting a new inclusive language when referring to women and men. Other denominations have found it more acceptable to use a multiplicity of linguistic images in any given service. For example, an ancient hymn may be sung using the original male language and images, while a contemporary song or the Scripture reading may use inclusive language.

While the matter of language sensitivity is an important factor for some,

253

it is not for others. The local church always faces the unpleasant possibility of offending someone through the use of language. It is not likely that the imagery of God will undergo any lasting change. For to change the language about God is to depersonalize God and change our understanding of God. However, change in the use of personal pronouns referring to women and men is important for many women in particular. Because a neutral gender language makes no fundamental change in the meaning of truth and because it is more inclusive of women and lest apt to offend the women of the congregation, gender language change will eventually become a permanent part of everyday speech and of the language of worship.[2]

MULTICULTURAL DIVERSITY IN WORSHIP

While America has always been the "melting pot" of the world, the dominant culture of America has been the white Anglo-Saxon. However, recent demographers have pointed to a significant shift taking place in the racial configuration of America. While the current white population is 83 percent, by the year 2010 the percentage of the population that is white will drop to 65 percent. In succeeding years the gap will continue to close. According to demographers, the African-American population will remain unchanged at 12 percent; Asians will increase to 5 percent; and Hispanics will double to 18 percent. Social scientists point out that when the dominant group is reduced to less than 70 percent of the population, conflict will result. A number of cities in the United States have already reached this point.

The implications of the rise of a diverse culture for worship are clear. Worshiping churches everywhere, and particularly in those cities and suburbs where there is strong ethnic diversity, must actively seek to build churches that reflect the ethnic diversity of their area. Building a church that expresses ethnic diversity means much more than having people from different cultures within worship; it means incorporating the music and the style of various cultures within the worship of the local church. If Asians, Hispanics, African-American, and whites all attend the same worship and the worship reflects a white style only, worshipers from other cultures will feel excluded. For this reason, it is imperative that white churches not only seek out worshipers from other ethnic groups but learn the music and style of other worshiping communities so that their worship reflects the cultural diversity of the church.

PASTORAL CARE

Sickness is no new issue to the church. In the Old Testament sickness was seen through the sovereignty of God and recognized as an opportunity for spiritual reflection and growth. In New Testament times sickness was understood in relation to the powers of evil. Jesus delivered the sick from their oppression and made them whole. Throughout the history of the church a tension has developed between theology and medicine. This conflict has caused many to separate care for the soul from care for the body.

Today, ministry extends to the whole person. All ministry, and particularly worship, can be an instrument of growth and healing. God ministers to us in worship and calls us to minister to each other.

Among Protestants, the charismatics have restored the rite of healing in worship. Because healing was a major element of Jesus' ministry, and because the church is to continue the ministry of Jesus, the debate over a healing ministry in worship has been renewed. Healing often takes place as the concluding act of worship. Some traditions have a threefold approach to the Sunday service: worship, teaching, and ministry. In charismatic and other churches that have adopted the fourfold pattern of worship, prayer for healing or the anointing of oil occurs at the same time as the Eucharist. After receiving bread and wine, the persons desiring healing proceeds to an appointed person who anoints them with oil, lays hands on them, and prays for them.

While many liturgical and traditional Protestant churches now have healing services, their pastoral care is usually performed within the context of new liturgical rituals. Catholics and every major mainline denomination have produced new liturgies for pastoral care. Liturgies have been developed for the healing of the mind, the body, and the soul; for abuse; divorce; and other traumatic experiences. Those liturgies and the power they exhibit to bring healing and a sense of peace to the ill and distraught have been the subject of considerable study and discussion in recent years.

The complexities of modern life and society, and the trauma these complexities create in the lives of all people are forcing the church to look closely at its pastoral care ministry. While counseling has been and still remains a vital element of pastoral care, churches that practice pastoral care in worship will add a new and helpful dimension to the worship of the local church.[3]

SPIRITUALITY

Renewal churches now recognize that worship makes a direct impact on the spiritual development of individuals. Contemporary liturgists and worship leaders recognize the priority of worship for faith and behavior. The ancient maxim (the rule of prayer is the rule of faith) points to the truth now being recovered that worship shapes faith and behavior. As the church worships, so it believes and so it behaves.

This means that the church must pay attention to the way its worship shapes faith and practice. Since the Word of God lies at the very heart of worship, new attention is being paid to the way the reading and preaching of Scripture actually influences the worshiper. Christians are called to live in obedience to the Word, an obedience that itself is an act of worship. The local church needs to develop ways to create more discussion of Scripture texts so that the message and ethic of these texts will actually take root in the lives of the worshipers. Ways adopted by some churches include talk-back sermons, Sunday school discussions, and home-study groups that discuss the sermon passages. These approaches encourage greater participation and ownership of the text of worship.

A second way that renewal churches are finding connections between worship and spirituality is through a renewed understanding and practice of the Eucharist. Spirituality is gaining a new empowerment through the recovery of the resurrection motif of the Eucharist. While contemplation of the death of Christ is still a part of the Lord's Supper, the recovery of the power of the Resurrection celebrated in the Eucharist empowers the Christian to live a new life. The Resurrection offers the power of Christ to enable the Christian to overcome evil and live a holy life. This is particularly true when the message of communion songs and the anointing with oil for healing and empowerment are experienced during the reception of bread and wine.

The renewal of baptismal vows is a third way of empowering spirituality through worship. Baptism is a renunciation of evil, a death to sin, and a new birth. The pattern of death and resurrection, which baptism enacts, is the Christian pattern of spirituality. Because of this, worship renewalists now advocate that all Christians live in recognition of the power of their baptism. One way of keeping a person's baptismal vows fresh is to renew the baptismal vows of all Christians at every baptism and to hold a service for the renewal of baptismal vows at least once a year.

Spirituality is also vitally related to the cycle of worship ordered by the Christian year. Even as every Sunday worship is a rehearsal of the death and resurrection, so the Christian year is an elongated experience of the weekly service. Congregational spirituality can be ordered by the Gospel that the Christian year celebrates as it experiences the hope of the coming Savior during Advent, the joy of his birth at Christmas, the manifestation of his salvation to the whole world at Epiphany, the journey toward his death during Lent and Holy Week, the joy of his resurrection during the Easter season, and the power of the coming of the Holy Spirit at Pentecost. These saving events, which the Christian year celebrates, are the events that order the spiritual walk of the worshiper into the very life of the Savior. When celebrated as evangelical events they not only organize congregational spirituality but empower the Christian life.[4]

EDUCATION

Educators are currently concerned with providing an education that forms character as well as informs the intellect. In contemporary worship, the most promising approach that combines worship and education is the new catechesis. While worship is the action of enacting the story that shapes the church spiritually, catechesis is the reflection on that story. Both are necessary for a healthy spirituality and for the formation of a person's character and values. The most valuable forms of catechesis are those that integrate education with weekly worship. These instructional sessions, which meet in the home, in family study, and in small groups during the worship service are ordered around the Christian year. Reflection on these texts and their implications for Christian living stimulates learning and prepares people for more meaningful worship. Accountability groups may be formed to inspire a commitment to a Christian way of life.

WORSHIP AND THE MINISTRIES OF OUTREACH

Recent studies in the field of worship have explored the relationship of worship to the ministries of outreach. Since worship is both the center toward which the church moves and the source from which all the activities of the church proceed, it is important for the church to recognize how worship empowers its outreach.

Hospitality

Hospitality is rooted in the character and the action of God. God is a hospitable God, a God who welcomes people. The only way a visitor to the local church may know that God is hospitable is if the people of God display his hospitality and demonstrate his love.

Worship must produce a welcoming environment. Symbols of care such as friendly parking lot attendants, courteous greeters, concerned ushers, helpful nursery attendants, a clean and inviting sanctuary, warm and affirming leaders, and a coffee social hour that allows people to become acquainted with each other help make people feel welcome.

Evangelism

In evangelism the church brings people to the point where they acknowledge Jesus as Savior and Lord. For evangelism to be appropriately related to the worship of the church, the church's worship must be celebrated in a way that is in keeping with the witness of the Gospel.

The Gospel is not only the Good News that God redeems us through Jesus Christ but the proclamation of God's reign over our lives and ultimately those of all people. To be evangelized then is to come to Christ for salvation and to put one's life under the rule of God.

Worship relates to evangelism through the effective proclamation of God's kingdom in the service of the Word and the celebration of the kingdom banquet in the eucharistic liturgy of the church. If worship is to regain its evangelistic emphasis, the notion of God's rule over all creation as proclaimed and enacted in worship must become central through Word and sacrament.

Renewal churches are regaining the evangelistic emphasis through ministers that catch the vision of the kingdom, through teaching about the kingdom, and through careful attention to the relationship of the kingdom to the enactment of the Gospel in worship.[5]

Social Justice

The relationship between social justice and worship is rooted in the biblical teaching of the kingdom. Jesus spoke of this eschatological vision in the Sermon on the Mount when he affirmed the new order of things for the poor and the hungry. Worship is a vision of what the world will be without the influence of evil. As an application of Christ's work to the entire creation, it summons up images of the world to come. Here nature is doing what it was created to do—give glory to God. People, too, are employed in service, doing what they were created to do.

Worship reveals the action the body of Christ must take to participate in the transformation of the world. The Lord's Prayer hints at this action: "Your will be done on earth as it is in heaven." In heaven God's will is fully carried out. The radical side of worship is clearly indicated as the worshiper prays that the earth may become a place where the will of God is also fulfilled.

In this sense the Eucharist contains a radical side. The Old Testament roots of the Eucharist lie in the liberation of the people of Israel from Egypt. This sense of liberation is also carried through in the Eucharist. For the Eucharist is the symbol of the potential liberation of the whole creation in Christ.

Paul tells us that the creation "was subjected to frustration, not by its own choice, but by the will of the one who subjected it, in hope that the creation itself will be liberated from its bondage to decay and brought into the glorious freedom of the children of God" (Rom. 8:20–21). The Eucharist is the sign of this liberation. The elements have a twofold reference. Both bread and wine represent redemption in Christ. When these two images are brought together, the relationship between redemption and creation is clearly seen in worship. The redemption accomplished by Christ transforms the entire creation.

This transformation first takes effect within the worshiping community, which may be called the eucharistic community. The vision of the earliest Christian community is one of a people who take the social implications of the Eucharist seriously. Theologian Tissa Balasuriya comments on the early Christian community in these words:

> The early Christians thus understood the deep meaning of the symbol instituted by Jesus. Its social impact was the main criterion of its value and credibility. That is why the early Christians were so acceptable to

many, especially the poor, and so detested by some of the powerful, particularly the exploiters. Christianity was then a dynamic movement of human liberation from selfishness and exploitation. All were to be equal in the believing community and this was symbolized by the eucharistic meal.[6]

The quest for us, of course, is a recovery of the social implication of the Eucharist. It was lost in the medieval period when the Eucharist was turned into an action to be observed. The Reformers tended to interpret the Eucharist in terms of personal devotion, a tradition still found among many Protestants (and also Catholics). More recently, the social and eschatological dimensions of the Eucharist have been lost in the notion of the Eucharist as a memorial. Contemporary liturgical scholarship, however, is helping today's church return to the full implications of the Eucharist through the study of ancient practices.[8]

CONCLUSION

Worship, as this chapter has demonstrated, has the power to minister to the worshiping community and to the world beyond. The challenge for pastors and worship leaders is to become sensitized to the way in which worship may touch the lives of the worshiping people and at the same time reach out to a hurting world.

---

1. For a complete introduction to these areas of worship studies see Robert Webber, ed., *The Ministries of Worship* (Nashville: Abbott Martyn, 1994).

2. For a study of this question see Brian Wren, *What Language Shall I Borrow?* (Grand Rapids: Eerdmans, 1991).

3. See Martin Israel, *Healing as Sacrament* (Cambridge, Mass.: Cowley, 1984); Francis MacNutt, *Healing* (Notre Dame, Ind.: Ave Maria, 1974); and Nelson S. T. Thayer, *Spirituality and Pastoral Care* (Philadelphia: Fortress, 1985).

4. See Don E. Saliers, *Worship and Spirituality* (Philadelphia: Westminster, 1984).

5. See Frank C. Senn, *The Witness of the Worshiping Community: Liturgy and the Practice of Evangelism* (Mahwah, N.J.: Paulist, 1993), and Robert Webber, *Liturgical Evangelism* (Harrisburg: Morehouse, 1992).

6. Tissa Balasuriya, *The Eucharist and Human Liberation* (Mary Knoll, N.Y.: Orbis, 1979).

7. See Kathleen Hughes and Mark R. Francis, 2ed., *Living No Longer for Ourselves: Liturgy and Justice in the Nineties* (Collegeville, Minn.: Liturgical, 1991), and James L. Empereur and Christopher G. Kiesling, *The Liturgy that Does Justice* (Collegeville, Minn.: Liturgical, 1990).

8. See also p. 196 on this issue.

Chapter 23

A Challenge to Evangelical Worship Renewalists

While *Worship Old and New* is an introduction to worship studies and applicable to the broad church, I have, because of my evangelical background and commitment, directed the message of the book toward evangelicals in particular. This final brief chapter is equally directed to all, but is especially aimed at the evangelical reader.

Evangelicals face a crisis in worship and theology. Evangelicals, who have a high regard for a theology that is biblical, need to be particularly concerned about their worship. If worship shapes believing, as has been suggested, then evangelicals, of all people, should be committed to a worship that is biblical.

The entire thrust of *Worship Old and New* derives from an evangelical commitment to a Scripture-driven worship that relates to the contemporary world. Unfortunately, many evangelicals are drawn to a market-driven worship that views worship in a mere functional, presentational manner. Eventually, such a worship will produce shallow believers. Hence, the urgency to perfect a biblically informed worship.

The closing remarks of this book are addressed to the evangelical reader. The challenge is organized around the concept of content, structure, and style. Many evangelicals are looking at style only and need to recover the content and structure of worship.

CONTENT

In this work we have developed a biblical theology of worship that defines worship in terms of the Gospel. This theology recognizes that the content of worship is the story of God's redeeming his creatures from the Evil One. This is expressed in his initiating grace toward Adam, Abraham, the patriarchs, Israel, and the prophets and culminating in the life, death, resurrection, and return of Jesus Christ. This message lies at the heart of everything done in the worship of the church. The voice of the Gospel is heard in preaching, in baptism, in the Lord's Supper, in hymns, psalms and spiritual songs, in prayers, in anointing, and in every conceivable act of worship. The content of worship is not negotiable. It cannot be changed, altered, or added to. A true biblical worship is this story of God's initiating a relationship with fallen creatures, a story that is remembered by God's people and for which they give thanks.

Evangelicals are familiar with this story. But, for the most part, evangelicals seem to be unaware that this story lies at the heart of worship. Evangelicals generally have defined worship in one of two ways, neither of which grasps the biblical imperative of worship. The first sees worship as ascribing worth to God. In this half-truth definition the burden of worship is placed upon the worshiping community. The community of worship, it seems, must originate words and feelings of praise through music and prayer that God will find pleasing. The second is a presentational approach to worship. Here worship consists of a series of packaged presentations to the "audience," so that they may hear the message. The error of both forms of worship is that they do not recognize the divine side of worship. In the divine side of worship, the God who has acted in history continues to act within the worshiping community in a saving and healing way as the community remembers, proclaims, enacts, and celebrates with thanksgiving. That is to say that God, who is the object of worship, is also the subject of worship. As God's saving action is recalled and enacted, God is worshiped through the response of thanksgiving.

When this biblical understanding of worship is firmly grasped, evangelicals will not only have a new appreciation of what the church does when it gathers for worship, but will begin to see baptism and the Lord's Supper not only as human responses but also as divine actions. And the Christian year will be seen not as a mere ritual but the festivals in which the church commemorates the particular saving actions of God, actions through which God continues to bring saving grace and nurturing power to those who remember and give thanks.

STRUCTURE

How one defines worship determines how one structures worship. If worship is defined as ascribing worth to God, then worship, as in the case of many contemporary churches, consists of twenty or thirty minutes of singing songs *to* God, followed by teaching and ministry, neither of which is defined as worship. If worship is presentational, then the worship committee thinks in terms of a package of worship items that will be presented: music, drama, dance, sermon.

Questions such as "Does it communicate? Is it relevant? Does it attract and hold the people?" become paramount.

Is there a structure to worship that delivers the content? Is there a way to order worship so that God's saving action is remembered, recalled, proclaimed, and enacted in a way that the people may give thanks and thus praise and worship God?

The general consensus of the church, rooted in the experience of the New Testament community and in the development of worship throughout the centuries, is that God's saving deeds are remembered primarily in the proclamation of the Word and in the thanksgiving of the church in the Eucharist. To these the church has added the acts of entrance and the acts of dismissal, both of which are rooted in the Scripture and attested to by the experience of the worshiping church.

What will it mean for the worship of the church if it seeks to structure its worship along the biblical and historical lines of the fourfold pattern? The church will experience a shift in structure from worship as a program to worship as a narrative. Programmed worship occurs when worship is seen as presentational, when the leaders are performers and the congregation is the audience. Generally, any worship that is dominated by entertainment, instruction, evangelism, or a particular theme is programmed worship. On the other hand, narrative worship recognizes that a meeting is taking place between God and his people. Worship narrates this meeting. It assembles people into the body of Christ. It orders and narrates God's communication with these people in the service of the Word. It narrates the proper response of thanksgiving at the table of the Lord. It narrates the people's movement out of worship and into the world to love and serve the Lord. This kind of worship is a participatory drama in which each person plays a part.

STYLE

Style is very different from content and structure. The content of worship is the Gospel. The structure of worship is the form that allows the Gospel to be remembered and enacted. Therefore, both content and structure are common elements to all worshiping communities. But style is open and flexible and relative to each culture, generation, and preference. One may speak of a liturgical style, a traditional Protestant style, an evangelical style, a charismatic style, or a praise and worship style. Or, one may experience worship shaped by an African-American culture, an Asian culture, a Spanish culture, or a Slavic culture. In each style the content is the same, and the structure may follow the biblical and historical fourfold pattern. But preferences such as the atmosphere, the music, or the use of the arts may vary greatly.

CONCLUSION

The challenge for evangelicals is to recover the content of worship, restore the ancient structure of worship, and integrate the evangelical style of worship. This is not only the challenge for evangelicals but the challenge for all worshiping communities. A worship that will have staying power is a worship that is firmly grounded in the old, yet aware of and concerned for new ways to respond to the old, old story.

Bibliography

REFERENCE WORKS

Davies, J. G., ed. *The New Westminster Dictionary of Liturgy and Worship*. Philadelphia: Westminster, 1986.

Fink, Peter E., ed. *The Dictionary of Sacramental Worship*. Collegeville, Minn.: Liturgical, 1990.

Lang, Jovian P. *Dictionary of the Liturgy*. New York: Catholic Book Publishing Co., 1989.

Thompson, Bard. *A Bibliography of Christian Worship*. Metuchen, N.J. & London: The American Theological Library Association and the Scarecrow Press, 1989.

Webber, Robert, ed. *The Complete Library of Christian Worship*. Nashville: Abbott Martyn, 1993 – 4.

Vol. I. *The Biblical Foundations of Christian Worship*.

Vol. II. *The Twenty Centuries of Worship*.

Vol. III. *The Renewal of Sunday Worship*.

Vol. IV. *The Role of Music and Arts in Worship* (Books One and Two).

Vol. V. *The Service of the Christian Year*.

Vol. VI. *The Sacred Actions of Worship*.

Vol. VII. *The Ministries of Worship*.

White, James F. Documents of Christian Worship. *Louisville: Westminster/John Knox Press, 1992.*

WORSHIP RESOURCE BOOKS

The Book of Occasional Services. New York: The Hymnal Corp., 1979.

The Book of Common Prayer. New York: The Hymnal Corp., 1977.

Book of Worship: United Church of Christ. New York: United Church of Christ, Office of Church Life and Leadership, 1986.

The Service for the Lord's Day. Philadelphia: Westminster, 1984.

Thankful Praise: A Resource for Christian Worship. St. Louis: CBP, 1987.

265

GENERAL INTRODUCTIONS TO WORSHIP

Allen, Ronald, and Gordon Borrow. *Worship: Rediscovering the Missing Jewel.* Portland: Multnomah Press, 1982.

Burkhart, John E. *Worship.* Philadelphia: Westminster, 1982.

Engle, Paul E. *Discovering the Fullness of Worship.* Philadelphia: Great Commission, 1978.

Erickson, Craig Douglas. *Participating in Worship.* Louisville: Westminster/John Knox Press, 1989.

Hayford, Jack W. *Worship His Majesty.* Waco: Word, 1987.

Hickman, Hoyt L. *A Primer for Church and Worship.* Nashville: Abingdon Press, 1984.

Hoon, Paul. *The Integrity of Worship.* Nashville: Abingdon Press, 1971.

Jones, Cheslyn, Geoffrey Wainwright, and Edward Yarnold, eds. *The Study of Liturgy.* New York: Oxford Univ. Press, 1978.

Kavanaugh, Aidan. *On Liturgical Theology.* New York: Pueblo, 1984.

Kendrick, Graham. *Learning to Worship as a Way of Life.* Minneapolis: Bethany House, 1984.

Liesch, Barry. *People in the Presence of God.* Grand Rapids: Zondervan, 1988.

Marshal, Michael. *Renewal in Worship.* Wilton, Conn.: Morehouse-Barlow, 1985.

Rayburn, Robert. *O Come Let Us Worship.* Grand Rapids: Baker, 1980.

Schmemann, Alexander. *Introduction to Liturgical Theology.* Scarsdale, N.Y.: St. Vladimir's Press.

Taft, Robert. *Beyond East and West: Problems in Liturgical Understanding.* Washington: Pastoral, 1984.

Wardle, Terry Howard. *Exalt Him!* Camp Hill, Penn.: Christian Publications, 1988.

Webber, Robert. *Worship is a Verb.* Nashville: Abbott Martyn, 1992.

_____. *Signs of Wonder.* Nashville: Abbott Martyn, 1992.

White, James F. *Introduction to Christian Worship.* 2d edition. Nashville: Abingdon, 1990.

Wiersbe, Warren W. *Real Worship.* Nashville: Oliver Nelson, 1986.

BIBLICAL STUDIES

Bradshaw, Paul F. and Lawrence D. Hoffman, eds. *The Making of Jewish and Christian Worship.* Notre Dame, Ind.: Univ. of Notre Dame Press, 1991.

Cullmann, Oscar. *Early Christian Worship.* London: SCM, 1973.

Di Sante, Carmine. *Jewish Prayer: The Origins of Christian Liturgy.* New York: Paulist, 1985.

Fisher, Eugene J. *The Jewish Roots of Christian Liturgy.* New York: Paulist, 1990.

Hahn, Ferdinand. *The Worship of the Early Church.* Philadelphia: Fortress, 1973.

Martin, Ralph P. *Worship in the Early Church.* Grand Rapids: Eerdmans, 1974.

Moule, C. F. D. *Worship in the New Testament.* Bremcote: Grove, 1977.

Peterson, David. *Engaging with God: A Biblical Theology of Worship.* Grand Rapids: Eerdmans, 1992.

Van Olst, E. H. *The Bible and the Liturgy.* Grand Rapids: Eerdmans, 1991.

HISTORICAL STUDIES

Adams, Doug. *Meeting House to Camp Meeting: Toward a History of American Free Church Worship.* Austin, Tex.: The Shering Company, 1981.

Deiss, Lucien. *Early Sources of the Liturgy.* Collegeville, Minn.: Liturgical, 1967.

Dix, Gregory. *The Shape of Liturgy.* San Francisco: Harper & Row, 1943.

Jasper, R. D. C., and G. C. Cumings. *Prayers of the Eucharist: Early and Reformed.* New York: Oxford Univ. Press, 1980.

Klauser, Theodore. *A Short History of the Western Liturgy.* New York: Oxford Univ. Press, 1979.

Maxwell, William D. *An Outline of Christian Worship.* Grand Rapids: Baker, 1963.

Oesterley, W. O. E. *The Jewish Background of the Christian Liturgy.* Glouchester: Peter Smith, 1965.

Rordorf, Willy. *The Eucharist of the Early Christians.* New York: Pueblo, 1978.

Thompson, Bard. *Liturgies of the Western Church.* New York: New American Library, 1974.

Wegman, Herman. *Christian Worship in East and West: A Study Guide to Liturgical History.* New York: Pueblo, 1985.

White, James F. *A Brief History of Christian Worship.* Nashville: Abingdon, 1993.

Willimon, William H. *Word, Water, Wine and Bread.* Valley Forge, Penn.: Judson Press, 1980.

WORSHIP AND THE ARTS

Music

Hustad, Don. *Jubilate.* Carol Stream: Hope, 1981.

Lawrence, Joy E. and John A. Ferguson. *A Musician's Guide to Church Music.* New York: Pilgrim, 1981.

A New Metrical Psalter. New York: The Church Hymnal Corporation, 1988.

100 Hymns, 100 Choruses. Laguna Hills, Cal.: Maranatha! Music, 1987.

Psalter Hymnal. Grand Rapids: CRC Publication, 1987.

The Worshiping Church: A Hymnal. Carol Stream: Hope, 1990.

Dance

Daniels, Marilyn. *The Dance in Christianity.* New York: Paulist, 1981.

Deitering, Carolyn. *The Liturgy as Dance and the Liturgical Dancer.* New York: Crossroad, 1984.

Gagne, Ronald. et al. *Introducing Dance in Christian Worship.* Washington: Pastoral, 1986.

Drama

Smith, Judy Gattis. *Drama Through the Church Year.* Colorado Springs: Meriwether, 1984.

For a brochure on materials available on Drama in Worship write: Meriwether Publishing, Ltd., P.O. Box 7710, Colorado Springs, CO 80933.

WORSHIP AND RELATED SUBJECTS

Church Year

Adam, Adolf. *The Liturgical Year.* New York: Pueblo, 1981.

Hickman, Hoyt, et al. *Handbook of the Christian Year.* Nashville: Abingdon, 1986.

Nocent, Adrian. *The Liturgical Year.* 4 vols. Collegeville, Minn.: Liturgical, 1977.

Evangelism

Senn, Frank C. *The Witness of the Worshiping Community: Liturgy and the Practice of Evangelism.* Mahwah, N.J.: Paulist, 1993.

Webber, Robert. *Liturgical Evangelism: Worship as Outreach and Nurture.* Harrisburg, Penn.: Morehouse, 1992.

Social Action

Webber, Robert, and Rodney Clapp. *People of the Truth.* Harrisburg, Penn.: Morehouse, 1993.

Prayer

Daily Prayer: The Worship of God. Philadelphia: Westminster, 1987.

Appleton, George. *The Oxford Book of Prayer.* New York: Oxford Univ. Press, 1985.

Rowthorn, Jeffrey W. *The Wideness of God's Mercy: Litanies to Enlarge Our Prayer.* 2 vols. New York: Seabury, 1985.

Webber, Robert. *The Book of Daily Prayer.* Grand Rapids: Eerdmans, 1993.

Index of Persons

Index of Subjects

Advent, 14, 26, 81, 126, 215, 225–26, 227, 258

Aesthetic, the: in Eastern Christian worship, 99–100

Agape feast: in *Didache*, 53; and the Lord's Supper, 57; origin of, 57; Pliny, and the, 52

Altars: proliferation of, in the Roman church, 104, 145, 211; replacement of by Cranmer, 112

Anabaptists, 112, 235–36, 245, 247–48

Ancient church: and the arts, 210; baptism in, 101–2; communion in, 114, 241, 250; source for modes of worship, 65; use of sound in, 199–200; worship in, 89, 172, 175–85

Anglican, 112, 116, 158, 170

Announcements: as an interruption of worship, 82

Apostles' Creed, 48, 76, 237

Apostolic: blessing, 194; constitutions, 182–83; importance of tradition, 48–49; literature, 155; teaching, 152

Aramaic Christian worship, 44

Ash Wednesday, 226

Baptism: Anabaptist view, 235–36; in the ancient church, 101–2; Christ as the minister of, 231–32; commemorative nature of, 232–37; as communicating spiritual reality, 115; as a dominical symbol, 43, 89; on Easter, 102, 225, 234; environment for, 141, 147–48; established by Christ, 87, 225; in the Holy Spirit, 123; Gnostic denial of, 86;

infant, 102, 234, 235; as an initiation, 28, 60, 232, 233–34, 251; and justification by faith, 235; and predestination, 235; preparation for in Lent, 226; preparation for the Eucharist, 184–85; renewal, 236–37; and salvation, 60–61, 114, 223, 235; and the sign character of worship, 29, 43, 47, 48, 60–61, 62, 67, 69, 73, 90, 137, 152, 258, 264

Baptists, 112, 114

Barnabas, Epistle of, 166

Basilica, Roman: use of space in, 143–44

Benediction, 152, 193–94, 198, 204

Bishop: increase of the power of, 142, 143, 144, 239; in the third century, 95, 98

Book of Common Prayer, 12, 112, 116, 125, 156, 158, 185

Calvinism, 112

Ceremony: of breaking bread, 56; consecration, 34; as covenant worship, 23; notions of, 74

Chants; in worship, 99, 100, 101, 102–3, 105, 106, 116, 169, 204

Charismatics, 13, 128, 257

Charismatic worship, 127–28, 133, 217

Christ: attitude of, toward worship, 42; and baptism, 232–37; as the content of worship, 35, 43, 47, 56–57, 58, 61; cosmic work of, 25, 48, 221; and the Eucharist, 238–51; as the mediator of Christian worship, 25; Old Testament forms of worship fulfilled by, 21–22, 24, 25, 34, 45, 221; presence of, in wor-

Index of Scripture